A FIERY FINALE TO THE WEEKEND

Philip Parker grabbed one side of the door and tried sliding it open. It wouldn't budge. He noticed a chaise lounge on the deck and turned to ask his cousin if he should throw it through the glass door. Phillips told him to wait until she got a fire extinguisher in case the flames shot out of the room when he broke the glass. While Phillips went around front to get the fire extinguisher, Parker got down on his hands and knees on the rear deck and looked inside to see if there was anyone in the room. All he could see was the faint outline of someone's feet. Parker jumped up and noticed that the other side of the sliding glass door was open slightly. Smoke was pouring out of the opening. Parker opened the sliding glass door all the way, crawled inside on his hands and knees and made his way to the person in the room.

The smoke was so thick Parker could only see about a foot in front of him . . .

An ACT of MURDER

LINDA ROSENCRANCE

PINNACLE BOOKS
Kensington Publishing Corp.
http://www.kensingtonbooks.com

For Jack, Jean, Marie, Ed, Danielle, Al, and, most especially, for Richard Montgomery, my favorite Chinese-language translator.

Acknowledgments

Many thanks to everyone who helped me with this project, including Talbot County court reporter Juanita Kohn, Talbot County Circuit Court clerk Mary Ann Shortall, Maryland State Police sergeant Joe Gamble, Steve's best friend, Mike Miller, and his wife, Maureen O'Toole-Miller, Deputy Fire Marshal Mike Mulligan, prosecutor Bob Dean, Assistant State's Attorney Henry Dove, jury foreman Curt Hutchinson, Kim's attorneys, Harry Trainor Jr. and Bill Brennan, Kim's mother, Lois Wolf, and Kim's biggest supporters, Cathy Rosenberger and Rachelle St. Phard. Thanks also to playwright Bobbi Benitz, who graciously allowed me to use her play *The Bride Who Cried* in this book.

I contacted the Hricko family a number of times, but they declined to be interviewed for this book.

Last, but not least, special thanks to my agent, Janet Benrey of the Hartline Literary Agency—there really is a special place in heaven for agents—and my editor, Miles Lott.

Author's Note

Some of the names in this book have been changed to protect the privacy of the individuals involved.

L.R.

There is nothing more dread and more shameless than a woman who plans such deeds in her heart as the foul deed which she plotted when she contrived her husband's murder.

—Homer, *The Odyssey*

Chapter 1

It was Saturday, February 14, 1998. Valentine's Day. After dropping off their eight-year-old daughter, Sarah (pseudonym), at a neighbor's house, Stephen and Kimberly Hricko began the seventy-mile drive from their home in Laurel, Maryland, to St. Michaels on the state's Eastern shore. They were planning to spend a romantic weekend at the Harbourtowne Golf Resort & Conference Center. The couple, married for eight years, had been having marital problems and were hoping to rekindle their relationship.

Kim, a hospital surgical technologist, and Steve, a golf-course grounds superintendent, were among one hundred couples who paid $239 for the overnight getaway. Around 3:00 P.M. on February 14, they checked into cottage 506. When they arrived, they were given a bottle of champagne. A highlight of the weekend was a dinner-theater murder mystery that the dinner guests were invited to solve. The title of the play was *The Bride Who Cried*.

The Hrickos and the other couples arrived in the main dining room around 7:30 P.M. The play began as the wedding party entered the room.

The wedding party consists of the bride and groom, the bride's parents—the groom's father has just been deported to Italy and his mother is deceased—and the best man. However, the maid of honor, the bride's best friend, Muffie, is so angry and confused at the weird wedding that she says she feels ill and leaves before the reception.

As the wedding party enters the hall, the groom, Bernardo Vittorio, puts his arm around Cynthia, his bride. She immediately pulls it away.

"I wouldn't do that, dear," he says.

"What are you going to do, have a member of my family killed," she replies.

Pamela Bartlett, Cynthia's mother, overhears the conversation and asks her daughter what she means by that statement.

"Nothing, really. You must have misunderstood me," Cynthia says.

But Pamela refuses to drop the subject. She turns to Fred, her husband, and repeats Cynthia's comments. Feeling very uncomfortable, Fred, too, tells Pamela she must have misunderstood their daughter.

Pamela now looks around for Muffie. Unable to find her, she asks her daughter where she is.

"Muffie is your dearest friend, I can't imagine your maid of honor not coming to your reception," Pamela says.

"Oh, she was ill and decided to go home," Cynthia replies. "And I don't blame her," she says to herself.

"I just don't understand any of this," says Pamela, looking rather pale, and leaning on her husband.

The wedding party now forms a receiving line

to greet the guests—including the Hrickos. Bernardo is preening. After all, he is now a member of a socially prominent Philadelphia family. Dino Gambino, the best man, is still wearing his dark glasses and the bulge under his coat is obvious. Most of the time he hovers close to Bernardo, except when he is following Cynthia like a lovesick puppy dog.

Pamela is in shock and Fred is extremely nervous. In the middle of the reception Cherie Chardonnay, the groom's jilted girlfriend, arrives to try and embarrass her former lover.

As the Hrickos and the other couples mingled with the wedding party and their invited guests, they learned a number of interesting facts about the main characters—facts designed to help them catch a killer. Here's what they found out:

In 1974 Fred Bartlett, self-made millionaire, met socialite Pamela Keaton Davis. A more unlikely pair you would seldom see. Fred left school at the age of fourteen and went to work for an uncle who owned a junkyard. A hardworking young man, Fred saved some money, bought a couple of antique stores, then some apartment houses. By the time he was twenty-three, when he met Pamela, he was a wealthy man.

Pamela was from an old Philadelphia family. While long on aristocracy, the family was very short on cash. Little by little, the family sold off the land surrounding the old mansion. Now it, too, was in danger of being sold. Always looking for a good deal, Fred decided to take a look at it. It was then that he met Pamela. It was, of course, love at first sight.

Fred married Pamela, and like a good husband, he paid off the mortgage on her family's home, and the couple soon moved in. They were very happy living there with their darling new daughter.

All went well for fifteen years or so. The '80s were good to Fred. He bought more and more real estate and built many office buildings around the country. Then the '90s hit and Fred was in financial trouble and desperate. A rather insecure man, and very aware of his lack of education and family background, Fred was frantic. He felt his life depended on the money he provided to Pamela and her family.

One of Fred's businesses, one of the few that was doing well, was importing tropical plants and birds from South America.

One day Bernardo Vittorio, the son of Mafia boss Gianini Vittorio, approached Fred in an attempt to convince him to "broaden" his import business and join the Vittorio organization. Although Fred was frightened of the Vittorio family, he accepted the "offer" in order to recoup his fortune.

Just as Bernardo was about to leave Fred's office, Pamela and Cynthia, the Bartletts' beautiful daughter, dropped by to have lunch with Fred. Cynthia didn't notice Bernardo, but he certainly noticed her. In fact, he called Fred later that day and told Fred he wanted to meet Cynthia.

"Absolutely not," said Fred, but soon changed his mind when Bernardo explained what happened to people who said no to a Vittorio.

So Fred told Bernardo he would be having lunch with his daughter the next day and arranged for Bernardo to run into Cynthia at the restaurant.

As luck would have it, Cynthia found Bernardo very amusing and charming. And when he invited her to dinner, she accepted immediately, much to her father's consternation and relief.

For the next couple of months Cynthia and Bernardo saw each other several evenings a week. He was unlike any other man she had ever known. He both fascinated and frightened her.

When her father told her that Bernardo wanted to marry her, she laughed. How completely ridiculous, she thought. But she stopped laughing when her father told her that Bernardo said if she didn't marry him, her mother would meet with a very bad accident.

At the wedding reception Fred confronts his son-in-law, saying, "Bernardo, something has to be done to stop this thing. My daughter looks so unhappy. You have to understand, she's my child. I love her. I can't stand seeing her so unhappy. And her mother is on the verge of a heart attack, I'm afraid. She's really not well, Bernardo."

Bernardo laughs and says, "Oh, come now, Fred, don't you think you're being overly dramatic? I wasn't so bad back when I took you into my import business and saved you from filing bankruptcy."

Fred is highly indignant.

"Now, just one damn minute. You didn't take me into your business—it was *my* tropical-plant business. And it was an honest business."

Bernardo looks around and says, "I would be careful what I say, if I were you, Fred. As the old saying goes, 'The walls have ears.' And I don't think you want your *honest* tropical-plant business to be investigated. As you said, it is *your* business. Just think how little Cynthia would take Daddy going to prison. And dear Pamela—that would knock her off the Social Register in a hurry. *If*, of course, she lived through it."

Pamela comes over to join the men.

"Have you seen Barbara's prize orchid?" Fred asks his wife, referring to the owner of the inn. "She just sent word that you must see it."

"I do so want to see it, but first I want to check on Cynthia. She just isn't looking all that happy," Pamela says, directing her last remark at Bernardo.

"Come. I'll go with you," Fred says.

Bernardo looks around and says to no one in particular, "Hmm, where is my lovely bride? Well, isn't that interesting?" he says upon seeing Cynthia and Dino with their heads together.

Bernardo walks over to them, and gets there at the same time as Pamela and Fred.

Not wanting to talk to Bernardo, Pamela excuses herself to go to the greenhouse.

Dinner was now served. The guests took their seats. Seated at the Hrickos' table were five couples, including Henry Dove, a Maryland assistant state's attorney, and his date. What the other guests didn't know was that on this night Dove was one of the actors in the play. In fact, he was playing a detective.

At the table with Dove and his date and the Hrickos was a couple from Gaithersburg, Maryland, who were probably in their thirties; another, somewhat older couple, from Preston, Maryland, in their sixties or seventies; and another couple, in their fifties, from Pennsylvania. Unlike the other couples at the table that were pretending to be friends of the bride, this couple acted as if they knew the groom and his family.

"The receiving line was pretty normal," Dove said later. "But the cast had to go around from table to table so people could hear about the story because most of the people were just not getting up from their tables—it works better that way. But Kimberly and another woman—the woman from Gaithersburg—went from table to table and really got into it. I just pretended I was there to enjoy it, like everyone else. That went pretty well, and then we got to the dinner, and while we're all seated, we talked about what we did for a living. I told them I was a state's attorney. I had a badge with me and I passed it around the table and Kim asked me some questions about it. It wasn't something you would notice at first, but in retrospect you'd think that she was a little more interested than normal."

At dinner Kim continued talking to Dove about herself. She told him about her work as a child advocate for Court Appointed Special Advocates (CASA). Stephen Hricko, however, hardly spoke a word. Most of the time all he did was stare at the head table. And he didn't seem to be drinking all that much.

"I couldn't even swear he had one beer, but maybe he did, but he certainly wasn't drinking heavily," Dove said. "The thing I remember most was that someone at the table brought their own bottle of wine, but it wasn't the Hrickos. As the show went on, Kim and the other woman did a lot of walking around and questioning—they'd go to the other tables and talk to the bride and groom and try to get more into it."

As the guests continue talking and eating, the wedding party is seated at the head table. Everyone is there, except Dino, who arrives several minutes later. Bernardo chastises Dino for being late.

"I'm so sorry," Dino says sarcastically.

Bernardo turns to Cynthia and asks why she's not eating.

"I'm not hungry," she replies, then excuses herself and leaves the table.

She soon returns and whispers something in her father's ear.

"Oh, yes. Thank you for reminding me, my dear," Fred says, then gets up and walks away.

"Where is he going?" Pamela asks her daughter.

"Oh, everything was done so quickly that no one selected the champagne. Daddy's going to check on it."

The guests continue to talk amongst themselves. Fred soon returns. Shortly a waiter wheels a bottle of champagne and some glasses over to the head table on a cart. The waiter begins pouring the champagne and passing the glasses around. Pamela knocks her glass over. There is confusion as everyone tries to mop up the spilled champagne. The waiter brings another glass for Pamela.

When things calm down, Bernardo asks Dino if he's going to make the traditional toast.

"I'm not too good at that sort of thing," Dino responds.

So Bernardo rises and toasts his beautiful bride. He sips his champagne, grabs his throat, and falls to the floor—dead.

In character, Dove, the detective, rushes over and puts his fingers to Bernardo's neck to see if he can get a pulse. Unable to do so, he looks up and says, "This man is dead. Don't anyone touch anything. Someone please call an ambulance. Will the people at this table please move to the side," he says, directing the members of the head table away from Bernardo's body.

"We finally get to the end of dinner, which is when [the] murder happens," Dove said. "At that point I'm trying to get the victim out so he can get away from everything and not just have to lie on the floor while we do the next hour of the show. But Kim followed me out of the dining room and asked if she could do anything to revive him and I said no and basically told her to go away. So she did go back in the room and

I get the actor playing Bernardo out of the way on a gurney and I go back in and start doing the questioning."

"There is no doubt that Mr. Vittorio has been poisoned," Dove says, speaking to the dinner-theater guests. "The grabbing of the throat and the convulsions that followed tell us that. The medical examiner will tell us more, but what we are concerned with right now is who put the poison in Mr. Vittorio's champagne. It had to be one of the people sitting in front of me, since they were the only ones who had access to the champagne. If the poison is strychnine, and I think it is, then anyone could have gotten it at the greenhouse."

Dove continues questioning the guests, "First, did anyone at the table see anything suspicious?"

No one answers.

"If anyone did see anything, would you tell me? Probably not—it doesn't seem to me that Mr. Bernardo Vittorio was very well-liked by you people," Dove says. "What about it, Dino, did you like your boss?"

"He was okay."

"Come now, Dino, you paid more attention to the new bride than you did to your boss," Dove says.

Turning his attention to the guests, Dove says, "Did anyone here notice anything suspicious about Mr. Gambino's behavior this evening?"

"Well, he certainly seemed to like Cynthia," a guest replies.

"I saw them whispering together a couple of times," says another guest.

"Saw who whispering?" Dove asks.

"Mr. Gambino and Cynthia," the guest says.

"That's very interesting," Dove says. "What were you whispering about, Dino?"

"I don't remember."

"C'mon, Dino, admit it. You paid more attention to the new Mrs. Vittorio . . ."

"Please don't call her that," Pamela says, interrupting Dove.

"Sorry, ma'am, but that is her name," Dove replies. "Now, Dino, tell us how you felt about your boss marrying the former Cynthia Bartlett. Did it make you angry?"

"It didn't look like it made her very happy," Dino responds.

"And that made you unhappy, right?" Dove asks. When Dino doesn't answer, Dove continues.

"How long have you worked for the late Mr. Vittorio?"

"He's my cousin—I mean, was my cousin. I've known him all my life, but I've only worked for him for a year or so," Dino says.

"Who hired you?"

"The Don—Bernardo's father."

"How long have you know Cynthia Bartlett?"

"About three or four months," Dino says.

"As long as Bernardo knew her?"

"Yeah."

"Did you go on dates with them?" Dove asks.

"They usually met at restaurants or theaters, and, yeah, I was along. I'm a bodyguard," Dino says.

"So you spent a lot of time with Cynthia and you became fond of her, right?"

"She's a nice kid."

"How far would you go to protect her?"

"Whaddya mean?"

"How many people have you killed in your

life, Dino?" Dove asks. "And isn't that a gun in your belt?"

"Hey, I'm getting me a lawyer. You can't accuse me of nothing."

"Calm down, Dino. I'll talk to you again later. Now, Mr. Bartlett, how well did you know Mr. Vittorio?"

"Oh, hardly at all," Fred replies. "I saw him at the house a few times when he came to pick up Cynthia."

"I thought Dino just said they always met at restaurants or theaters," Dove says.

"Oh, well, maybe I'm confused. There's so much happening," Fred says.

"Come now, Mr. Bartlett, where did you meet Mr. Vittorio? You obviously knew him," Dove says.

Turning his attention to the guests again, Dove says, "Did anyone overhear Mr. Bartlett talking to Mr. Vittorio?"

"I saw them talking, but I couldn't hear what they were saying," a guest says. "Fred seemed very serious, though, and Mr. Vittorio just smiled."

"Is that right?" Dove says. "What were you talking about, Mr. Bartlett?"

"Well, Cynthia told me that Bernardo was taking her to Italy for an extended stay and I was trying to convince him that they shouldn't stay too long," Fred says. "Cynthia's mother is not well and she would be very unhappy if Cynthia were away too long."

"I see. What did he say to that?" Dove asks.

"Well, he, um, he said he would think about it."

"Dino, where did you first meet Mr. Bartlett?" Dove asks.

"In his office with Bernardo."

"Whose office?"

"Mr. Bartlett's."

"Mr. Bartlett, what was a well-known Mafia figure doing in your office?" Dove says, putting Fred on the spot.

"Well, he asked me to include him in my tropical-plant import business, but, of course, I said absolutely not."

"Oh, you expect me to believe you refused to go into business with this man, yet you allowed your only daughter to marry him," Dove says. "It just doesn't make any sense, Mr. Bartlett."

"All right, all right. I had lost a great deal of money in real estate. In fact, I was in real trouble. The Vittorio family heard about it and came to offer me a great deal of money if I would have my plant exporters in South America turn their heads, so to speak, when my cargo was being shipped here. I did it. I was afraid I would lose everything—my wife and my daughter—everything," Fred says, crying.

"So that's how he married your daughter—he blackmailed you. But then he would have to incriminate himself," Dove says.

"Just how did Bernardo force you to marry him?" Dove asks Cynthia.

"He was going to have my mother murdered."

"Just when did you get this bit of information, Mr. Bartlett?" Dove asks Fred.

"He told me he wanted to marry my daughter about a month ago," Fred replies. "I told him he was crazy. That's when he said my wife could meet with a fatal accident. He knew all about her schedules—when she went to the beauty shop, when she went to the garden club. Everything.

He said it would probably be a hit-and-run accident, or maybe faulty brakes on her car. I knew he wasn't kidding, so I told Cynthia. You see my wife has a bad heart, so even a slight accident could cause her serious problems. He was an evil man," Fred says, putting his arm around Pamela, who begins to cry.

"I don't think anyone would argue that point, but you don't go around taking the law into your own hands, Mr. Bartlett," Dove says. "Did you murder Mr. Vittorio?"

"No, but I wish I had."

"Oh, Fred, poor Fred. You were always afraid that we would lose everything. I've always been able to depend on you," Pamela says.

Dove turns his attention to Cynthia again.

"When did you hear about Mr. Vittorio's threat on your mother's life, Miss Bartlett?"

"Father told me right away. Bernardo had mentioned marriage to me and I just laughed at him. Then he told me I should ask my father what he thought about it," Cynthia says.

"You know, I can't think of anything much worse for a parent, or a would-be suitor, than having a girl you love forced to marry scum like Bernardo Vittorio and know he was taking her away to a foreign country so you would not even be able to help her if she needed you," Dove says.

"The only thing I can think of that would be worse, is to be that girl; to have to put up with his slimy hands on you; to be taken away to a foreign country—away from your family and friends. That would drive you to do almost anything to keep out of his clutches, wouldn't it, Miss Bartlett? We would all understand why you killed your husband. You did kill him, didn't you, Miss Bartlett?" Dove asks.

Before Cynthia has a chance to answer, Pamela speaks up.

"Just a minute, sir. I know that horrible person had threatened to kill me—I overheard Cynthia saying something about killing a member of her family and I quickly put two and two together. I figured that would be the only thing that would make my baby marry that monster."

Dove considers Pamela's comments for a minute, then speaks.

"That puts a different slant on matters. So you knew that Bernardo was threatening you, but you didn't find out until today, so you couldn't have planned to poison him ahead of time. But your husband could have, your daughter could have, and certainly Dino could have. It pains me to say this, but I just don't see Dino knocking Bernardo off with poison. That just wouldn't be his style. As much motivation as you had, Mr. Bartlett, you just don't fit the killer stereotype. But Cynthia—Cynthia has always had everything she wanted," Dove says.

At this point someone comes into the room and whispers something to the detective.

"Don't anyone leave," Dove tells the guests. "I have to go to outside for a minute. I'll be right back."

Soon Dove comes back into the dining room.

"Well, now we know what the poison was—it was a poison found in insecticides. Mrs. Henry, the owner here, said she has a container of the insecticide inside her greenhouse. Now, who went to that greenhouse to see an orchid? We know Mrs. Bartlett went. Who else had the opportunity to slip around the building and go to the greenhouse?" Dove asks the guests.

"Everyone at the head table left at some point during dinner," a guest says.

"Yes, I saw each of them leave, myself," Dove replies. "So we have opportunity and motive. They all had the opportunity, so the motive has to point to the killer. Everyone had a strong motive to want Mr. Vittorio dead. But the question is, who had the strongest motive? I still feel that Cynthia Bartlett Vittorio had the strongest motive. Cynthia, I'm arresting you for the murder of your husband."

Pamela quickly speaks up.

"Oh, you are so wrong—don't you know a mother's love is stronger than anything? You must arrest me, too, because my motive was as strong as hers," she tells Dove.

"Well, now, isn't that interesting," Dove says. "I have one murder and two killers. There is one thing missing—someone should have a container with the remnants of the poison in it. Could I see your purse, Mrs. Bartlett?"

Pamela pulls the purse away from Dove and a brief scuffle ensues, but Dove wins out. He takes her purse, opens it, and discovers a vial that smells of poison.

"You were wrong about one thing, Mrs. Bartlett. I did know a mother's love was stronger than anything. I just had to let you prove it."

Then Pamela is handcuffed and led out with Fred and Cynthia following close behind, trying to comfort her.

"When we finished the show, I still hadn't eaten my dessert, so I sat down to eat that and most of the rest of the table stayed and kept talking to me for about another half hour, even though the rest of the crowd had broken up," Dove said. "The Hrickos stayed at the table with at least two other couples and me and my date."

Soon the Hrickos went back to their room, stopping to buy a couple of beers to take back with them.

At 1:21 A.M. Kimberly Hricko walked into the hotel's main lobby to report a fire in her room.

What happened when the Hrickos got back to their room is unclear, but here's what Kim had to say about the events of that weekend, some of which she told police.

Kim didn't work Friday, February 13, because she had a doctor's appointment at 8:30 A.M., as well as errands to run. The doctor's appointment was for a sigmoidoscopy. This is a procedure that enables a physician to look at the inside of the large intestine from the rectum through the last part of the colon, called the sigmoid or descending colon. The test left her feeling completely drained.

Later that night she met her friend Jennifer Gowen for dinner at Mi Rancho in Silver Spring, Maryland. She didn't sleep well Friday night and awoke exhausted. She wasn't really excited about the weekend.

It seemed she really hadn't been looking forward to going to Harbourtowne since Steve told her about it. In fact, she spoke with her counselor about Steve's plans for a romantic weekend, saying that she was very tired and didn't want to go away. Kim told her counselor that she didn't think it would be a very pleasant weekend.

On Saturday, February 14, after dropping Sarah off at a friend's house to spend the night, Kim and Steve drove to St. Michaels. Kim slept most of the way there. Kim knew Steve was taking her to Harbourtowne, but she didn't know exactly what he had planned.

"On our calendar at home, Steve had marked the day with 'Keep open,'" Kim said.

After checking into the hotel, the couple drove to their room. Kim still had no idea what surprises Steve had planned for the evening. When they got to their room, Kim noticed what looked like a wedding invitation on a table. After reading it, she discovered they would be taking part in a murder-mystery dinner theater. Now she knew why Steve told her to pack something nice to wear.

"Steve and his friend Mike [Miller] planned the dinner. The weekend was a surprise for me," Kim said. "Steve and Mike had been friends since grade school. They had been talking more recently because Steve was falling apart. He was under so much pressure at work to do a good job. He really let it get to him. Our marriage was strained, too," Kim said.

The room was freezing, so Kim started a fire in the woodstove with the log provided by the hotel. She also made a pot of coffee and spread out on one of the room's two beds with the Sunday newspaper.

Steve opened the complimentary bottle of champagne and poured each of them a glass.

"I didn't like mine because it tasted cheap and didn't drink any more," Kim said. "Steve drank the rest of the bottle."

Because they had missed lunch, Steve drove to a convenience store, where he purchased two hot dogs, Tastykakes, and soda. While he was gone, Kim unpacked and hung a pair of wet pants, which she had washed at home that morning, out on the deck.

"We spent some time watching TV and enjoying the

view from our porch," Kim said. "It was extremely windy and the water was choppy. It was damp and gray—too cold to stay outside long."

Before the couple went to dinner, Steve took Effexor, medication for his depression—he had been on the drug for about two weeks and the dosage had recently been doubled. Steve took the medicine at the same time every day. He only brought enough medication for the weekend, not the entire bottle. Steve also took Xanax, used to treat anxiety, and Flexeril, a muscle relaxant, at some point during the evening. The couple took their time getting ready for dinner.

"When we went into dinner, they had a receiving line just like a real wedding," Kim said. "We had more drinks. We joined three other couples at our table. One person at our table had ordered a bottle of wine and shared it with everyone. We ordered several rounds during dinner and put one round on our room number. There was a cash bar outside [the dining room] and Steve and I got several beers there after the play and we took them back to our room."

During dinner, while the murder-mystery play was under way, Kim and another woman from her table got up and walked around, interacting with the actors.

"The actors encouraged us and seemed somewhat disappointed that everyone seemed to stay planted in their chairs. This lady and I teamed up," Kim said. "Before leaving the lobby [after dinner], we got a second log for the fireplace."

When the Hrickos got back to their room, they turned on the television and watched *Tommy Boy*, with Chris Farley. Steve changed into a T-shirt with a logo on it and lightweight sweatpants and had a chew. Steve had chewed tobacco for years. Steve heated some water in the coffeemaker for his Theraflu and drank it. The whole family had had bronchitis and strep throat. Steve still had it because he was the last to get it.

"By the time I took my Zoloft, all Steve's pills were gone," Kim said. "After we watched the movie, Steve was showing some signs of having a little too much to drink. He normally does not give any indication that he has had too much to drink. The movie made us laugh, but still we did not talk about our problems."

The Hrickos had a brief, but not loud, argument over sex—Steve wanted it, Kim didn't.

"We had both been seeing counselors and along with our counselors the decision had been agreed to in advance that the weekend getaway would be just to relax with each other and have a good time," Kim said. "It had been agreed that we would not be intimate on this weekend. It had been many months since we had been intimate."

After the movie Steve approached Kim for sex. Kim got upset and left the room. She got into her car and drove around Easton. But she wasn't sure where she was because she had been sleeping on the trip to Harbourtowne and had only been to the resort once before, three years earlier with her friend Maureen Miller, who drove to the hotel from her home in Easton.

Kim thought of driving home but decided against it because then Steve would have no way to get back to Laurel. As she drove around—she told police she was trying to find the Millers' house in Easton—she got lost. She was trying to find Route 50, the main drag in Easton, but every road she hit had a "3" in it. She stopped to ask for directions but was still unable to find her way. She was very tired and getting more confused.

"I have always been very poor with roads and directions and always seemed to be lost. I could have crossed over Route 50 and not have known it," Kim said. "I think I asked three people for directions—one person was in a white Volvo. I saw a mixed-race couple in Historic Easton and I remember the woman was holding a single rose and I thought, 'How sweet.' I asked them how to get to Harbourtowne and Route 50. The couple told me that the two were in opposite directions and asked me which one I wanted. So they gave me directions back to the hotel and I eventually found my way back to the resort."

When Kim got back to her room, she realized she had forgotten her electronic room key. She didn't want to knock because it was so late, so she went around back, because she remembered the sliding glass door had been opened. It was still unlocked. As Kim opened it, thick, oily smoke and intense heat poured out. She couldn't see her hand in front of her face. There was no light, nor was there a smoke alarm sounding. Panicking, Kim ran to the surrounding units, knocking on the doors, waiting for someone to hear her. But there were no sounds or lights in any of the rooms. When no one responded to her pleas, she jumped in her car and drove to the lobby. It was approximately 1:15 or 1:30 in the morning. As she drove, she called 911 on her cell phone.

When she reached the lobby, which was in a separate building, she parked the car directly in front, partly on the sidewalk. She ran into the building screaming for help while still on the cell phone with emergency personnel, who were asking her to calm down so they could get the pertinent information from her.

"So when I walked into the lobby, I was already involved with the emergency operator, giving them the exact location and directions to my room," Kim said.

"They just keep saying over and over, 'Calm down,' and kept asking questions. I understand a woman said I walked in calmly and a man said I walked in hysterical. I was hysterical! Everyone present left and I didn't know what to do, so I ran on foot to the unit because I was too upset to drive. I know I left the keys and purse in my car and I think I left the motor running."

Kim followed people from the lobby back to her room.

"The police were at the cottage with cars. A lady held me back, pushing my head onto her shoulders and squeezing me. I heard over the police car radio, 'We have a white male, DOA.' From that information I knew that Steve was deceased without anyone telling me. The voice probably came from around on the porch side of the cottage over a walkie-talkie or radio. I never went into our room or saw Steve before I was taken away. I tried to get away from the lady and a policeman, and was screaming, 'I want to see him.' I understand the lady misquoted me saying, 'I want to see his body.' No one offered to help take me to the hospital to meet with the doctors or see if there was anything that I could do for Steve."

Chapter 2

It was nearly 1:00 A.M. and Elaine Phillips, Harbour-towne's banquet manager, had just finished up for the night. After working a twelve-hour shift she was glad for some downtime, which she spent socializing with her aunt, Bonnie Parker, her cousin, Philip Parker, and his girlfriend, who were spending the weekend at the resort. Phillips and her family had just called it a night and were walking through the lobby when Kim entered and said she needed to speak to a Harbourtowne employee.

"A woman walked into the lobby. She had a cell phone up to her ear. It was turned upside down. She was just listening into it," Phillips said later. "She walked over to us, my cousin and I, and she said, 'I need to speak to someone who works here.' My cousin, who was about a step ahead of me, kind of directed her to me. I asked her, 'May I help you?' And she said, 'My room is on fire.'"

Phillips immediately asked Kim what her room number was, but Kim didn't answer. So Phillips then asked her what her name was and Kim said Hricko. Remembering the spelling of Kim's name, Phillips spelled it out for another Harbourtowne employee, who looked up the Hrickos' record and shouted out that their room number was 506.

Phillips immediately called 911 to report the fire, while her cousin asked Kimberly if she was okay. The emergency operator told Elaine Phillips that the fire already had been called in.

As soon as she got off the phone, Phillips ran out of the lobby after her cousin, who was already on his way to the Hrickos' room. When Parker got outside, he could smell smoke and started following his nose to the fire. As soon as Phillips caught up with him, she pointed him in the direction of room 506. When the pair arrived at the grouping of rooms that included 506, Parker couldn't quite tell which room was on fire, so he started banging on the front doors of all the rooms. Then he went around to the back of the building, where he could see the smoke in the Hrickos' room through the sliding glass door.

First Parker grabbed one side of the door and tried sliding it open. It wouldn't budge. He noticed a chaise lounge on the deck and turned to ask his cousin if he should throw it through the glass door. Phillips told him to wait until she got a fire extinguisher in case the flames shot out of the room when he broke the glass. While Phillips went around front to get the fire extinguisher, Parker got down on his hands and knees on the rear deck and looked inside to see if there was anyone in the room. All he could see was the faint outline of someone's feet. Parker jumped up and noticed that the other side of the sliding glass door was open slightly. Smoke was pouring out of the opening. Parker opened the sliding glass door all the way, crawled inside on his hands and knees, and made his way to the person in the room.

The smoke was so thick Parker could only see about a foot in front of him. When he finally got to Steve's body, which was lying faceup on the floor in between the room's two beds, he started beating him on his stomach, trying to wake him up. Steve didn't wake up, so Parker decided the only way to help him was to get him out of the room. He tried grabbing Steve by his arms, but when he did, his hands just slid off. He couldn't seem to get a good grip, so he tried dragging Steve out by his feet. Parker got Steve's body to the edge of the sliding glass door, but couldn't pull him over the raised threshold. Parker yelled for his cousin, who also grabbed Steve and helped pull his body out onto the deck. Once outside, Parker and Phillips saw that the upper part of Steve's body was very badly burned. It was obvious to them that Steve was dead.

As soon as Parker got Steve out onto the deck, he remembered that his fiancée had been right behind him when he was running to the Hrickos' room. He remembered when he was inside he could hear her yelling to him through the sliding glass doors. He didn't want her to see Steve's body, so he grabbed hold of her and tried to rush her around the corner of the villa. When the couple reached the side of the building, they saw Officer Patrick Sally and Officer Stephen Craig, St. Michaels police officers, getting out of their cars.

"As I arrived and got out of my vehicle, I observed two individuals, later identified as Philip Parker and Elaine Phillips, waving and yelling that there was a man down in the back," Sally testified later.

Sally, Craig, and their sergeant raced around the corner to the back of the building. As they approached the back porch, they observed Steve lying there on his back with his left arm sticking straight up in the air. He was wearing a pair of light blue pajama bottoms that were pulled down, exposing his penis, and pulled up high on his shins. He was also wearing what appeared to be a white T-shirt, which had been burned. His chest and head were severely burned. It was obvious to the officers that Steve was dead. Sally checked Steve's body temperature and found that it was elevated but not hot. His upper torso was stiff, either from the heat of the fire or from rigor mortis. His left arm was sticking straight up in the air and bent slightly backward. Sally attempted to take Steve's pulse, but felt nothing.

Officer Sally now went inside room 506 to make sure no one else was inside and determined it was empty. As he looked around, he noticed that there was a lot of smoke damage to the room. He saw that the mattress closest to the bathroom was smoldering and completely burned, exposing the springs. The headboard was charred and the carpeting around the bed was melted and charred. As Sally was looking around the room, members of the St. Michaels Fire Department, as well as members of the Talbot County Sheriffs Department and the Maryland State Police, arrived and Sally apprised them of the situation. Sally then secured the perimeter of the villa and stayed there until 5:00 A.M.

While Sally was checking the room out, Officer Craig went around to the front of the building to help evacuate other guests and to speak with Philip Parker, who said he was the person who pulled Stephen Hricko out of the room and onto the deck. As Parker and Craig were talking, Kimberly approached Craig. She was holding her cell phone in her left hand. She kept saying she wanted "to see the body," although she hadn't yet been told that Steve was dead.

Craig told her that the rescue squad was with him. He said Kim was at times hysterical and then despondent.

"She was very upset and could not stand without assistance," Craig said.

Craig put her in his police car and tried to calm her down. Philip Parker told Craig that he could bring Kim to his room so police could talk to her. With the help of Philip Parker's mother, Bonnie, Craig brought Kim to room 1016 in the main building. Once in the room, Kim asked Officer Craig to call Steve's best friend, Mike Miller, which he did. Craig told Miller that the fire marshal would be coming to speak to Kim about the fire. After several minutes Kim went to lie down on one of the beds and fell asleep briefly. When she awoke after a few minutes, she again began to ask about her husband's condition.

Also on the scene in the early-morning hours of February 15 was state police trooper Clay Hartness, who was assigned to the Easton Barracks. Hartness arrived at Harbourtowne around 1:30 A.M. and immediately went to the back of room 506, where he spoke with members of the St. Michaels Fire Department, who informed him of the death of Stephen Hricko. Hartness looked around and saw the badly burned man lying on the back porch with his head partially inside the open sliding glass doors. Hartness then went inside the room and surveyed the damage. After exiting the room, Hartness was met by Deputy Scott Kakabar, of the Talbot County Sheriffs Department, who initially contacted the state police. Kakabar brought Hartness up to speed on the investigation. Several hours later, the state police took over the investigation.

Hartness contacted Father Paul Jennings, the state police chaplain, and the two men went to room 1016 to notify Kim formally of her husband's death. When they got there, they discovered that the Parkers were in room 1016 and Kimberly was in an adjoining room, standing near the glass windows at the far end of the room. Jennings introduced himself and Trooper Hartness and asked Kim to sit down on the edge of the bed so he could talk to her. When she was seated, Jennings knelt down in front of her so he could talk to her face-to-face. He told her Stephen was dead.

"I found her in an agitated state and apparently slightly intoxicated," Hartness said. "Upon learning of her husband's death, she exhibited little reaction beyond a few muffled sobs and moans."

Jennings agreed that Kim showed very little emotion.

"Her response was not very emotional," Jennings testified later. "I was kneeling and Trooper Hartness was standing next to her and then he asked her what happened and she proceeded to tell us her version of the story."

Kim told Hartness that after leaving the murder-mystery production, she and Steve bought some beer from the bar and returned to their room. Once in the room Steve began pressuring her for sex, she said. When she refused, Steve became "pushy" and was "groping" her. She said she continued to resist Steve's advances and then they started arguing. She told Hartness "I didn't want to get into it, so I got my keys and my purse, got in the car, and left." She said she drove to Easton looking for the home of some friends, but she said she wasn't familiar with the area and never found the house. She said she couldn't even find Route 50 and had to get directions back to St. Michaels. Kim told Hartness that when she got back to Harbourtowne, she realized she didn't have her electronic key card to get back into her room.

She said she remembered that she and Steve had

been using the sliding glass door and thought it might still be unlocked, so she went around to the back of the complex. Kim said she pushed the door open and was confronted by thick smoke. She said she screamed, pushed back the curtain, and felt around for the light switch, but couldn't find it. She told the trooper she ran to the other rooms and knocked on the doors, screaming for help, but no one answered. Next she drove to the main building and went into the lobby, screaming that her room was on fire. She said several people who were in the lobby quickly ran to her room. She told Hartness she tried to go back to the room, but she was stopped by "someone in a uniform."

While Hartness and Jennings were with Kimberly, Deputy Scott Kakabar arrived to speak with her. After listening to Kim's version of the events leading up to Steve's death, Kakabar called the Maryland State Police Criminal Investigation Division and the Maryland State Police Crime Laboratory.

Fire investigator Mike Mulligan, a bomb technician and a canine handler, was also called to the scene before the state police arrived to take over the case. Mulligan came to Harbourtowne, sometime after 2:00 A.M., with Bear, a black Lab, trained to detect explosives and accelerants at a fire scene.

Mulligan was called because the fire investigator in charge of the scene, Paul Schlotterbeck, was suspicious of the fire from the beginning. Schlotterbeck thought there was a possibility that the fire was set and that Steve had been murdered. That was the reason he called in the state police and the sheriff's department, as well as Mulligan and Bear.

Schlotterbeck thought something just wasn't quite right. And it had something to do with the way Kim conducted herself when the investigators initially talked to her. When Mulligan arrived at the scene about an hour after he was called, he conducted a test to make sure Bear was in the mood to go to work—and he was.

"What you do with a scent-detection dog is you put out a sample to see if they're working," Mulligan explained. "What I had was an eyedropper with evaporated gasoline in it and I put a drop out somewhere in the parking lot in front of the [building] and then I took the dog out of the car and took him for a little walk to see if he could detect any petroleum-based accelerants in the vicinity. And he gave me a hit where I put the drop of accelerant. The way he let me know that there was an accelerant present is he sat down and looked at me. He was on play reward, not food reward, which means I threw a little ball for him, and that was his reward for doing that work."

Next Mulligan took Bear into Kim and Steve's room. When he first entered the room, he stood for a minute in the foyer and noticed that there was a heavy deposit of soot in the room, and he knew that the room had been filled with a lot of smoke. He looked around and noticed that although the windows were black, they had not been burned by the fire.

"There wasn't much flame damage to the room—not as much as I would normally see in the course of my work," Mulligan said. "You usually find a room has burned further than this one. This fire smothered itself out because there was a [low level of oxygen] and therefore the fire damage was relatively minor."

When Mulligan walked into the main room, which was approximately twenty feet by thirteen feet, he observed two double beds that were separated by a nightstand. The headboards were attached to the front wall. A wooden entertainment center with a television in it was located against the back wall and there was a masonry hearth in front of the first bed. There was a small metallic wood-burning stove sitting on the hearth. The doors to the stove were open and Mulligan could see the remains of a store-bought "easy light" log wrapper among the warm embers in the stove.

Past the hearth and wood-burning stove, along the back wall, was a sliding glass door that led to a covered wooden deck. In the corner, past the sliding door, was a padded chair. A heating unit/air conditioner was on the side wall behind the padded chair. There was a window with curtains on the side wall. There was also a desk located close to the heating unit.

When Bear first entered the room, he indicated he detected an accelerant on the sliding door. Mulligan later found out that when Parker dragged Steve out of the room, he left him near the sliding door for a short time before dragging the body out farther onto the back deck.

"I suspect that was what the dog was smelling," Mulligan said.

Bear then detected some kind of petroleum-based accelerant at a spot in between the room's two beds, which Mulligan later determined was the fire's point of origin. However, because lab tests did not detect any accelerant—Mulligan said it probably evaporated—he was not able to testify at trial as to what the dog detected.

"Dogs are like people—they get up on the wrong side of the bed some days and they don't want to work, so you have to go on the handler's ability to read the dog—whether he's working well, or not," Mulligan said. "That day I think he was on the money—he had something there. Either I didn't collect the evidence properly, or I didn't recover enough of it so the lab could identify it, or it sat in the lab too long and it evaporated—but I think something was there. The dog's ability to detect parts per million is more sensitive than some of the equipment they have in the lab."

Mulligan explained that the minute a light accelerant—like the fluid in a cigarette lighter, or almost any type of petroleum-based accelerant, whether it's gasoline, or diesel fuel, or kerosene—is exposed to the air, it starts to evaporate.

"The lighter it is, the faster it's going to evaporate," he said.

And once you put a match to it, that type of accelerant will burn up in the resulting fire.

Both Mulligan and the state police believed Kimberly staged the scene to make it look as if Steve, who was drinking heavily, she claimed, had been masturbating. When Steve was found, his pants were down slightly and his penis was exposed—and it looked like he accidentally had set himself on fire. And there was a copy of *Playboy* magazine next to him. They later theorized she got him in a compromising position by promising him sex, then injected him with a powerful muscle relaxant, succinylcholine chloride, which is rapidly processed by the body and therefore undetectable.

"I think his heart was still pumping, but the drug shut down the ability of the diaphragm to pump air in and out of his lungs," Mulligan said. "The drug stops his ability to breathe when she shoots him up with it, but even though his lungs aren't working, he had a certain amount of oxygen in his bloodstream, in his brain, so his heart is going to keep pumping. Just think how long you can hold your breath underwater—at least a minute or two. Steve could have known what was happening, but it depends on how soon she set him on fire after she injected him with the drug. If she waited four or five minutes before she lit him on fire, then there was a good chance he was unconscious before she sets him on fire. But if she gives him the shot, and as soon as he's immobilized, she torches him up, [and] then she burns him alive, he's conscious," he said.

"My suspicion is she used something like that, like lighter fluid, and poured it on his face, and right around the pillow his head was on, to get the fire going," Mulligan said. "I think it's backed up by the way his shirt was burned. It seems to me she hated him— she just didn't want to kill him, she wanted to embarrass him in death as much as she could. It fits—the head of his penis was pulled out above his pajama bottoms, like he was masturbating and the fact that she placed a *Playboy* next to him—it fits to me."

In the Hrickos' room Mulligan worked Bear around the far wall, up around the far bed and then in between the two beds, and when he came to what he later determined was the point of origin of the fire, Bear gave him a hit.

"It was a real hard show that he was detecting some kind of petroleum-based substance right there," Mulligan said. "I gave him a reward and worked him through the rest of the room, as small as it was, but he didn't give me more indications that there were accelerants there."

When he was finished, Mulligan took Bear back outside and walked him around the parking lot and the dog again hit on the sample Mulligan had left out there originally—indicating that he was indeed working well. Mulligan then put Bear back in the car.

In the meantime the state police were beginning to show up and a couple of them went to interview Kim.

At this point Schlotterbeck asked Mulligan to determine the fire's point of origin, which he concluded was the spot between the two beds where the dog detected some kind of accelerant. Schlotterbeck also asked Mulligan to figure out what caused the fire.

"By that time our supervisor, Jake Kinhart, had arrived on the scene from his home in Salisbury, and with Jake's help I did the origin-and-cause investigation of the room," Mulligan said.

"You're looking for where the fire began, and once you determine the point of origin, you look for what the ignition source was. And the way those investigations are done is you go from the amount of least damage to the amount of most damage—the theory behind that is where the most damage is the fire has burned the longest," Mulligan said. "A least-to-most assessment of the fire damage [in the Hrickos' room] led to a point approximately three inches from the corner of the double bed nearest the bathroom."

Mulligan noticed an accumulation of burned debris at the foot of this bed, in the center aisle between the two double beds. At this particular point the fire had burned down through the carpet and padding. Mulligan also observed deep charring on two wooden blocks that kept the legs of the bed off the carpet. The charring was on the side of the blocks closest to the center aisle.

"There were two-by-four blocks that they used to hold the bed up and the sides of the two-by-fours that were facing where Stephen's head was lying were charred and the char on that side nearest the center aisle was much deeper than the char on the other side," Mulligan said. "The wooden bottom framing of the box spring had deep char from the corner nearest that point and for approximately fifteen inches toward the head of that bed. It was scorched from one corner almost to the corner near the wall separating the main room from the bathroom."

Mulligan said the bedspread was destroyed by the fire except for the portion that was farthest away from the point of origin. There was a narrow scorch on the headboard of this bed along the wall and through a glass picture frame on the wall. The scorch mark began on the mattress at the spot where a pillow would normally be placed. The heat cracked the glass in the scorched picture frame. The fuel source for the fire creating this scorch was traced to a pillow left on the bed. This was confirmed by the melted remains of the fiberfill used in the pillows that Mulligan observed on the carpet and the base of the headboard below the scorch.

"I believe Kim took [two] pillows and put [them] under her husband's head, but one of them was left on the bed at the headboard," Mulligan said. "There was a burn pattern on the wall and the heat from that pillow burning cracked the picture frame that was right above it. And when we looked on the floor under that burn pattern, we found a brown glop, like melted plastic. And there was also that same melted plastic at the point of origin and we had a suspicion that that was probably from the melted pillow."

Later that morning, Mulligan, Kinhart, and State Trooper Richard Fey, from the crime lab, used one of the other pillows in the room that hadn't burned to see what would happen if it was exposed to a flame.

"We did a burn test on it that morning. Out in the back, on the water side of the complex," Mulligan said. "At first we held a match under it or a cigarette lighter, or something like that with a small flame—and nothing happened. And somehow in the parking lot we found a newspaper and we rolled the newspaper in the shape of a torch, set the newspaper on fire, and then held that under the pillow; and when we did, the pillow burned very hot and it melted into the consistency of what we had found at the point of origin and also under the headboard."

In the room Mulligan also observed two nearly full bottles of beer, as well as a wallet, keys, and an electronic key card on the nightstand in between the two beds.

"Significantly, a plastic Pepsi-Cola soda bottle with a paper label was centrally located, away from the front wall, on the nightstand," Mulligan said. "The heat radiating from the point of origin melted this plastic soda bottle to a degree that it folded over toward the point of origin, so that the top of the soda bottle would point in the direction of the point of origin. This plastic soda bottle serves as a pointer from the nightstand to the fire's point of origin."

Mulligan and his team looked at all the burn patterns in the room and decided the scorch spot on the rug in front of the woodstove and between the two beds was where the fire started. When Mulligan looked closer at the burned debris at the point of origin, he noticed a circular swatch of what appeared to be cotton gauze, approximately two inches in diameter. That brown gauzelike fiber—later determined to be a piece of the pillowcase—was connected to the brownish ceramic-looking deposit, which Mulligan determined was the remains of a pillow.

"The approximately two-inch circular section of unburned pillow fiber matched up with an area on the rear of the victim's head," Mulligan said. "An approximately two-inch-in-diameter area of the victim's hair was not burned off the back of his head."

Fire damage in the room was confined to the bed, the headboard, and the wall above the headboard. The carpet was scorched or burned by a piece of the burning bedspread that had fallen down onto the floor. It appeared the burned debris on the floor was the remains of two pillows, Mulligan said. Stephen Hricko was burned from his chest up to the top of his head. The well-insulated room contained the smoke and smothered the fire before it could spread any farther. An unburned pillow—the fourth in the room—was found near the fire's point of origin. A *Playboy* magazine was opened on this pillow at the time of the fire. Mulligan knew this because the pillow was covered with soot except for the area that had been covered by the magazine. The *Playboy* was opened to a page revealing the photograph of a nude woman. Beneath the pillow Mulligan discovered an eight-pack of Backwoods cigars. One cigar was missing from the package.

Later, after looking at a photo of the scene, Mulligan made an eerie observation.

"I noticed from a black-and-white photo of the scene that you could see the silhouette of where Stephen was lying. The soot that came down during the fire fell everywhere in the room, but where he was lying, not as much soot fell there because it was protected by his legs. . . . And when you look at the photograph, you can see this eerie shadow of where he was lying, which put his head right at the point where that scorch mark was," Mulligan said.

Chapter 3

Around 4:00 A.M., on February 15, Corporal Keith Elzey, the on-call criminal investigator for the Easton State Police Barracks, and Sergeant Karen Alt, also a state trooper, arrived at Harbourtowne to take over the investigation. At that time the state police did not have a homicide unit, but rather a special investigative unit that assisted the local barracks.

After getting briefed by fire and police personnel, Alt and Elzey went into the lobby of Harbourtowne and interviewed Philip Parker and Elaine Phillips, who told the officers what transpired earlier. Alt also spoke with Bonnie Parker, Philip's mother. Bonnie told Alt about something that happened that she found a bit odd.

According to Bonnie, when she arrived at the Hrickos' room, Philip's fiancée, Traci, was already there waiting in the parking lot in front of the room for Philip and Elaine, who were around back. When Bonnie went up to Traci, the young woman whispered in her ear that the victim was dead. Bonnie told Alt that she didn't think Kimberly, who was standing at the front door of the room, was close enough to hear what Traci said. She said she thought it was strange that Kim kept saying she "wanted to see his body," rather than saying she wanted to see Steve or Stephen or her husband, especially since no one had told her Steve was dead. Bonnie also told Alt that she thought it was unusual that Kim stayed in the front of the building, rather than go around back because that's where Philip and Elaine entered the room.

While in the lobby, Elzey also spoke with Steve's best friend since junior high, Mike Miller, who was Harbourtowne's golf-course grounds superintendent.

Mike and his wife, Maureen, were supposed to watch Sarah while Steve and Kimberly were at Harbourtowne, but at the last minute Kim called to say Sarah was going to spend the night with a friend and she and Steve were coming down by themselves. Kim told the Millers they didn't have to worry about watching Sarah.

"I was pregnant at the time—it was early in the pregnancy and I wasn't feeling all that well, so we were going to just stay in anyway," Maureen said. "When we found out we weren't watching Sarah, we went out to dinner and we were thinking about going down to Harbourtowne—we hadn't been seeing them much as a couple—to see if everything was going okay. We thought we'd have a drink with them, but then we thought, no, let's just let them be, and if things go as planned, it will be a nice romantic weekend for them. So we just went back to the house."

Shortly after 1:30 A.M., on February 15, the Millers' telephone rang. Thinking something was wrong with Mike's dad, Maureen quickly answered it. The caller asked for Mike. It was someone from Harbourtowne who told Maureen that there'd been a fire at the resort and that Steve had been badly injured. The caller said Kim was asking if Mike could go to the resort to be with her. Maureen handed the phone to Mike, who said he'd be right there. Mike hung up the phone and started getting dressed. But since old habits die hard, Mike turned on the television and started searching for a weather report.

"It's this thing with golf superintendents that whenever they leave the house, they have to know what the weather is, and Mike was so out of it that he turned the TV on looking for the weather," Maureen explained. "I said, 'What are you doing? You have to get down to Harbourtowne.' He said, 'I don't know what I'm doing, I'm half-asleep.' So he finished dressing and left."

Not knowing what was going on, Maureen started worrying about Kim. So she called Mike back into the house—he was outside scraping the ice off his windshield—and called the general manager of Harbourtowne to ask what was happening.

"Maureen, I think he's dead," the general manager told her.

Maureen put the telephone down and told Mike to hurry and go to Harbourtowne because Steve was probably dead. She asked Mike to call her as soon as he got there. Later, she realized she should have let Mike find out about Steve's death when he got to Harbourtowne so he wouldn't have to think about it while he was driving.

Mike ran back outside, jumped in his truck, and flew down to Harbourtowne, getting there in half the time it would normally take him. All the while he kept thinking how weird it was that there was a fire in the Hrickos' room.

In shock Maureen got back on the line with the general manager and asked him what happened. Instead of answering her, the general manager started questioning her about Steve's behaviors.

"Did Steve smoke cigars?" he asked.

Maureen said no, Steve would never smoke.

"Well, apparently he was smoking tonight and fell asleep and lit the room on fire and he died in the fire," the general manager said.

Maureen told him Steve would never smoke, ever. The general manager explained that Kim said he'd also been drinking a lot that evening.

"That doesn't sound like Steve, either," Maureen said. "I've never known him to be drunk."

"Something's not right here, Maureen, and Mike needs to get here," the general manager said.

Maureen told him Mike was already on his way.

Maybe Steve was drinking too much and maybe he was smoking cigars, Maureen thought. After all, the Millers hadn't seem much of him lately and he was under a tremendous amount of pressure because of his marriage. But even though the Steve that Maureen knew would never have done that, she just put the general manager's questions out of her mind.

Around 2:30 A.M. or so, Maureen decided to call Mike's parents in Pennsylvania to ask them to come down to Easton. She knew if Steve was dead, Mike was certainly going to need his parents. Mike's parents left their home in State College about an hour after Maureen's call. Maureen also called Mike's friend Ken and asked him to go to Harbourtowne so Mike wouldn't be alone.

When Mike arrived at Harbourtowne, he parked his truck in front of the main lobby. As he got out of his truck, he saw people standing outside the hotel.

"Somebody from Harbourtowne was there and said that there was a fire down in the room, that

Steve was in the fire, and that Kim had come into the lobby to report the fire, and at that point she was up in one of the other rooms," Mike said. "They told me Elaine Phillips and her cousin, Philip Parker, pulled Steve out. Philip's family was at Harbourtowne for the weekend and they had a suite of rooms, and Elaine told me Kim was in her aunt's room."

Immediately Mike ran up to the room and knocked on the door. Elaine Phillips's aunt Bonnie Parker opened the door and Mike asked for Kim.

"It was all kind of surreal. I was trying to figure out what the hell went on and what was going on," Mike recalled. "And I walked into this room and I didn't recognize these people and this woman said Kim's in there and pointed to an adjoining room. And then she asked me if I wanted a drink. I don't remember if I took a drink or not. And when I walked in—it was cold. Something felt wrong when I walked in that room."

As he stood in the room, Mike flashed back to something that had happened several hours earlier. While Mike was washing dishes at home, he picked up a sharp knife and had a weird feeling that somebody was hurt, or somebody had been stabbed with a knife, and all he wanted to do was put the knife down.

"It was just a weird feeling," he remembered. "And then to have this happen."

When Mike went into the room where Kim was staying, he noticed that she was lying on her side, her back toward him, on the bed farthest away from the door. Mike walked over to Kim and she sort of got up and looked at him.

"Oh, thanks for coming," she said as she started toward him.

Mike was struck by Kimberly's utter lack of emotion. Sure, people grieve differently and maybe she was in shock, but it didn't seem like that was the case—she was totally unemotional.

"You would have thought, knowing how long we'd known each other, there would have been more there," Mike said. "She didn't even give me a hug when I hugged her, she just stood there. She was just cold. She was void of any emotion. It didn't feel right, something was wrong. Something weird or evil."

Mike sat with Kim for a bit, but she didn't say anything to him and he didn't know what to say to her. Soon she went back and lay down on the bed and eventually fell asleep—which Mike also thought was weird. Mike then went downstairs to talk to the people from Harbourtowne to find out what was going on and whether or not Steve was alive. Mike soon learned that his best friend since junior high was dead.

"Somewhere along the way someone said something about Kim saying Steve had been smoking cigars and I said that's impossible because he doesn't smoke," Mike explained. "And so I started hearing these things that she was feeding to these other people. But to me it just wasn't clicking—something wasn't right—what she was trying to say was Steve was just not Steve and that he had been smoking cigars and he had been drinking. I said there's just no way."

The more Mike heard about what Kim was saying regarding the events preceding Steve's death, the more he knew something just wasn't right—and the more he began to think Kim had something to do with Steve's death. In fact, Mike had a gut feeling the moment he walked into her room that she was somehow involved with the death of his best friend.

"When I told Elzey [that] Steve didn't smoke cigars, he said, 'Really?' And I said, 'No, he didn't.'"

Elzey told Mike that during the investigation of

the Hrickos' room, officers found a package of cigars, an empty bottle of champagne, and some empty beer cans. But Mike again told him that Steve just didn't smoke. And, he said, there was no way he would have been drinking heavily that weekend.

"Steve told me on the phone before they went to Harbourtowne that he wanted to do this for Kim—it would be something special to rekindle the relationship," Mike recalled. "Steve viewed it as their first date and he wanted it to be special and he wanted to take her down there and show her a nice time, and he told me, 'I'm a red-blooded male and Kim and I haven't been together sexually for a long time, and it is in the back of my mind that that's what I want to do, but it's probably one of the farthest things from my mind as well. It's just a chance for us to get away and kind of rekindle our relationship.'"

Steve told Mike if sex with Kimberly happened, it happened, but that really wasn't the reason he planned the weekend. And, according to Mike, contrary to what Kimberly was telling police and anybody else who would listen, Steve never said he and Kim agreed not to have sex while they were at Harbourtowne.

Steve also told Mike he was on medication for his depression and he wasn't drinking because of the medication. So when Mike started hearing that Steve was smoking cigars and drinking and trying to force himself on his wife, and then turning to *Playboy* when that didn't work out, he knew Kimberly was lying.

"This was all about Steve trying to start up the relationship, so why would he go down there and totally blow it?" Mike asked. "Why would he get all liquored up and force sex on her? It just didn't add up."

The whole *Playboy* thing was ludicrous, Mike said.

And the way the *Playboy* was laid out next to Steve's body really smacked of a setup.

"I had never known Steve to view pornography. I mean, I can remember in high school, but he wasn't an addict and he never viewed it online," Mike said. "And I know they were given a bottle of champagne and Kimberly said he drank it, but Steve drinks beer and he chewed tobacco—Skoal—that's the only tobacco product he used. He never smoked in the time I knew him. From junior high school to high school to college, I can't recall him smoking a cigar."

A little after 5:00 A.M. Alt and Elzey, along with Deputy Fire Marshal Paul Schlotterbeck, went up to room 1016 to interview Kimberly, who had been sleeping most of the morning. After she woke up, Kimberly told the officers pretty much the same story she had been telling everyone else, but with a few additional details.

Kimberly explained that she and Steve had been having marital problems for about three months and decided to attend the Valentine's weekend hoping to revive their marriage. According to Kim, Steve got "sloppy drunk" during the evening, drinking all but one glass from the complimentary bottle of champagne that was left in their room, as well as drinking wine at dinner, more champagne, and beer. And, after the dinner show, the couple purchased more beer to drink back at their room. Kim told the officers that Steve was taking several types of prescription medicine for his depression, including Xanax. She said he was also taking the over-the-counter liquid cold medicine Theraflu. According to Kim, Steve took the Xanax and Theraflu around 7:00 P.M., just before they went to dinner. Kim also told the officers that her husband regularly chewed tobacco and always smoked cigars when he drank. However, she said she didn't think Steve bought or brought any cigarettes or cigars with him to Harbour-towne. She said she didn't, either.

Kim said when she and Steve got back to their room they watched the movie *Tommy Boy* and then started watching the 11:00 P.M. news when Steve began "pawing" her. Kim said she was surprised because she and Steve had agreed there would be no sex during the weekend. She also said she was surprised at her husband's advances because when he wanted sex he usually turned to pornography, not her. She said she left the room because of the fight over Steve's drunken behavior, adding that it wasn't a physical fight. Kim explained that Steve had never been physically abusive toward her.

As Kimberly was relating the rest of her story, Alt asked her if she was able to continue and let her know that the officers understood that she had been through a great deal. Alt gave Kim a glass of water and asked her if she wanted anything else, or if she needed to use the bathroom. Kim didn't take any breaks when offered, nor did she ask for any herself. Both Alt and Elzey said that Kim didn't seem to be either emotional or in shock.

"During the interview with Kimberly, I noticed that she exhibited little reaction," Elzey said. "However, she was continually holding a damp face towel to her mouth while she periodically sobbed and moaned."

Alt noted that Kimberly offered very detailed information to police—information that they had not asked for, and that was very unexpected.

"Kimberly told us that her husband smoked only when he had been drinking and then he smoked cigars," Alt said. "She made a point of saying that she had seen no cigarettes or cigars in there, but added, 'I did not pack for him.' This information was given like the information about the pornography, it was unasked for and a very unexpected detail."

Deputy Fire Marshal Schlotterbeck was also present while Alt and Elzey questioned Kimberly. When they finished interviewing her, it was Schlotterbeck's turn to ask her some questions about the fire. First he asked her if she or Stephen had used the wood-burning stove. Kimberly said they had burned two logs, each of which was in a wrapper. She said they lit the logs with matches that were in the room. Kim told Schlotterbeck that when she got back to her room and tried to enter through the patio door, she was hit with a blast of heat. However, she didn't see any light or glow in the room. She added that the smoke "stunk bad" and that it had a "burned plastic synthetic smell." Kim also told Schlotterbeck that Steve hadn't been smoking anything in the room.

When the interviews were completed, Kimberly told Alt that she wanted to see Steve's body. Even though Alt discouraged her, Kimberly insisted, so Alt went back to room 506 to arrange a viewing. When she got there, another officer gave her the open package of Backwoods cigars, which was minus one cigar. Alt returned to room 1016 to talk to Kim again, but she had to wake her up first. Alt showed Kim the package of cigars and asked her if it looked familiar. Kim said she had seen the package at home, but not in the room at Harbourtowne. Alt then mentioned to Kim that Mike Miller said Steve didn't smoke. Kim responded that Steve had been doing a lot of things over the previous two months that he had never done before. In fact, Kim said it was like living with a stranger.

"Her expression and tone indicated this was not a favorable change," Alt said. "She mentioned Stephen 'smothering' her recently and this seemed oddly negative in time and expression, also especially considering the proximity of his corpse."

Alt again asked Kim if she wanted to see Steve's body, telling her that she wouldn't want to see her husband under the same circumstances because it would be very unpleasant. When Kim didn't answer, Alt told her straight out that Steve had been burned very badly. Kim looked away and said she didn't want to see him then. Alt then returned to the Hrickos' room and helped the funeral home personnel move Steve's body to their van so they could take it to the medical examiner's office in Baltimore. Alt returned to the Easton Barracks to prepare a press release for the media about Stephen Hricko's death, while troopers Elzey and Fey were assigned to witness the postmortem exam. They provided Dr. David Fowler, the medical examiner, with a brief synopsis of the events leading up to Steve's death.

About 8:30, on Sunday evening, Elzey, who was off-duty, received information pertaining to Steve's death from Sergeant Tom Williams, of the Maryland State Police. Williams told Elzey that one of Kim's friends had called him to say that Kimberly might have killed her husband by injecting him with a drug that would paralyze his muscles, preventing him from moving and leaving him helpless. After talking with Williams, Elzey called the on-duty officer, advised him of the situation, and asked him to tell the medical examiner not to release Steve's body.

Chapter 4

Shortly after Mike's parents arrived at the Millers' house around 8:00 or 8:30, Sunday morning, Maureen drove to Harbourtowne to take care of Kim. At this point Maureen knew that Steve was dead.

"I had made a couple more phone calls and Mike told me Steve had died. He said they were [in the Hrickos' room] and they were going to have to go through all this stuff, and Kim was up in another hotel room waiting for me, and could I please come and take her home," Maureen said.

When Maureen got to Harbourtowne, she went straight to the Parkers' room, where Kim was staying. The first thing she noticed was Kim's brother, Matt (pseudonym), sitting in between the two beds, crying hysterically. What struck her was that Matt was completely falling apart—bawling and crying—while Kim, on the other hand, was sitting in a chair at the far side of the room, absolutely still. It was almost as if she were catatonic.

"I was hysterical to a point that I ran to her to try to comfort her and put my arms around her. But she walked right by me and walked into the bathroom and started like dry heaving. And then she came out and said, 'Can you take me home?'" Maureen recalled. "And I'm like, 'Are you okay, do you want to talk about this?'"

Kim told Maureen she was fine and that she just wanted to go home. Now Maureen was beginning to think Kim was acting really weird. She asked Matt what was going on, but he was so hysterical he couldn't even answer her. So she told Kim to pack up her things so they could leave. Kim told her everything was already packed up and ready to go. She said she and Mike and Matt had retrieved the Hrickos' belongings from room 506 before Maureen arrived.

On the drive home Kimberly didn't say a word. She didn't even cry. It was as if she were dead, but in a live body, Maureen said. The only time Kim opened her mouth was when Maureen needed directions to get from the highway to Kim's house in Laurel. When they arrived at the Hrickos' house, Maureen took Kim inside and unloaded the car. The pair then had to figure out how to get Sarah, who, they thought, was still at her friend's house, and bring her home. Kim's brother had called their mother, Lois Wolf, and she was on her way to Laurel, so they decided to wait for her to arrive before making arrangements to pick up Sarah. They also contacted the counselor Kim had been seeing and asked her to come to the house to help Kim tell Sarah about her dad.

While they were waiting for Kim's mother and the counselor to arrive, Kim still wasn't talking much. She just sat on the couch and started rocking back and forth. Finally Kim spoke to Maureen and told her what happened before Steve died.

Kim explained that when she and Steve went back to their room, they got into an argument. After that, she left Harbourtowne, but didn't know where to go. She said she got confused and couldn't find the Millers' house.

"And I said, 'Kim, you were just at my house two-and-a-half months ago, how could you not find my house?'" Maureen said. "Why didn't you call me to find the house?"

"I didn't want to wake you up," Kim responded. "I couldn't find your house, so I just drove around for a while."

"But you would have woken me up when you got here," Maureen said.

"That was a red flag—that she got lost—because she had driven to my house from the club the night of the bachelorette party two-and-a-half months before. Not to mention, her brother lived down the street from my house," Maureen said.

Kim said when she couldn't find the Millers' house, she decided to go back to Harbourtowne.

"When I got back to the hotel, I remembered I forgot my key. And I remembered we had been walking in the back, so I walked around back to the sliding door, hoping that it was still unlocked and I could get in that way," Kim told Maureen. "But when I went and pulled the door open, this huge heat rush came out and I knew the room was on fire. So I drove to the lobby and I ran inside and asked for help, and everybody just ran past me and I went down there and nobody would tell me if he was hurt, or if he was alive, or if he was dead, or what was going on."

"Didn't you go into the room to see if Steve was okay?" Maureen asked.

"No. I knew the room was too hot."

Then Kim said something that caught Maureen off guard.

"They think that I did it," she said. "They wouldn't let me see him. They wouldn't even tell me how bad he was hurt, or if he was dead or alive. They treated me like I was a criminal."

Maureen thought it odd that Kim could only focus on herself.

"It was all about her," Maureen said. "About her and how mean they all were to her. I'm looking at her and I'm thinking, 'Man, everybody really does grieve differently.'"

Maureen just kept telling herself that Kim was in shock and she had no idea what she was saying. But Kim still wasn't crying and she just kept saying she was tired and she wanted to go to sleep, so she fell asleep on the couch before anyone else arrived. While Kim was sleeping, Maureen cleaned up the house. When she was done, she found Kim's address book and started calling people she thought should know about Steve.

"I called her work and said she wouldn't be there. I called CASA because she was a child advocate and said she wouldn't be available for a while. I called all her friends I could remember," Maureen said. "I called Jenny Gowen. Jenny acted really weird on the phone and said she couldn't come right over because she was busy. I said. 'Fine, come when you can.' Then I spoke with Rachel McCoy. I told Rachel that something really, really bad happened at Harbourtowne the night before—that there was a fire and Steve was killed in the fire. I asked her if she could come over and help me take care of Kim. Then there was total dead silence on the phone and Rachel asked me to tell her what happened one more time, so I told her again, and then she said she couldn't talk to me right then and she hung up."

Maureen was really confused about the reactions of Jenny and Rachel.

"I'm thinking, 'What is wrong with these people?' My God, where are all these people who are supposed to be her friends? What's going on here? Am I the only friend she has?"

Kim also called Jenny Gowen to tell her about Steve and ask her to come to see her. Jenny said she'd be over later. Immediately after speaking with Kim, Jenny called their mutual friend, Norma Walz, who now lived in Washington State, to tell her that Stephen Hricko had died in a fire.

Jenny told Norma that Kim had called her to tell her about Steve's death and she was on her way to Kim's house with her husband, Sean, and she'd call Norma back with more information as soon as she could.

"Do you think Kim did it?" Norma asked Jenny before hanging up.

"Yes," Jenny replied.

"At this point, and with very little information—Jenny and I didn't know any details—our immediate conclusion was Steve's death was not an accident and Kim must be involved," Norma said.

As soon as she finished talking to Jenny, Norma called the Maryland State Police and spoke with Sergeant Karen Alt. She gave Jenny's contact information to Alt and explained that they were scared that Kim had killed Steve and wanted to come forward with the information.

Coincidentally, about an hour before Kim called Jenny to tell her Steve was dead, Norma and Jenny had been discussing Kim's recent behavior. Jenny, it seemed, was really bothered by the way Kim had been acting toward Steve over the past two months or so. During their conversation Jenny shared something with Norma that made her skin crawl.

"Jenny said Kim was feeling like she would never be able to divorce Steve and it would be easier if he were dead," Norma said. "I told Jenny that people say things like that, thinking it would be easier, but it wouldn't. And the likelihood of Steve dying at thirty-five years old just wasn't going to happen."

Jenny told Norma she just didn't know if she could continue being Kim's friend.

Jenny, Norma, and Kim met at Holy Cross Hospital in Silver Spring, Maryland, where they worked in the main operating room as surgical technologists. They had been friends for several years. When they were together, the three friends often discussed what made them, and other people, tick. But Norma felt that she and Jenny shared a stronger bond of friendship and trust than she shared with Kim.

"I've always described Jenny and I and our conversations as being able to think out loud with each other," Norma said. "Jenny and I don't have to worry about saying something stupid to each other because we know each other's hearts and there is a trust that exists—a trust that has not existed the same way with Kim."

Still, Norma said Kim had always been a great friend to her and Jenny.

"I would describe Kim as a strong, intelligent woman who knows what she wants and doesn't stop until she is satisfied with the outcome," Norma said.

And Norma and Jenny admired Kim for her know-how and "go-get-'em" attitude. For example, Norma said because Holy Cross Hospital was a Catholic hospital, it had refused to pay for any type of birth control products for its employees, regardless of an employee's insurance plan.

"Kim thought this was outrageous and unlawful and spent may hours contacting women's groups to get the policy overturned," Norma said. "Kim was always very aware of her rights as an employee and gave Jenny and I advice sometimes on some management problems we had at work. Jenny also noted how well Kim could work the system and could beat people at their own game."

Nevertheless, Norma said, there was a lot about Kim that she and Jenny just didn't understand and a lot they didn't know.

"There was a lot of things Kim didn't share—her marriage to Steve was one of them," Norma said.

Norma recalled a time early in their relationship when she invited Kim and her family over for dinner. Norma was really surprised when Kim showed up with Sarah, but not Steve.

"She made some excuse that he had family in town or he was tired, I don't remember the exact excuse, but I remember how odd it seemed that he wasn't with her," Norma said.

Norma and Jenny often discussed Kim's relationship with Steve, and why he was not really a social person, but they didn't feel they could talk about it with Kim.

"Kim would say things like 'he's shy,' or 'he gets up early, so at the end of the day, he's tired and he just likes to chill out at home,'" Norma said.

Norma and Jenny, though, concluded that people could be shy, but when they were adults, they just needed to "get over it" and at least be social.

"Jenny and I found Steve to be rude and antisocial— the complete opposite of Kim," Norma said.

Whenever Norma or Jenny would try to talk to Kim about her marriage, she would just blow them off, saying she and Steve got along great. Even though they were different, she said, they complemented each other and they understood each other. To Norma and Jenny, it seemed Kim was always on the go and Steve was always at home, if he wasn't at work.

"Jenny and I would often marvel at Kim's energy and we would often wonder how she managed to do it all," Norma said. "We would also wonder if she was trying to fill some void by filling up her time, so she didn't have time to stop and think about something she didn't want to think about."

In October 1996 Norma and her husband moved to Washington State, but they still kept in close contact with Kim and Jenny by phone. The three women still maintained their great friendship. In fact, Norma and Kim were both in Jenny's wedding to Sean Gowen on November 29, 1997. Kim was the matron of honor and Norma, who stayed at the Hrickos' town house while she was in Maryland, was a bridesmaid.

During her first year in Washington, Norma and Jenny often talked about Sean's cousin Brad Winkler, who was in the marines and living at Sean's parents' house. Jenny always spoke very affectionately of Brad and how she thought he was a great guy and fun to be around.

Brad was very involved in his cousin's wedding plans and was at Jenny's bridal shower at the Hrickos' house. Like Jenny, Norma found Brad to be warm and funny and felt comfortable with him. While Norma was in Maryland, she, Kim, and Brad spent a lot of time together doing last-minute errands for Jenny's wedding. Once, when the three were together, Brad told them about his bad marriage and subsequent divorce.

"Looking back, I see how sympathetic Kim was to Brad," Norma said. "I remember her saying to me, 'That's too bad that happened to Brad, he's such a nice guy' and 'The girl who gets him will be lucky.'"

About two weeks after Norma went back home to Washington, Kim called to tell her that she and Brad were having an affair. Kim asked Norma not to be angry with her.

"She said things between her and Steve had been bad, and she asked him to go to a counselor in August, but he missed his appointment and just blew it off," Norma said. "I remember saying I didn't know things had been that bad in her marriage and I reminded her that this was a subject she would never discuss before— even with me, a good friend."

Kim admitted to Norma that she had been living a lie for a long time and she was really miserable, but she added she wasn't sure she wanted to throw away ten years of marriage. Norma encouraged Kim to stop seeing Brad until she made a decision about what she wanted to do with her life.

"It was important to her that I didn't judge her," Norma said. "I wasn't mad. I wanted her to be happy, even if it meant that she divorced Steve. But if they could work things out, that's what I wanted for her. I wasn't in a position to tell her what to do, and all she wanted was for me to listen and be a shoulder to cry on. I was willing to do that."

Although Norma wasn't angry with Kim over her affair with Brad, Jenny was really upset with her. And Kim was furious with Jenny for not supporting her. Kim felt Jenny was only worried about how the affair would affect her and her marriage to Sean. She didn't seem to care about what Kim wanted.

But Jenny was also concerned about how Kim's

affair with Brad would affect Steve. She didn't like the fact that Kim was deceiving her husband.

"Kim's point was that the affair really had nothing to do with Jenny and Jenny wasn't a 'player' in the affair," Norma said. "Kim felt Jenny's responsibility was to be a friend. So Kim felt somewhat betrayed by Jenny because she felt Jenny was being selfish."

Kim asked Norma to talk to Jenny on her behalf, which she did. Although Norma was on Kim's side, Jenny helped her see the situation in a different light. Jenny felt Kim had never been completely honest about her marriage to Steve. Now, however, Kim was sharing information with her friends that put Steve in a bad light so they would be supportive of her and her affair with Brad. Because of that, Jenny felt manipulated by Kim.

"Kim slept with Brad for the first time at Jenny and Sean's home while they were away on their honeymoon," Norma said. "Jenny was angry about this and felt she was being put in uncomfortable situations to cover for Brad and Kim. And I agreed that things were not as simple for Jenny in this situation, as Kim would like to believe."

Sometime in late December 1997, or early January 1998, Kim told Norma she was going to ask Steve for a divorce. She was planning on doing it on a particular weekend when Sarah was going to be out of town. On Sunday of that weekend, Norma called Kim, but Steve answered the telephone and said Kim wasn't home. Norma was surprised that Steve sounded so pleasant and thought maybe Kim had changed her mind about asking him for a divorce. That wasn't the case. When Kim called Norma back, she said she had asked him for a divorce and that he broke down in tears when she told him.

"He wrote her a letter later that weekend begging for a chance to change—to work things out," Norma said. "I was very impressed by the letter—she read it to me—and I was hopeful that their marriage could be saved. She told me he canceled some kind of business trip on Monday so he could get into his doctor to get a referral to a counselor."

Kim told Norma she gave Steve a week to make an appointment to see a counselor. Even though Norma thought Steve seemed sincere in his efforts to make the marriage work, Kim wasn't impressed. Kim didn't think Steve could change and she felt he was smothering her, so she continued to see Brad.

During one conversation with Kim Norma told her about an annoying life-insurance salesman who was trying to sell her family a universal life-insurance policy, when they were set on purchasing term life insurance. Kim told Norma she should buy life insurance through the insurance agency she used. Kim explained that she took out a $250,000 term life insurance policy on Steve and said it was very inexpensive, even for a smoker's policy. Norma was surprised by Kim's comments because she knew Steve didn't smoke. Kim explained that because Steve chewed tobacco, she had to get a smoker's policy.

Shortly after talking with Kim about life insurance, Norma spoke with Jenny about Kim's continued affair with Brad. Jenny was extremely frustrated because Kim was still seeing Brad and not even giving Steve a chance to change his behavior. Jenny felt like Kim was playing Steve for a fool by letting him think their marriage had a chance to survive, when it was obvious, by her actions, that Kim wanted out of the marriage. Even though Kim said she would stay married to Steve if he changed completely, she didn't mean it.

If she had meant what she said, she wouldn't have continued sleeping with Brad.

"I could hear in her voice that she couldn't stand to be around Steve," Norma said. "In my last conversation with Kim before Steve died, she sounded tired, like she was worn down by Jenny's disapproval of her actions. She said she had been in contact with some old college friends who were being more supportive of her and her position than Jenny was."

While Maureen was waiting for Kim's mom and the counselor to arrive, she was walking around Kim's place, trying to figure out what to do next. She remembered that before she and Kim left Harbourtowne, Kim wanted to go to the funeral home to see Steve.

"In fact, she was almost angry that no one would let her go to see him," Maureen said. "She wanted me to take her, but I refused. I told her that Steve was burned in the fire and that's not the way she wanted to remember him. I told her she didn't need to see him and that she could wait until the funeral home did what they needed to do before she saw him. But she was really mad. So while I was waiting, I called the morgue to see what was happening."

After Maureen finished talking with the people at the morgue, Rachel called back.

"I said, 'Oh, good, are you coming over?' But she said no and that she needed to talk to Kim immediately," Maureen said.

Maureen asked Rachel why she wasn't coming to be with Kim, but Rachel said she didn't want to talk about it and repeated her request to speak with Kim. So Maureen woke Kim up and told her Rachel was on the phone. When Kim found out that Maureen had initiated the call to Rachel, she was none too happy.

"Why did you do that?" Kim asked.

Maureen explained that she needed someone to help her take care of Kim and Sarah. Kim angrily pulled the telephone out of Maureen's hand, stormed up the stairs, went into her bedroom, and slammed the door shut.

"I'm thinking this is the strangest shit," Maureen said. "I could not figure out what was going on."

While Kim was on the phone with Rachel, Maureen called Mike on her cell phone to see how he was doing. Although Maureen wanted to go home to help her husband deal with the death of his best friend, she knew she couldn't leave Kim alone. She had to wait until Kim's mother arrived from Pennsylvania.

After almost an hour Kim emerged from her bedroom and went downstairs. She was visibly pissed off.

"She thinks I killed Steve," Kim said to Maureen.

"What would give her that crazy idea?" Maureen asked.

"Because we were out in a bar one night and I was drunk and I was mad at Steve about a fight we had and I said I wanted to kill him," Kim said. "So she thinks I killed him."

"She's crazy and that's nuts, Kim," Maureen responded. "Why would she think that over just a stupid drunk conversation? Just forget about it."

But Kim couldn't seem to forget about it. Still angry, she began to pace around the house like a caged animal. And once again she started talking about no one letting her see Steve. She was acting really crazy, but she still wasn't crying, Maureen said. Finally Kim's mother showed up with Sarah. Lois and her husband had picked Sarah up at the hospital, where she was taken after injuring herself at the home of the babysitter.

"But her mom is kind of a nervous Nellie and she was no help at all," Maureen recalled. "All she could do was talk about how high her blood pressure was and how she was going to have a nervous breakdown, and she kept saying, 'Oh, my God, what are we going to do?' And I'm thinking, 'I'm never getting out of here.'"

At long last, the counselor arrived, and Kim, her mother, and the counselor took Sarah into the family room to tell her about her dad. Wanting to let them have some privacy, Maureen went into another room.

"To this day I have never heard anything more horrible than the way Sarah cried," Maureen remembered. "She screamed so loud. It was so horrible I put my hands over my ears and hummed so I couldn't hear her."

After hearing that her father was dead, Sarah went up to her room. For the rest of the day Kim slept. Maureen couldn't understand how she could sleep at a time like that, but she figured maybe she was mentally exhausted. While Kim slept, Lois and Maureen sat around and talked. Jenny finally showed up with her husband and daughter in tow—something Maureen thought was a bit strange. But she was kind enough to bring food for everyone.

"I found out the reason Jenny wanted her family along was because she knew that Kim knew that Jenny knew that Kim killed Steve because she had told Jenny the plan beforehand," Maureen said. "And Jenny wouldn't come over alone because she thought if Kim could really go through with killing her own husband, who's to say she wouldn't kill Jenny as well to keep her quiet. She was terrified and she didn't want to come over unless her husband was with her.

And Rachel didn't want to see Kim at all because Rachel was the person Kim laid out the entire plan to and she didn't know what to do."

Like Jenny, Rachel never thought that Kim actually would go through with her plan to kill Steve. She was in a total state of shock. In fact, after Maureen called Rachel to tell her about Steve's death, Rachel called a friend who was a state trooper and asked for advice. The trooper said she had to turn Kim in.

"That's when Rachel called Kim back to say she knew Kim killed Steve," Maureen said. "But Kim denied it and said it was a total coincidence that Steve died in the same way as her plan. Kim told Rachel she didn't do it."

Sunday evening didn't go much better than the day had at the Hrickos' house. Maureen soon realized that Kim's mom wasn't in any condition to take care of Kim or Sarah, so Maureen decided to stay the night. Although she was worried about Mike, she knew that his parents would take care of him and their children.

The next day, Monday, Maureen made calls to the morgue, the funeral director, and Steve's family.

"That was not pretty," Maureen said. "I called the funeral director and told him we needed to make arrangements for the funeral. But he said he'd been in contact with the Hrickos and they were having a problem because Kim wanted Steve cremated and the Hrickos didn't, because he was Catholic."

Maureen had no idea what the funeral director was talking about, so she told him she'd talk to Kim and call him back.

Kim explained to Maureen that Steve wanted to be cremated.

"We were at Steve's grandmother's funeral and she had been cremated. While we were at the funeral,

Steve said that's what he wanted. It was clean. It was neat. It was closure. And that's what I want to do for him," Kim said.

Maureen bought Kim's explanation hook, line and sinker, so she called Steve's sister Jennifer and told her what Kim said.

"So he'll be cremated because Kim's his wife and that's what she's saying he wanted," Maureen told Jennifer. But Jennifer insisted that Steve must not be cremated, because that wasn't what the family wanted.

"I thought I was doing Kim a favor being the liaison, because she was acting like she didn't want to talk to anyone because she was too upset," Maureen recalled. "But I think it was really because she didn't want to fight with Jennifer."

After going a few rounds with Jennifer, Maureen called the morgue again and asked when the medical examiner was going to release Steve's body, so Kim could make the final funeral arrangements. Maureen was surprised when the medical examiner said he wasn't releasing Steve's body immediately because he was going to do a postmortem examination of the body in order to determine the cause of death.

"Isn't it obvious? He died in a fire," Maureen said.

The medical examiner explained it was just standard procedure and he wouldn't be releasing the body until Tuesday. Maureen then went upstairs and told Kim the medical examiner wasn't going to release the body until he performed an autopsy.

Kim went nuts. She just started flipping out.

"Why are they doing that? He was burned in a fire," said an extremely agitated Kim. "They think I killed him. They think I did something."

"Kim, they don't think you did anything, and, if anything, this will protect you, to make sure you didn't do anything," Maureen said, trying to calm Kim down. "All they're trying to do is determine what the actual cause of death was and once they determine that, it will be fine. It's not a big deal."

Even as she spoke, more little red flags were starting to go up in Maureen's mind, but she tried to put them out of her head.

"And all this time Mike's telling me something's not right here, Kim did something," Maureen said. "But I said, 'No, she didn't, Mike. You're Steve's best friend and she's his widow, and you need to operate like this is a terrible accident—you're just trying to make sense out of a bad situation.'"

Maureen, however, wasn't sure she believed her own words.

"I never told Mike about what Kim told me about the fact that she told Rachel that she wanted to kill Steve," Maureen said. "But I felt so uncomfortable about it that I called another friend and told her the situation with Rachel was making me really nervous and I didn't know what to do. I asked her if I should tell Mike and she said no, all it was going to do was add fuel to the fire that she did something, and right now we all had to just get through the funeral."

Knowing her friend was right, Maureen decided to wait before she talked to Mike about the whole Rachel issue.

Chapter 5

Michael Miller and Stephen Hricko first met when they were about ten years old. Their fathers were in the same bowling league in State College, Pennsylvania.

"I went there one night with my dad and Steve was there with his dad, who was a doctor at the Pennsylvania State College Infirmary," Mike recalled. "We had to be in fifth grade, but we went to different elementary schools. I didn't really talk to him. We said hello to each other and that was it."

Mike and Steve really got to know each other in seventh grade, when they attended the same junior high school, Wesley Parkway Junior High School, in State College.

"We kind of formed a bond in seventh grade, where we became best friends," Mike said. "In seventh, eighth, and ninth grade we played basketball and football. Steve was very bright."

To prove his point, Mike recalled the day when Steve, who was probably around fourteen years old, started spouting off some complex medical terms.

"We were sitting around with a couple of other guys and talking about whether one guy's mom had a certain condition, I don't remember exactly what condition," Mike said. "And Steve rattled off the condition. We wanted to know how he knew it and he said he read his dad's medical books."

Stephen Hricko was as big as he was bright, and he could be intimidating, according to Mike. But, on the other hand, he was a big softy who'd do anything for his friends.

"He was [about] six feet two inches tall, but if you knew him, you knew he was pretty softhearted," Mike said. "He'd do anything for you. But don't try to BS him—he'd see through you. He didn't care for that too much. If you were genuine, then Steve would have something to do with you—he'd want to be friends with you."

Mike and Steve shared a very special bond—maybe it was their love of sports or maybe it was because each of them had three sisters and no brothers. Whatever the attraction, Mike and Steve remained best friends until the day Steve died. They even followed the same career path. They graduated from State College Area High School in 1981. While they were in high school, they both worked at the Pennsylvania State University golf courses. Mike got a job there because his great-grandfather and grandfather were involved in Penn State golf. Then Mike got Steve a job at the golf courses.

"So we basically worked there during the summers," Mike said. "We maintained the golf course, cutting greens, weed eating, raking bunkers, pretty much anything that needed to be done. We worked there all through high school and part of college."

After high school the friends parted ways for a while. Mike went to Allegheny College in Reedville, Pennsylvania, for about two years, then transferred to

Penn State in 1985. He graduated in 1987 with a bachelor's degree in photography and graphic arts. He met Maureen O'Toole, his future wife, while he was at Penn State.

While Mike was away at Allegheny College, Steve stayed at Penn State and continued working at the golf courses. In the early 1980s Steve enrolled in the Penn State Turf Grass Manager program, a training program for golf course superintendents. From 1987 to 1989 Mike tried to make a living doing freelance photography for a local newspaper in State College, and also working for a local company doing graphics work, but he eventually decided that wasn't the career he really wanted. Mike talked to Steve about his future and Steve convinced him to enroll in Penn State's Turf Grass program.

"He said if he could get through the turf grass program, any dummy can get through it," Mike said. "But he was a little brighter and he understood all that scientific stuff."

However, Maureen and Mike—who married in June 1989—talked it over and he decided to go for it. Mike entered the two-year program in September 1989.

Maureen met Kim Aungst in 1988 while she was going to college and working as a waitress at a Hoss's Steak and Sea House in Altoona, Pennsylvania. Maureen was twenty-three and Kim was twenty.

"I actually didn't have a whole lot of interaction with her until her cat died one day and she was very upset and hysterical and I tried to help her out," Maureen recalled. "And I took her home because she was just too upset and we became friends from that point."

Kim had been attending college, but really never took it seriously, so at that point she was working full-time with the intention of going back to school, but she never did, Maureen said.

"She was quite the partyer," Maureen said.

Soon Maureen and Kim, who was also a waitress at the restaurant, started going out together after work.

"We started spending a lot more time together," Maureen said. "I was dating Michael at the time and she was just in one bad relationship after another— she'd fall madly in love with somebody and they'd just treat her like crap. I think it was probably because she was meeting them in the wrong places. She was kind of looking for a nice relationship, so we fixed her up with one of Mike's friends, Steve Hricko."

Maureen and Mike figured that Steve and Kim would either really, really like each other, or really, really hate each other. They were complete opposites—Kim loved to party and socialize, Steve kept pretty much to himself. He wasn't really very outgoing, nor was he someone who would walk into a room and light it up with his presence. People would notice him because of his size and stature, but he wasn't the type of person who would make a grand entrance into a room. How their relationship fared depended on how much Kim really wanted to straighten her life out.

"If she really wanted a serious relationship, then she was going to have to mature a little bit," Maureen said.

Steve and Kim started dating around the middle of 1988. They had been dating for four or five months when she got pregnant. Steve did the right thing and asked her to marry him. They decided to have their wedding in March 1989.

"He was head over heels in love with her. There was no question about it, and she was in love with him," Maureen recalled. "However, I think if the relationship was allowed to take its own course, I don't know if he would have married her, only because at that time Kim was trying to mature. She was trying to straighten out her life and I don't know whether or not that was something she was truly going to end up doing."

When Maureen found out that Kim and Steve were going to get married, she was just about finished making arrangements for her June marriage to Mike, so she told Kim she'd help her plan her wedding.

"I had the thing planned from beginning to end in three days," Maureen remembered. "I made all the phone calls—I did mostly everything by the phone."

Everything went off without a hitch, except for one small matter—Steve was deathly ill. The night of his wedding he was running a temperature of 103 or 104. He sweated bullets through the entire wedding, but he never let anybody know he was sick.

Steve and Kim got married at the Eisenhower Chapel at Penn State. Mike was Steve's best man and Maureen was Kim's maid of honor. Maureen recalled a humorous moment during the ceremony.

"Steve had forgotten the ring, so I ended up taking off my engagement ring and slipped that to him instead and he used that to put on her finger," Maureen said. "It was kind of a funny thing."

The newlyweds had their reception at the Fire Hall in Boalsburg, a small town next to State College. The Hrickos didn't really have much money in those days, so their honeymoon was an overnight stay at a local hotel.

When they got married, Steve was working at Toftrees Resort & Four Star Golf Club, a golf course and conference center hotel complex, in State College. He worked there as an assistant superintendent and eventually became a golf-course superintendent at Iron

Masters, a golf club near Hollidaysburg, Pennsylvania. Beginning on Memorial Day, 1991, Mike worked as an assistant superintendent at Medford Lakes Country Club in Medford Lakes, New Jersey. During the two-and-a-half years he worked there, Steve was working at Iron Masters.

"Steve was very, very busy at work and there was a little bit of conflict between the two of them (Kim and Steve) before Sarah was born," Maureen recalled. "They were getting the nursery ready and it seemed to be taking forever and Kim was a little frustrated with trying to get things done around the house."

Sarah was born in August 1989—the busiest time of year for a golf superintendent. At first Steve was very intimidated by his daughter's size. She was so small and he was so big. He was very clumsy around her. Although he loved her very much, he just didn't know what to do for her. It didn't help that Sarah was an extremely fussy baby. Nevertheless, everything seemed to be going along just fine. When Steve got the job at Iron Masters, the Hrickos moved from State College to Hollidaysburg.

At the time Maureen was working as a sales representative for Bell Atlantic and was very busy at work and Mike was going to school, so the two couples would only see each other occasionally. But Mike and Steve talked on the phone quite a bit. And Maureen would sometimes travel to Hollidaysburg to see Kim.

"We didn't talk to each other every day, or as much as we had when they lived in town. And I really missed them," Maureen said.

But things didn't go well for Steve at Iron Masters.

"He had a problem with some of the board members," Mike said. "Some of the older members wanted one of the older guys who worked under Steve to be superintendent. They felt this older guy could do the job as well as, if not better than, Steve—and do it for less money. They were looking to bump Steve out, but the younger guys knew that Steve had an education and they knew that he had done a lot for the course. So there was a little rift there and I don't remember if he was fired or stepped down, but he said enough is enough. He was tired of all the politics."

So the Hrickos moved back to State College and into an apartment in Steve's parents' house. For six months to a year, while Steve was looking for another job, he stayed home and took care of Sarah while Kim went to school to get her surgical technologist license. As Steve became more comfortable with his role as a full-time dad, the clumsiness he once felt taking care of Sarah completely melted away. He spent every moment with her, reading to her, playing with her, and just doing everything for her. Steve truly fell in love with the idea of being a dad. He was like a big burly teddy bear.

"He was big and macho, but he even let Sarah put makeup on him," Maureen said. "They'd play games and at one point he even said he could really get into being a full-time dad all the time."

But when Kim graduated from school, the Hrickos ended up leaving State College and moving to the Baltimore area, where Steve took a job as an assistant superintendent at Sparrows Point Country Club in Dundalk, Maryland. After the Hrickos moved, the Millers, who were living in New Jersey, started seeing less and less of Steve and Kim, but they would get together when they could. Steve and Mike, however, always stayed in touch.

When Mike got a job at Harbourtowne as the golf-course superintendent and the Millers moved to

Easton, they would sometimes spend the weekends with the Hrickos.

"Kim and I stayed friends with the girl she roomed with in college—Rachel McCoy," Maureen said. "Kim stayed in touch with Rachel because she was in the Baltimore area and had married a distant cousin of Kim's. So they spent a lot of time with each other when Kim was living in Dundalk because they were both living and working in the Baltimore area. And they had become closer friends than Kim and I were at the time."

During this time Mike and Steve would get together occasionally to play golf while Maureen stayed at the Hrickos' house visiting with Kim.

"Everything seemed to be good in their marriage," Mike said. "He never said at that time that there was anything different. But sometimes Kim would get a little perturbed with him when he would go out and stay out late, but we didn't stay out that late. Steve was a homebody. He wasn't one to go out and get liquored up and raise Cain, or anything like that. But he liked to go out and have an occasional beer with the guys, play a little golf, that kind of thing."

In June 1995 Steve got a job as the golf superintendent at Patuxent Greens and the Hrickos moved to Laurel, Maryland, where the course was located. Although Laurel was only about seventy minutes away from the Millers' home in Easton, the couples rarely got together.

"Our two kids and Sarah were getting older, and as we got more involved with our kids, we didn't see them as much because Maureen and I were both working and it got a little more difficult to spend time with each other," Mike said. "But Steve and I talked on the phone at least three or four times a week—

he'd call me about something in the business, or he'd call me about whatever, and we'd talk from ten to fifteen minutes to an hour depending on what we were talking about."

Mike also would see Steve when he traveled to Baltimore to attend work-related seminars. And sometimes Steve would drive to Easton to play golf with Mike.

"Kim wouldn't always come along," Mike said. "It got to a point where we weren't seeing or hearing a lot from Kim. I remember Maureen saying she had tried to keep in touch with Kim, but Kim wasn't returning her calls. So Maureen said if Kim didn't want to keep in touch with her, she wasn't going to keep wasting her time trying to get a hold of her. She'd call and leave messages and Kim wouldn't call back."

Even though Kim was distancing herself from the Millers, Steve never gave Mike any indication that anything was wrong with his marriage.

But in the winter of 1997, Mike discovered that the Hrickos were having some serious problems.

"From my perspective it happened really fast," Mike said. "I don't think Steve even realized how bad things were until Kim asked him for a divorce. Around wintertime Steve called me and said Kim wanted a divorce. He was very upset. I don't ever recall Steve being that upset, to the point of crying."

Part of the problem centered around the personality differences between Kim, who was a very outgoing woman, and Steve, a more introverted kind of guy.

In her job as a surgical technologist, Kim became friends with a number of doctors and she would often invite these doctors home for dinner or drinks. But Steve didn't like Kim's work friends. He thought they were phonies.

"He felt they kind of put on airs and having these

people over just wasn't his cup of tea," Mike said. "Kim would get a little perturbed when she would invite these people over and Steve would say fine, invite them over, but he wasn't going to say up all night and entertain them because he had to get up early— around four A.M.—to go to work. So when eight P.M. rolled around, Steve would get up and say he was going to bed and he'd go to bed."

As time went on, the relationship between Kim and Steve seemed to deteriorate even more. Maybe it was because Kim felt that Steve just wasn't outgoing enough for her. But, even so, he was a great husband and father.

"He'd go to work and bring home a paycheck," Mike said. "He wasn't out drinking. He was a family man. He loved Sarah."

Although Mike and Steve continued to keep in touch, Kim and Maureen drifted apart.

"Closer to when this [was] happening, I hadn't talked to her for a very long time," Maureen recalled. "She wasn't coming down with Steve anymore to visit and she wasn't really calling much anymore. It was almost like she was really distancing herself. I think what ended up happening is they started having trouble in the marriage, and she, knowing that Steve and Mike were so close, was very limited in what she was sharing with me, knowing it would probably get back to Steve."

Then one day in November 1997, out of the blue, Kim called the Millers and told Maureen she wanted to come to Easton for a visit. Maureen thought that was odd because she had asked Kim to visit on several occasions, but she always turned her down. But Maureen was happy that Kim wanted to come to Easton.

"Mike was going to be out of town. He was going

home to State College for a turf-grass meeting and he always took the kids with him. I was going to have the house to myself, so I made plans with Kim," Maureen said.

Several days before she was supposed to arrive, Kim called to tell Maureen that they would be going out with a bunch of her friends because it was a bachelorette party for her friend Jenny, who had grown up in Easton. Maureen soon figured out the real reason Kim contacted her was because she needed a place for all her friends to stay while they were in Easton.

"So they came down for the bachelorette party and that was my first meeting with Brad Winkler," Maureen said. "Brad came down with Kim and his cousin's fiancée, Jennifer—it was her bachelorette party."

Maureen had a previous engagement and caught up with the group at a local watering hole around 11:00 P.M.

"Everybody was completely sloshed and most of the people at the party had already left, except Kim, Brad, Jennifer, and a couple of [other people]," Maureen said. "We stayed until one or one-thirty in the morning and visited and then we went back to my house. We played football outside for a while and then everybody went to bed and in the morning they got up and left."

Before Kim left that morning, she and Maureen were sitting around the kitchen table catching up.

"You have the perfect life," Kim said.

"Why do you say that?" Maureen asked, a bit taken aback by her friend's remark.

"Because you have the perfect job, the perfect house, the perfect husband."

"Honey, are you forgetting you and I work almost in the same business—you're a surgical tech, and I'm a drug rep. Our houses are pretty much the same thing and our husbands are pretty much duplicates of each other," Maureen said. "So why is my life so different from yours?"

"It's hard to explain," Kim responded.

Maureen couldn't figure out why Kim was saying those things because she had never before compared their lives. Although Maureen thought Kim's comments were a bit strange, she just put them out of her head.

In January the news that Kim had asked Steve for a divorce completely blindsided Maureen, because Kim had never even told Maureen her marriage was in trouble the last time they were together.

But Maureen began putting the pieces of the puzzle together.

"The whole time we were out with Brad at the bachelorette party, he was talking to people about his failed marriage—he had only been married six months and his wife fooled around on him and broke his heart," Maureen recalled. "And Kim was talking about Brad—not just telling me his story, but going on and on about his story and how if she was only ten years younger . . . and I told her she seemed to be forgetting that she was married."

At the party Kim couldn't seem to stop talking about Brad. She kept telling Maureen that he was the sweetest guy she had ever met. But Maureen hadn't put two and two together.

"He wasn't a man I would look twice at. I have no idea what she saw in him, but I think she was totally attracted to his personality," Maureen said. "He really was a nice guy, caring and genuine."

Around the end of 1997 Kim asked Steve for a divorce. He was devastated. Steve called Mike in January 1998 to tell him Kim had asked for a divorce and he didn't know what to do. He didn't want to lose his wife and daughter. They were everything to him. Steve told Mike he'd do anything to keep his marriage together, including going to counseling.

"I told him early on Maureen and I had gone to counseling and I said it's not that big of a deal. You go to counseling and talk things out and it can't hurt," Mike remembered.

Mike went to Laurel in January to visit Steve. The friends sat and talked about everything, except Kim and their marriage.

"It seemed like old times. Steve didn't seem upset and he never really brought up the problems in the marriage. It kind of didn't occur to me that he had just called me and said Kim wanted a divorce. I didn't want to pry, either, but it was odd thinking back on it," Mike said. "Then Kim came back from bringing Sarah home from soccer and she came downstairs and sat on the couch next to Steve. I was on another couch in the corner and Steve was talking and Kim was sitting on the couch next to him. Steve had his arms on the back of the couch and she was kind of nestled in next to him with her hand on his knee. I didn't think anything of it, but after the murder happened, I thought how odd it was that he was all upset about her wanting a divorce and she came in and sat next to him like everything was peachy keen. I think at that time he told me, in his opinion, things were better."

Steve really did think his marriage was on the right track again. He and Kim were going to counseling together and they were each seeing a counselor one-on-one. In addition, Steve was taking medication for depression. Mike said he never thought his friend was that depressed, although he admitted Steve was under a lot of pressure at work.

"In his situation as a golf-course superintendent, the owners didn't have a lot of money, but they wanted top-rate conditions," Mike said. "But there's only so much you can do without money. So he was working a lot of hours and he was under a lot of stress. I don't know if that had anything to do with making him depressed, but I know he was looking to better himself and get out of that situation and make the situation better for his family."

Sometime between the middle of January and the end of that month, Steve called Mike to ask if he had any ideas for romantic things to do for Valentine's Day. Steve told Mike he had talked to the counselor regarding doing something with Kim and the counselor said it was up to Kim to decide if she wanted to do anything.

Mike told Steve about the Valentine's Day weekend getaway at Harbourtowne, which included a murder-mystery dinner-theater production. Steve thought that sounded like a good idea and he set the weekend up.

"Steve talked to Kim's friends about it—I think he told her he was planning this little getaway, but I don't think he told her where it was, because he didn't want to upset her if she didn't want to do it. I think one of her friends told her where they were going," Mike said. "But she gave him the impression that she was cool with it. Maureen and I offered to watch Sarah for them, but Kim said no, which thinking back on it was odd. As close friends as we were, all they would have to do was zip down to our house in Easton, drop Sarah off, and then go out to the resort. But she didn't want to do that. She was either going to leave Sarah with a friend in Laurel, or her mother would travel to Laurel to watch her."

Chapter 6

Kim and Maureen made all the funeral arrangements and purchased a cemetery plot on Tuesday, but the fighting with the Hrickos over the disposition of Steve's body continued. They insisted they didn't want him cremated—according to their religion, he wouldn't be able to be buried in consecrated ground then.

"It was a nasty scene," Maureen said. "The Hrickos were upset, understandably so, and they were fighting tooth and nail on every decision Kim made because it went against their faith. But Kim didn't care and kept saying that was the way it was going to be. And now we all know why she was doing it. And there I was thinking she was telling me the truth."

While Kim and Maureen were making arrangements with the funeral director, something else happened that Maureen thought was a bit odd.

"We had to talk about how we were going to pay for this thing, and after I had talked to the funeral director, I told Kim that it was going to be expensive and asked her how she was going to pay for it," Maureen recalled. "I asked her if she had life insurance on Steve and she said there was a life insurance policy. I asked her if she knew where it was, because I don't know where our policies are, and she said it was in the dining room."

Maureen asked Kim what it was doing there and Kim told her it was sitting in a cardboard box in the corner of the room. Kim explained that she had taken it out for some reason a couple of weeks earlier and hadn't had time to put it back yet. So Maureen went into the dining room, located the box, and opened it.

"The life insurance policy was laying on top of all the paperwork," Maureen said. "And I'm thinking this is the weirdest thing—that she would know right off where the policy was. That was one of the other red flags that went off."

After spending two days with Kim, Maureen finally told her that she needed to get home to her husband. She told the Hrickos she was going to send Kim to State College and they could continue to fight over the funeral arrangements when she got there.

So on Tuesday, Maureen sent Kim, her mother, and Sarah to State College to stay with the Hrickos; then she went home. Once there, Maureen asked Mike what he knew about the events leading up to Steve's death. Mike told Maureen what he had learned from police and others at Harbourtowne.

"He said Kim told police that they had gone to the dinner theater, where they drank beer and wine. Kim told police Steve had taken his antidepressants, as well as some muscle relaxant, because his back was bothering him. When they got back to their room, they got in a fight and Kim stormed off and Steve lit a cigar and had fallen asleep," Maureen said. "Mike said they had found a *Playboy* next to him. So we figured that he and Kim argued because he had taken a *Playboy* with him to Harbourtowne."

The Millers speculated the *Playboy* was the cause of Kim and Steve's argument because they knew how much Kim hated pornography.

"When they were living in Hollidaysburg, Kim ran across a collection of *Playboy* magazines Steve had from when he was a teenager, probably from his father. They were very old—probably collectibles. Well, she came across them in the bottom of a closet in their house in Hollidaysburg and she flipped out," Maureen remembered. "We happened to be visiting that weekend and she was still very upset about it. And she discussed the argument over the *Playboy*s with me. Kim had a very religious upbringing and she abhorred pornography and thought it was absolutely abhorrent that any man would possess it. And what did that make her feel like if he was going and looking at the big, bodacious women in the magazine and then coming and making love to her? It was so insulting to her that she told him that if she ever, ever saw a *Playboy* in their house again, their marriage was over."

So when Mike told Maureen that there was a *Playboy* found near Steve, another red flag went up. Maureen started thinking that something was wrong because it just seemed too obvious that there was a *Playboy* in the Hrickos' room.

"I knew that Steve would never, in a million years, have taken a *Playboy* on his romantic getaway weekend to save his marriage," Maureen said. "I knew about how she felt about it and I knew the ultimatum that she had given him."

That was the first time Maureen started thinking that something just wasn't right. But she decided to take the advice she had given to her husband—stop trying to make sense out of nonsense.

While the Millers were packing and getting ready to head to State College on Wednesday, Maureen called the Hrickos to see how things were going and to check on Kim. Maureen was shocked to hear that Kim was nowhere to be found. The Hrickos told Maureen that the last they had heard, Kim and her best friend, Rachelle St. Phard, were planning to go back down to St. Michaels and Harbourtowne because Kim said she needed to be with Steve. Maureen told the Hrickos that Kim should stay away because the media were swarming all over Harbourtowne.

"But they said, 'She's on her way and you can't stop her, we tried,'" Maureen said.

In the meantime Kim called Maureen, who quickly told her not to go to the resort. But Kim was determined and insisted that she was going, no matter what. Maureen told Kim she was going to call her husband at work at Harbourtowne and she'd call Kim back. Maureen explained to Mike that Kim was dead set on going to St. Michaels.

"Mike said to tell her to go to the maintenance shop and he'd keep her there until it got dark and then he'd take her down to the water," Maureen said.

Kim agreed and she and Rachelle drove to Harbourtowne to meet Mike.

Rachelle St. Phard met Kim Aungst when she was in ninth grade and Kim was in tenth grade.

"I ended up at the school she was attending, Calvary Baptist Christian Academy in Altoona, Pennsylvania," Rachelle said. "I knew her vaguely, but we really weren't friends until we went bowling one night and we kind of started playing jokes on one another. That was the beginning of our friendship—we really just clicked. We'd spend nights in one another's houses. We played basketball and soccer and softball and we were cheerleaders. Her parents were divorced when I met her. She was pretty young, around four, when they got divorced. She lived with her mom and stepfather. Her last name was Aungst— her dad's name. He lived about fifteen or twenty minutes from Hollidaysburg, where she lived. I lived in Altoona, about fifteen or twenty minutes away. She had one brother, a half brother, who was younger than her."

Rachelle said Kim was very friendly and very outgoing. She was someone who liked to joke around and have fun, even though she had a pretty strict upbringing—they both did.

"We weren't allowed to do a whole lot of stuff. In some respects her mom and stepdad let her do a few more things than I was allowed to do, but there were things that weren't allowed in her house," Rachelle said. "Her stepdad put a lot of weird restrictions on things. One example sticks in my head. She was only allowed to use the iron once a week. If she didn't have all her clothes ironed at that point, she wasn't allowed to go get the iron again. He wasn't very kind back then. [Now] he's a different person and a more kind person than he was back then. Her mom, she tried. She did her best to raise the kids in the best way she saw fit. I think Kim was slighted in her house, more so than her brother, because her brother was her stepdad's natural child. He was definitely favored more."

Rachelle and Kim remained friends through college, although they didn't go to the same school.

Rachelle went to the University of Pittsburgh and Kim's first year of college was spent majoring in communications at Messiah College, a Christian college in Grantham, Pennsylvania. When Kim came home for the weekend, she often stayed at Rachelle's house rather than her own.

"I think because of her stepfather's interesting rules, she chose to come to my house," Rachelle said. "She really was like a part of our family. My mom and dad were real close with her and she took family vacations with us."

After her freshman year Kim decided to enroll at the Altoona branch of Pennsylvania State University. After a year there she transferred to Penn State's main campus in University Park and continued majoring in communications, Rachelle said.

When Kim met Steve, Rachelle was living outside Philadelphia. Kim called Rachelle and told her that she was pregnant.

"But I didn't even know she had been dating anyone," Rachelle said. "She felt pretty strongly that Steve was the one. She wanted to spend her life with him and have a home with their child. When she met Steve and they had Sarah, she hadn't finished school, so later she decided to pursue a health career and she enrolled in a local college that offered a surgical technologist program."

Rachelle said although she didn't know a whole lot about Kim's marriage, she did have some concerns about their relationship.

"Steve was not the most outgoing of people," Rachelle said. "I sensed that there were issues. I wrote her a couple of letters asking if everything was okay because it just felt weird throughout the marriage. He wasn't particularly my cup of tea. Maybe it was because he was so introverted and I tend to be more out-going as well. The few times I did visit them when they were married, I didn't see much of him because he was holed up in their basement working out, or watching TV, or whatever, but I really didn't see a whole lot of him."

Rachelle said shortly before Steve died, Kim called her and whispered into the telephone that she wanted to get a divorce. But she couldn't elaborate because Steve was nearby. Rachelle said she found out about Steve's death from Maureen O'Toole-Miller.

"Maureen called me and told me that he had died in a hotel fire and that Kim was okay," Rachelle said. "So I told my husband I have to go. I called Maureen back and she told me Kim was going to State College to the Hrickos and I packed up my stuff and went and stayed with my mother in Altoona. Then I went to the Hrickos' house and hung out with her. She was pretty numb. She didn't really say a whole lot. She definitely cried, but numb is the best word to describe it."

Rachelle said Kim told her all the details surrounding Steve's death and she believed her.

"I didn't have any reason to believe otherwise," Rachelle said.

When Kim said she wanted to go back to St. Michaels the day before Steve's viewing, Rachelle wasn't comfortable letting Kim go back by herself. She was afraid Kim would take her own life.

"So I went with her," Rachelle said.

Rachelle said the first thing Kim did when they got to Harbourtowne was to go to room 506. Kim got out of the car, but Rachelle didn't go with her.

"She wanted to go back to the room to see where

he had died, because they got her out of there so fast that night," Rachelle said. "She might have picked up some rocks or something to take back with her. Then she got back into the car and we went to see Mike Miller. The TV was on in the shop and there was a report about her possibly being a suspect and we talked about how crazy it was. That's the first I knew they were looking at her."

When night fell, Mike drove Kim back to the water's edge behind the cottage where Steve had died. Mike didn't know that Kim had already been to the room when she first arrived. When she got to the water, she told Mike she wanted to be alone. She got out of the car and walked along the riprap next to the water and then walked back again, all the time looking at the ground.

"Mike's watching her and he's thinking this is so freaking weird and he's trying to keep her hidden so nobody will see her," Maureen recalled.

Then Kim and Rachelle drove to Kim's town house in Laurel.

"I had a three-month-old baby at the time, who was at my sister's house, and I needed to get back to him, but Kim wanted to spend the night at the house," Rachelle recalled. "I was uncomfortable leaving her there alone, so I made her swear and promise that, for me, she wouldn't do anything to herself because I couldn't live with myself for leaving her there if she did. I don't know if that was what saved her at that point or not."

Rachelle went back to Pennsylvania that evening. The next morning, Thursday, Kim headed back to State College.

Mike and Maureen drove to State College on Thursday morning, the day of Steve's viewing, and went straight to Mike's parents' home. When she arrived, the first thing Maureen did was telephone Kim, who was at the Hrickos' house.

"I told her I'd pick her up and we'd go over to the viewing early, just her and I. And she said, 'I'd like that,'" Maureen said.

Later that afternoon as Maureen was getting ready for the viewing, she turned on the TV and started watching the local news. Soon the station started reporting a story about Steve's death—but as a homicide, not an accident.

Infuriated, Maureen called the state police investigator in Easton to find out what was going on, but he wouldn't give her any information. She then called the TV station and demanded to talk to the reporter, who explained that his information that Steve was murdered came from the Maryland State Police.

"I said, 'You better make damn sure this is correct because we're going to sue you,'" Maureen said. "This is an hour before Steve's viewing. I was so flabbergasted that they would have the balls to lie and say it was a murder an hour before people were showing up for his viewing and they're all going to be looking at Kim and wondering if she did it. The timing of it was really bad."

Trying to put the news story out of her mind, Maureen picked Kim up at the Hrickos' and took her to the viewing at the Koch Funeral Home.

"When I picked her up, I asked her if she knew they were reporting Steve's death as a murder and she said she did," Maureen said. "I asked her what she was going to do and she said nothing because it wasn't true and she was just going to the viewing."

As they walked into the funeral parlor, they noticed that the funeral director had set up two rooms—the first room contained flowers, as well as a photo display of Steve's life, and the second contained more flowers and Steve's casket. Even though Steve was cremated, the Hrickos decided to put a casket there for Sarah's benefit.

Kimberly went into the first room and moved from one bouquet to the next, checking the cards to see who had sent the flowers. Next she went through the second room, where the casket was, and again began looking at cards in the flower bouquets.

"She started at one bouquet and went to two or three bouquets, then walked right by the casket and kept looking at flowers on the other side of the room. And she still hadn't shed a tear," Maureen said. "And I asked her if she wanted to kneel down and say a prayer and she said, 'Oh, okay.' So we went over and sat down and I started crying and she started crying a little bit and I'm thinking, 'Finally we get some emotion out of her.'"

Soon friends and family began arriving. At one point during the evening people got up and talked about Steve.

"It was pretty emotional and Mike and I and Mike's parents were sitting in the front row of the first room and Kim and her mother were in the front row of the other room—there are sliding doors that open, so it was really one big room," Maureen said. "And there was this awkward moment when everyone was waiting for Mike to speak. He was the last person who was supposed to speak. But he couldn't do it because he was too emotional."

What happened next really caught Maureen and others off guard. Kim got up and went to the podium, instead of Mike, and began telling people that if Steve were alive, he'd be surprised that half of them came to pay their last respects and how much she appreciated everybody being there.

"It was almost like she was at a party," Maureen recalled. "She was sort of pretending to cry. I'm thinking she has some guts to get up at the funeral of her own husband and maintain her composure and say something. I'm thinking, 'Is this appropriate at the viewing?'"

After Kimberly finished, there was another pregnant pause while the visitors were waiting for someone else to get up and speak about Steve.

Mike was so upset he couldn't do it. He sat in his chair with his elbows on his legs and his head hanging between his knees. Maureen told him he had to get up and talk, but he just kept saying he couldn't.

"But he had to—he was Steve's best friend forever," Maureen said. "So I got up and I talked instead. The thing I do remember I said, and I am so ashamed about it now, is, I said, that Mike and I would always be there for Kim and Sarah—no matter what happened."

When the viewing was over and everyone began leaving the funeral home, they were met outside by a barrage of reporters and television cameras, including a crew from the tabloid television show *Hard Copy*.

As they made their way out of the funeral home, Maureen shielded Kim with her umbrella and her coat to prevent the reporters from filming her. When Kim got back to Steve's parents' house, around 10:00 P.M. she called Norma in Washington to say hello. Norma asked if Jenny was with her and Kim responded, "The Jenny who won't support me. The Jenny who won't talk to me."

Norma asked Kim what she meant.

"Jenny called me the day after she came to see me and said, 'I cannot support you through this right

now. I'm sorry, but there are too many questions,'"
Kim said.

"What questions?" Norma asked.

"I don't know," Kim replied.

"You don't know," Norma said.

"No," Kim said.

Norma told Kim she had talked with Steve's mother,
Mary Esther Hricko, in State College the previous day.
She said Mrs. Hricko told her that Kim had gone back
to Maryland and would be back for the viewing.
Steve's mom also said the family had been getting
some weird telephone calls.

Kim explained that the media had picked up on the
story because of the murder-mystery dinner-theater
angle. She said the local papers, as well as the *Washington Post,* had reported on Steve's death. As for
why she went back to Maryland, Kim said one of her
friends took her back to Harbourtowne so she could
get a handle on the "realness" of Steve's death.

Not wanting to press Kim on her trip back to Maryland, Norma asked her what the newspapers were
saying about how Steve died. Kim said one media
report mentioned that accelerants had been used,
but Kim told Norma that one fire marshal said that
wasn't true.

Kim said she called the state police because she
hadn't heard anything about how the investigation
was progressing and also because she thought some
trooper might be leaking information. According to
Kim, a trooper told her one officer was talking to the
media because he was trying to make a name for
himself and was trying to look important. Kim also
told Norma the initial coroner's report said Steve died
of smoke inhalation and thermal burns, but the autopsy report wouldn't be back for a couple of days. She

said she was going to meet with the state police at the beginning of the next week to discuss it.

Soon their conversation turned to Jenny again. Kim said Jenny was just being selfish and thought everything revolved around her (Jenny). For the second time Norma asked Kim why Jenny would have questions about Steve's death.

"I don't know. I don't know," Kim said.

After a long pause Kim continued.

"About a thousand years ago Jenny and I joked about how we would have to kill Steve, but we were just joking. And I told her I could never do that," Kim said.

"Even if I found you with a smoking gun standing over your husband's body, I would be at the prison gate on the last day yelling, 'I know what it looks like, but Norma didn't do it,'" Kim said, referring to the fact that Jenny believed she had something to do with Steve's death and refused to support her.

Kim then went on voluntarily to tell Norma what happened the night Steve died—or at least her version of the events.

"She started by saying that she and Steve went back to their room and took two beers back with them after the show," Norma said. "She said the movie *Tommy Boy* was on and Steve got into his pajamas. She then backtracked and said he had a whole bottle of champagne and a couple beers through dinner."

Kim told Norma that she had brought a "shitload" of Xanax with her. According to Kim, Steve's doctor had doubled his depression medication and he had also been taking her Xanax.

"She said he made some kind of advances toward her and she was repulsed and left," Norma recalled. "She said she drove around for what seemed like hours. She said she thought of going to her brother's house or her friends' house on the Eastern Shore, but realized she was a lot farther away then she originally thought," Norma said. "Then she thought about going home, but couldn't find Route 50. She said she was out in this Podunk town, where everything closed at eleven or eleven-thirty P.M., so she decided to go back to the resort."

Although the first part of Kim's story didn't quite jibe with what she told police, the rest of it pretty much adhered to the story she had told investigators.

When Kim was finished with her account of the hours before Steve's body was found, Norma asked her how the fire started.

"Kim said she didn't know," Norma said. "She said they showed her the box of cigars and asked if she recognized them. She said they had been sitting on her kitchen table for about a month, but she didn't know Steve packed them, because they packed their own things separately."

Again Kim told Norma she had packed a "shitload" of Xanax, as well as Flexeril, but she said when she got back the contents of their room, all the pills were gone. Kim told Norma what must have happened was that Steve decided to have a cigar, but he must have passed out because of all the alcohol and medication he consumed and then caught on fire. Kim speculated that there must have been a lot of toxic fumes in the room from all the flame-retardant materials, but she said he probably didn't breathe them in if he was already dead.

"She said this in a way that sounded like she was thinking out loud to herself," Norma said.

A few minutes later, the phone call ended.

The next day, Friday, Steve's burial service was

held at the funeral home—it couldn't be held in church because Steve had been cremated.

When the family arrived at the cemetery, *Hard Copy* was waiting.

Kim's brother, Matt, tried to keep the *Hard Copy* crew from trailing the family into the graveyard. In fact, he almost came to blows with the reporters.

Undeterred, the *Hard Copy* team followed the Hrickos to the graveyard and tried to take pictures of Kim at Steve's grave site. Once again the family tried to shield Kimberly with their umbrellas, and after the burial they escorted her back into the waiting limousine. When the funeral director drove away, family and friends blocked in the *Hard Copy* car so the crew couldn't chase Kim's car.

The funeral director took the back roads and drove Kim to Mike's parents' house.

"Kim didn't go to the reception at the Hrickos' house, she came to ours instead to try to get away from *Hard Copy*," Maureen said.

During the burial Mike's mother stayed at home to get things ready for the reception her family was hosting. Before the guests began to arrive, Kim went into the Millers' kitchen, pulled the plastic wrap off the lunchmeat tray, and started gobbling the lunchmeat down like she had never eaten.

"I looked at her and I said, 'Hey, Kim, are you hungry?' and she said, 'I'm starving,' and then she realized that I was looking at her like she had two heads and she immediately said, 'I don't know, I guess it's because I'm nervous'; then she started making excuses while she was still gobbling down lunchmeat right after she buried her husband."

About an hour after the Millers' reception began,

Maureen took Kim back to the Hrickos' house. Before she left, she told Kim to call her the next day.

The next morning Maureen got a frantic telephone call from Kim.

"She was hysterical," Maureen said.

Kim told Maureen the Hrickos were being mean to her and she needed to get out of their house.

"I'm sure they were horrible to her because they didn't hide their emotions," Maureen said. "And at this point I'm sure they thought Kim had done something. But I don't know when they found out that Kim might have had something to do with it, because nobody would tell me anything. Later, I found out the police thought I helped her kill him and that's why no one would tell me what was going on."

During the early stages of the investigation, the police suspected Maureen because she was a pharmaceutical representative. They thought Maureen helped Kim obtain the succinylcholine. They couldn't understand how Kim could have done everything by herself.

"Because I was taking care of her and because I was filtering all the messages from everybody else, the police thought that I was being way too protective of her. They thought I helped her," Maureen said. "So I said [to Kim], 'Why don't you come to the Penn State basketball game with me and Mike and Mike's family.'"

But Kim said no way. "I would rather have bamboo shoots shoved up under my fingernails than go to a basketball game," she told Maureen.

Maureen was a bit confused. She figured if Kim was that desperate to get out of the house, what difference did it make where she went? So Maureen told Kim she'd get her a ticket for the game, but Kim said she'd rather get a massage instead.

"I said call me and I'll check on you later when we get back from the basketball game, but she was pretty much expecting me to cancel my plans with Mike and the family to take care of her again," Maureen said.

Kim called Maureen back about an hour later and asked if she could meet her at the massage studio after the basketball game, which started at noon. After the game Mike dropped Maureen off at the massage salon to meet Kim, then left planning to come back in an hour to pick Maureen up. After the massage, as they walked out to meet Mike, Kim told Maureen she had broken a nail and needed to get it fixed.

"Will you go with me to the mall to get my nail fixed?" Kim asked Maureen.

"I'm looking at Mike and thinking, 'Oh, my God'— so I say, 'Okay, I have to go to the mall anyway, it's Jenny's birthday and I have to get her a gift. I'll take you to the mall.' So we went in Kim's car and I made arrangements with Mike to pick me up later at the Hrickos' house," Maureen said.

When they got to the mall, Maureen brought Kim to the nail salon; then she went to the Lane Bryant store to get Jenny's gift. When Maureen finished shopping, she went back to the nail salon to get Kim.

"When I got back to the nail salon, there she is talking like Chatty Cathy, like there's no big deal, like she didn't bury her husband the day before. And she's carrying on like it's social hour. And not only did she have her nail fixed, she was having her nails done— all of them," Maureen said. "I'm trying to make excuses for her, like she's going over the deep end and she doesn't know what she's doing, and I have to wait for her to get all her nails done while my husband is waiting for me at home. And I've spent like maybe twenty-four hours with him since his best friend died."

The Millers were scheduled to drive back home together the next day, Sunday. But first they had to figure out how to get Steve's truck back to Laurel from State College. The problem was that when Kim left State College to go back to St. Michaels with Rachelle on Wednesday, they went in Rachelle's car. However, because Rachelle left Laurel before Kim did, Kim had to drive Steve's truck back because her own car was still in State College.

So the Millers and Kim decided that Mike would drive Steve's truck and Maureen would follow in their car.

"It killed him having to be in Steve's truck and smell him and see all his stuff that had been there the day he died," Maureen recalled.

After the Millers dropped Steve's truck off at the Hrickos' house in Laurel, Mike and Maureen drove back to Easton together.

Chapter 7

The day after Steve died, Kim's friend Rachel McCoy contacted Corporal Keith Elzey. She was scared and crying. Rachel told Elzey that she didn't think Steve's death was an accident. In fact, she believed Kim killed her husband. Ultimately Elzey set up an interview with Rachel at her workplace in Baltimore for the next day, Tuesday, February 17, at 11:00 A.M.

After speaking with Rachel on the telephone, Elzey called Dr. David Fowler at the medical examiner's office and told him there might be new evidence pertaining to the death of Stephen Hricko.

Norma Walz also called the state police on Monday regarding the Hricko case. Norma told Sergeant Karen Alt she believed Kimberly played a part in her husband's death. Norma then directed Alt to call Jennifer Gowen, who had more information about Kimberly's possible involvement. Alt contacted Jennifer and made arrangements to interview her and her husband, Sean, at their home in Silver Spring, Maryland, that evening.

During the interview Jennifer said that although

Kim often talked about how bad her marriage was, she always made it seem like she had everything under control. But in the months before Steve's death, Kimberly became increasingly negative about her relationship with him. She even told Jennifer she was thinking of asking him for a divorce. Kimberly said the only way she would stay in the marriage was if Steve completely changed his ways. Jennifer thought Steve did just that, but apparently Kim didn't.

"Her opinions about him became more that he was like pathetic and she didn't think he would be able to go on if they got a divorce," Jennifer said. "She came to see him as a nonperson and she said several times that she had no feelings for him. During many of our conversations she said he would be better off dead because there was no way that he would be able to maintain a life without her and Sarah."

Kim was also afraid that if she divorced Steve, he might turn Sarah against her, or make her life miserable in other ways.

"Kim said many times that . . . she thought that this whole situation could be best reconciled if Steve was dead, and she told me that she would like my support as far as being there for her unconditionally, no matter what happened," Jennifer said. "And she said things like, 'If I knew that I could kill him and get away with it, I would do it tomorrow.' She would say that Steve needs to die. She said that she was tempted to tell Steve about the relationship she was having with Brad, so that he would get mad enough and kill himself because he had mentioned suicide in the past."

But even if Steve committed suicide, Kim still wouldn't be happy, because she wouldn't be able to collect on his life insurance, Jennifer told Alt.

"So I think she really felt that the best way out of the situation was indeed to kill him," Jennifer said.

Jennifer told Alt she and Kim were both surgical technologists. In fact, she said, that's how they met. Jennifer explained that their jobs consisted of getting the operating room set up for surgery, assisting the surgeon during an operation, breaking down the room after the surgery was completed, and preparing the room for the next case. As part of their jobs she and Kim had access to numerous drugs, Jennifer said.

"Did there come a time when you and Kim discussed drugs that could be used potentially to kill people?" Alt asked.

"Yes. I always thought it was an interesting fact that there was a drug so readily available, a nonnarcotic, or a noncontrolled substance, that was just sitting around on almost any anesthesia cart, that could be used as a weapon or as a drug, that, to the best of my knowledge, could paralyze someone's muscles, all of them, and they could die from a small amount of that drug," Jennifer said. "We had discussed it, when Kim said, 'Yeah, I need to get some good anesthesia drugs or Sodium Pentothal,' and I said, 'Well, hey, if you're going to do it, I heard [about] a drug called succinylcholine,' and I related to her how I had heard of that drug used in the past as a weapon."

Jennifer then explained how succinylcholine worked when given intramuscularly.

"To the best of my knowledge . . . I guess what could happen is that the person would lose muscular control over their functions, and for a time they're aware of what is going on because it takes a while for all your muscles to stop working. That would include the muscles that you use to breathe, and you stop breathing. Eventually you would be starved for oxygen and you would die because you couldn't take in a breath," she said.

Jennifer said about a month before Steve's death, Kim talked about how she could use this drug to kill him.

"I know that Kim told me on [a] Friday night that she wanted my unconditional love . . . and that she didn't understand why I couldn't just accept the affair [with Brad] as something that people do," Jennifer said. "She wanted to know why I couldn't accept the lying to Steve and why I couldn't accept that this is what she needed to do and she wasn't necessarily ready to end it—the whole relationship with Brad—in a quick manner, or to go back to Steve and try to reconcile their marriage."

Alt asked Jennifer to explain Kim's definition of "unconditional love."

"Kim felt that her definition of unconditional love was . . . that I could do anything, including—specifically—kill someone, and she would support me, and she asked that I support her in that way. . . . She didn't ask for me to support her in something she was going to do, but she asked me [if] I would support her, no matter what happened. And she ended the conversation by saying, 'If you killed someone tomorrow, I would support you,'" Jenny said.

Later in the investigation Alt spoke with Kim's friend Teri Armstrong. Teri, who now lived in Pennsylvania, had lived next door to the Hrickos in Laurel for about two years. Sergeant Alt met with Teri at the state police barracks in Waterloo, Maryland.

Teri said she and Kim used to see each other every day until the Armstrongs moved away in August 1997. After that, Teri would spend every other weekend at

Kim's house and they would also talk on the telephone several times a week.

Teri told Alt about a conversation she had with Kim the New Year's Eve before Steve died.

"She told me that she was going to be asking Steve for a divorce. I asked her if Steve had a girlfriend and she said no. I asked her if she was seeing anybody and she said yes, in a roundabout way," Teri said. "And I asked her if they kissed and how they met and if they were having an affair, sexually, and she said no about that, but they had kissed. She said they weren't going to be seeing each other until the divorce was final, which I agreed with. She told me it was one of her friends' cousin and later I found out his name was Brad and he was in the military."

Kim told Teri that when she asked Steve for a divorce, she knew he was going to try and take Sarah from her, but she wasn't going to let him do that.

"But in my heart I didn't believe Steve could do that," Teri said. "I knew Kim enough to where I didn't find that to be true."

It seemed to Teri that Kim just didn't want to deal with the hassles of a divorce—hassles from her parents and his family as well.

"She gave me the impression that she was under a lot of torment . . . but I just found this all to be out of sync," Teri said.

Kim also told Teri that she had been thinking about several different ways of killing Steve, basically for the insurance money so she and Sarah could live well. Teri said a couple of months earlier, Kim had started feeding her negative information about Steve—about their sex lives and how he was raised and that his parents let him look at pornographic magazines.

"She said once when she came home from a trip,

she caught him with things all over the house, sex magazines, and she was really embarrassed because she was with her girlfriend," Teri said. "[Kim] also found out, without him knowing it, that he had been getting off with computer online [pornography]. Things like that. Like he only wanted to have sex in the morning—he didn't want it at night. He only wanted it when he wanted it. I didn't see Steve to be like that, but she never mentioned any of that stuff before. I just found it really strange, all of a sudden."

During the interview Teri told Alt that she had spent some time alone with Steve about a month before he died. It was January 16 and Teri was supposed to meet Kim at the Hrickos' house. When she arrived, Steve told her that Kim wasn't home, so Teri spent about ninety minutes talking with Steve in the kitchen.

"He was a nervous wreck," Teri said. "He was so upset. He was crying. He was just really sad."

Steve told Teri that he wanted his marriage to work. He said he loved Kim and Sarah and really wanted to do better, and he promised he would do better. He said he was seeing a psychologist and taking antidepressants.

"I always told him that if he ever needed to talk to me, to do so," Teri said.

While they were waiting for Kim, who was at Jenny's house, Steve called the Gowens to find out when she was going to be home. However, there was no answer, so he left a message. He called a couple of times more, but he hung up when no one answered, rather than leave more messages. Steve also called Kim's cell phone, but it was turned off. When Kim did finally come home, she looked like she had been crying.

Her eyes were red and puffy. Although she looked tired and drained, Teri had a feeling she was faking.

"She was overdoing it. [She gave] me the impression that she was faking this, being ill, but she wasn't crying," Teri said.

Soon Steve went to bed and Teri tried talking to Kim, but Kim really didn't want to talk about anything. Teri, though, wouldn't take no for an answer.

"Things had been bothering me because her relationship [with Steve] wasn't like it was before, and I had to let her know how I felt about the situation because we had always talked about things," she said.

Teri told Kim to go easy on Steve—after all, he was trying. If she gave him a chance, he might even become the man he was when she fell in love with him. On the other hand, Teri told Kim to do what she needed to do. However, all the conversations Teri had with Kim in the weeks leading up to Steve's death led her to believe Kim wanted a divorce.

"She didn't want to work it out. She wanted to leave, but she knew that there was really no way out [by] getting a divorce," Teri said. "She knew she was going to get a lot of hassles. . . . She was not wanting to hear what other people had to say, but she did ask my opinion of the relationship."

Teri told Kim she thought the relationship was an unhealthy one. It seemed that Kim was always on the go, while Steve just sat around doing nothing except getting fat. According to Teri, Kim took care of everything around the house, including the bills. She said Steve was a couch potato.

"He watched television lying in bed," Teri said. "And he was rude to a point—lazy rude. Even when I would come over and [he would answer] the door and I would say, 'Is Kim here?' and he would say,

'Yeah, she's upstairs,' and he would go and sit back on the couch, or his favorite chair. He never went to get her. I had to ask him if I could go get her."

Teri last saw Kim and Steve together on Friday, February 13, the day before they left for Harbourtowne. Even though Teri arrived at the Hrickos' house late in the evening, she and Kim sat at the kitchen table and talked for about three hours. Steve went upstairs to bed and Sarah fell asleep downstairs, watching television.

"I didn't know what to say anymore. I didn't know how to handle it," Teri said. "I didn't know what was going to be the right thing or the wrong thing because she just seemed to be a totally different person at this point. The Kim I saw that night . . . I mean, she just seemed to be changing every two weeks that I did see her. She was completely cold. She was cold."

On Monday, February 16, Dr. Fowler had called Elzey and told him the autopsy indicated that there was no carbon monoxide in Stephen Hricko's blood, nor was there evidence of soot or burns in his trachea or related injuries to his lungs. That meant that Steve was either not breathing, or dead, before the fire in his room started. Fowler also said that, contrary to Kim's statements that Stephen had been drinking heavily, there was no alcohol in his blood. Fowler told Elzey he was awaiting the results of other tests to determine exactly how Steve died.

After speaking with Fowler, Elzey called Scott Patterson, the state's attorney for Talbot County, to update him on the Hricko case.

Later that afternoon Elzey and other members of his team, as well as members of the state police crime lab, went to Harbourtowne to do a search of the Hrickos' room and the surrounding area. While they were there, they also searched room 1016, where Kimberly was taken after the fire.

That evening Elzey got a call from Kimberly's friend Marsha Carter (pseudonym). Marsha had taken care of Sarah while the Hrickos were at Harbourtowne. Marsha told Elzey about Kim's affair with Brad Winkler. She said a couple of weeks before Steve's death, she and Kim went to a pub in Laurel, where Kim met up with Brad. When they left the pub, they all went back to Marsha's house, and Kim and Brad went upstairs to the bedroom and had sex.

Elzey also got a phone call from Marsha's boyfriend, who was unaware that she had already called the police. The boyfriend provided Elzey with essentially the same information that Marsha had.

The next day, Tuesday, Elzey and another state police trooper met with Rachel McCoy at the Baltimore bank where she worked. Rachel told them that she and Kim had been friends since 1986. They met when they worked at Hoss's Steak and Sea House. They quickly became best friends and roommates. Over the years they remained in touch, although they lost contact with one another for about a year-and-a-half when Rachel moved to Baltimore in 1988. They reestablished their friendship again shortly after Sarah was born. When the Hrickos moved to Maryland in 1991, Rachel and Kim once again became best friends. They talked on the telephone at least three times a week, went shopping, and went out to eat and to the movies.

Rachel said that sometime in the fall of 1997, Kim told her that she was looking into divorcing Steve. Then one day, several weeks before Steve's death,

Rachel and Kim had lunch together and Kim confided in Rachel about the state of her marriage. She explained that she didn't feel Steve was very helpful around the house. And it bothered her more and more every year that he didn't like to go out and do things with her. Kim also told Rachel that when she asked Steve for a divorce, he cried and promised to go to counseling to keep their marriage together. Steve kept his promise, but Kim still wasn't happy. In fact, she was quite annoyed at the "new" Steve.

"We talked about [the fact] he had started seeing a counselor and that he was talking more and being more outgoing in their relationship. But he was talking to her all the time and that was driving her crazy," Rachel said. "He wanted to talk to her all the time and talk about their feelings. And she told me that she was seeing somebody else."

When Rachel asked Kim if the relationship with Brad was serious—and was she going to leave Steve for Brad—Kim said no.

"This is just about sex," Kim said.

After lunch the women went shopping. In the car on the way to the Marshalls department store in Laurel, Rachel and Kim were joking about putting their husbands in Steve's truck and going up to Pennsylvania and pushing the truck off a cliff.

"It would be so much easier if Steve were dead," Kim said.

On Thursday, January 29, Kim made plans to visit Rachel in Baltimore the next day. After work on Friday, Rachel went out with a coworker. She called Kim to see if she was still planning to visit. Kim said no, but asked Rachel to telephone her when she got home. When Rachel returned home about 10:00 P.M., she discovered that Kim had left five messages on her answering machine asking Rachel to call her as soon as possible.

"The messages were gradually sounding more panicky," Rachel said. "She said, 'I really need to talk to you. Please, please call me. I just really need to talk to you. Call me as soon as you get in.'"

When Rachel called her, Kim said she needed to talk to her and asked her to drive to Laurel right away, which she did.

"She said, 'Rachel, you need to come down here now. I need you. Do you remember when I saved you in State College? I need you. You have to come here now,'" Rachel said. "And I said, 'Give me fifteen minutes to let the dog out and I'm on my way.'"

Rachel arrived at Kim's around 11:30 P.M. The first thing she noticed was that Kim was very nervous and it was obvious that she had been drinking. Rachel asked Kim where Steve was and she said he was upstairs sleeping and Sarah was at a friend's house for the night. Rachel and Kim went into the kitchen. Rachel sat at the table, while Kim sat on the floor across from Rachel. Kim was very upset.

"She seemed very drunk to me, because she just kept running her fingers through her hair, crying," Rachel said. "I'm like, 'Just talk to me, tell me what's wrong. I'm here.'"

Kim then told Rachel that she had a plan to kill Steve and no one would ever find out that she had done it.

"She said she either had a drug or could get a drug at work that she would inject in Steve that would cause his muscles to become paralyzed and stop him from breathing," Rachel said. "Kim said the drug couldn't be traced."

To make it look like an accident, Kim said, she

would light a cigar or candles and set the curtains in the house on fire and burn the house down with Steve in it. That way it would appear that he died as a result of the fire and smoke. Kim told Rachel that her life would be so much easier. Rachel was terrified and tried to talk Kim out of killing Steve, saying she would surely get caught, especially since Steve didn't smoke cigars.

"I tried to poke holes in the story," Rachel said, "I tried to say, 'Where are you going to get this drug, and what if your house burns to the ground, your brand-new house? And what if your neighbor's house catches on fire?'"

But Kim had an answer for all of Rachel's concerns.

"She told me that she could get the drug at work very easily—that it was in every hallway or every operating room," Rachel said. "She said that they used it for trauma victims to stop their breathing so they could put a tube in their throat to put them on oxygen. She said it wasn't traceable in the blood. She told me the house wouldn't burn down because there's always neighbors up in that neighborhood and they would see the fire before the house burned and call the fire department."

Kim also told Rachel she had taken out a smoker's life-insurance policy on Steve so people would think he was a smoker. She reasoned, albeit illogically, that because Steve chewed tobacco, she could use a cigar to start the fire and investigators would be none the wiser. And she reminded Rachel the drug she planned on using couldn't be detected in Steve's system.

At this point Kimberly was sitting on the floor in a daze. Rachel was really scared, so she called Karen Porter (pseudonym), one of her neighbors in Baltimore, and told her about the conversation she just had with Kim. As she was talking to Karen, she noticed Kim walking upstairs. Worried that Kim was going to kill Steve right then, Rachel told her neighbor she was going to hang up, but if she called back in a few minutes—Kim's telephone number would register on her caller ID—and then immediately hung up again, Karen was to call the police and tell them to go to the Hrickos' house. After hanging up, Rachel ran up the stairs and found Kimberly in her bedroom standing over Steve while he slept.

"Kimberly was standing there staring at Steve with the strangest look on her face—a look I'd never seen before," Rachel said.

Rachel told Kim they should go back downstairs, but she got no response. Finally Rachel got Kim's attention and they headed back to the kitchen, where they stayed for a couple of hours. Rachel wanted to go home, but she didn't know if she should leave Kim alone with Steve. Kim finally went upstairs to bed. Rachel waited about twenty minutes, then left. She got back home around 3:00 A.M.

Rachel called Kimberly at 9:00 the next morning to see how things were going. Kim said everyone was okay, but she couldn't talk because she wasn't feeling well. Around 3:00 that afternoon, Kim called Rachel to tell her again that everything was fine. Rachel asked Kim if she was really going to kill Steve. Kim said she didn't know what she was going to do. That was the last time Rachel spoke to Kim before Steve's death.

During the interview with police Rachel told Elzey that Kimberly wanted her to support her plan to kill Steve. She also told the police that she had never seen Steve smoke—only chew tobacco. And he very rarely drank—but when he did, he only drank Budweiser.

Rachel told police that on February 15, 1998, Kim

left a message on Rachel's answering machine asking Rachel to call her at home as soon as possible. When Rachel called back, she spoke with Maureen Miller, who informed her about Steve's death. Rachel said Maureen asked her if she would come to the Hrickos' because Kim needed her, but Rachel said she wasn't able to do that. Later that afternoon Kimberly called Rachel and asked her to drive to Laurel to be with her. Kim told Rachel that the police and the fire marshal had interrogated her and she was really upset. She said she needed Rachel's support. Again Rachel refused.

"Kim then told me she knew what I was thinking," Rachel said. "And I said, 'You know what I'm thinking?'"

When the interview at the bank ended, the police went back to Rachel's home to continue talking with her. While there, they spoke with Rachel's neighbors Karen and Tom (pseudonym) Porter, who confirmed the fact that Rachel had telephoned them the night Kimberly first laid out her plan to kill Steve. The neighbors said Rachel called them at midnight on Friday, January 30. As the call came in, the caller ID displayed the Hrickos' telephone number, a number neither Karen nor Tom recognized. They let their answering machine pick up the call. When they heard Rachel's voice, Tom immediately put the telephone on speaker mode so both he and Karen could hear. Rachel told them that she was concerned about her friend Kim, who said she was planning to kill her husband.

The Porters said Rachel told them that Kim was going to use a cigar or cigarette to burn down her house with her husband inside. They said Rachel told them that Kim was drunk, so she didn't know whether to take her seriously or not. Tom told police he could hear Kim laughing in the background, reacting to what Rachel was saying. The Porters said

Rachel told them how Kim had talked about using a drug to paralyze Steve. Before the call ended, the Porters told Rachel to call them back if she needed help or if she wanted them to call the police. Rachel did call them back an hour later from her car phone to tell them Kim had passed out and she was on her way back to Baltimore.

The next day Elzey contacted Dr. Fowler at the medical examiner's office to tell him that police believed that Kim used succinylcholine chloride, or a similar drug, to stop Steve's breathing before setting him on fire. Fowler, who was familiar with the drug, said it was normally used as a muscle relaxant during surgery and/or to facilitate endotracheal intubation. Fowler said the drug should only be administered intravenously in those situations. When injected into the body, it would take between four and six seconds to paralyze a person's skeletal muscles and for the person to stop breathing and then die.

Later that day Henry Dove, the assistant state's attorney for Talbot County, called Elzey to provide him with his firsthand information of the Hrickos' behavior during the murder-mystery dinner-theater production at Harbourtowne. Dove, a cast member, said he was sitting at a table with the Hrickos and three other couples. According to Dove, although Kimberly was friendly and participating in the play, Stephen appeared to be bored or not interested in the play at all. Dove added that he didn't think Steve had much to drink.

Elzey also spoke with other couples in rooms adjacent to room 506. The couple in room 501 said they went back to their room after dinner and sometime between 1:00 and 1:30 A.M. a man started banging on their door, yelling, "Get out, get out, fire." The couple in room 504 said they returned to their room around 10:50 P.M. after the dinner and play. At approximately 1:10 A.M. a Harbourtowne employee named Elaine was banging on their door, yelling, "Get out, fire." The people in room 502 said they returned to their room around 11:00 P.M. They said sometime around 1:00 A.M. someone knocked on the door, but never said anything. A short time later, someone began banging on the door, yelling, "Fire."

Elzey made a mental note that the statements of these people directly contradicted Kimberly's statement that after she discovered that her room was on fire, she started banging on the nearby rooms, screaming for help.

On Thursday, February 19, Elzey and Alt met Kimberly's friend Marsha Carter at her job. Marsha, the woman who had watched Sarah while the Hrickos were at Harbourtowne, told police pretty much what she had told them over the telephone. She said that about two months before Steve's death, Kimberly had met a United States Marine named Brad Winkler. She said they had started seeing each other after the wedding of his cousin, Sean Gowen, to Kim's friend, Jennifer Moore.

Marsha said that on February 6, while Stephen was home babysitting Sarah, she and Kim went to the Green Turtle Pub in Laurel, where Kimberly met Brad. Later that night, after leaving the pub, the three friends went back to Marsha's house. As soon as they got there, Kim and Brad went upstairs to the bedroom to have sex, Marsha said.

During the interview Marsha told Elzey that several months earlier, Kimberly had told her that she had asked Steve for a divorce. And sometime in January, Steve had called Marsha to tell her he wanted to work things out with Kimberly and that he was going to be a better husband. Although they were friends, Marsha thought it was very odd that Steve would call to talk to her about his feelings toward Kim.

While Marsha was babysitting Sarah on February 15, Sarah injured herself as she was playing. Marsha took her to the hospital and was met there by Kim's parents, who then took her home. Around 5:30 that afternoon, Marsha told Elzey, Kimberly called her to tell her about Steve's death. Kim told Marsha that Steve started drinking heavily as soon as they arrived at Harbourtowne and continued drinking through dinner. When they got back to their room after dinner, Steve wanted to fool around, even though Kim specifically had told him she had no intention of having sex over the weekend. The couple started arguing and she left the room, hoping to find her way to the Millers' house, she explained to Marsha. But she got lost and decided to go back to the resort, she said.

However, she soon realized she didn't have her electronic key card with her, so she walked around back to try to get in through the sliding glass patio door. That's when she was hit with a wall of smoke and discovered the room was on fire. She told Marsha she ran around front and began banging on the other doors, yelling, "Fire." When no one responded, she drove to the lobby to get help. She said she called 911 on her cell phone as she drove to the hotel's main entrance. When the firefighters and police arrived, they found Steve's body, she said.

Kim also told Marsha that when she finally got home she called Rachel McCoy, but Rachel refused to come to the house to help her. Marsha said when she asked why, Kim said something like it was because one night

when she was drinking she told Rachel she wished
Steve were dead.

When Elzey got back to the office, he learned that
Dr. Fowler had called earlier to tell him that Steve's
blood alcohol level was 0.00. Fowler said he conducted several tests to confirm this result. That meant,
contrary to Kim's statements, that Steve had not been
drinking heavily, if at all, before he died.

A couple of hours later, Elzey received information
that Kim had asked Ken Burgess, a former coworker
at Holy Cross Hospital in Silver Spring, Maryland, to
kill Steve for her for either $5,000 or $50,000—
Burgess couldn't remember the exact amount.
Burgess had contacted the state police at the Salisbury
Barracks to tell them his story. Corporal Joseph
Gamble, of the Easton Barracks, and another state
trooper made plans to meet with Burgess on February 22 at his home in Chantilly, Virginia.

As part of their investigation police subpoenaed the
Hrickos' cell phone records from Bell Atlantic, but
they garnered no important information from those
records. They also subpoenaed any applications for,
or purchases of, life insurance on the Hrickos within
the past two years from the Medical Information
Bureau.

On February 21 Kimberly telephoned Elzey to ask
about the status of the investigation into Steve's
death. During their conversation Kim told Elzey that
she was being harassed by news reporters and reporters from *Hard Copy*. Kimberly also asked for an
update on the medical examiner's report. Then she
said she wanted to go back to Harbourtowne and to
room 506 to see where Steve died. Elzey told Kim that
he didn't have the results of the autopsy yet, but he
did have Steve's wedding ring, which he received

from the medical examiner's office. Elzey asked Kim to meet him and Sergeant Alt at the state police barracks in Easton on Monday, February 23, to retrieve the ring. Elzey said he and Alt would then take her back to Harbourtowne.

Chapter 8

At the time of Steve's murder Joseph Gamble, now Detective Sergeant Gamble, was a corporal with the Maryland State Police. Gamble headed up the unit that did the background investigation on Kim.

Around noon, on February 22, Gamble and Corporal Jason Merson interviewed Ken Burgess at his Chantilly, Virginia, home. Burgess was one of Kim's former coworkers at Holy Cross Hospital in Silver Spring, Maryland. Burgess, who had worked as a surgical technologist at Holy Cross for about two-and-a-half years, started his job about the same time as Kim. The two first met at a hospital orientation class they attended together.

As certified surgical technologists, their duties at Holy Cross Hospital included setting up the operating room, handling surgical instruments, physically assisting the surgeon during a procedure, and then cleaning the room to get it ready for the next case. During the interview with police Burgess described Kimberly as smart, articulate, and a respected surgical technologist. He said she resigned from Holy Cross sometime in December 1997 to take a higher-paying job with a temporary placement agency, and he hadn't spoken with her since she left the hospital.

Burgess told police that just before Kimberly resigned, she approached him in the hallway near the operating room and asked him to help her kill her husband. He said she asked if he would do it, or if he would find someone to kill Steve for her, for either $5,000 or $50,000. Initially Burgess wasn't sure of the exact amount, but he later said it was $50,000.

"We were in the middle of a construction phase at the hospital and I was standing in the back hall that went into the women's locker room. That's where we kept the scrub caps and booties and that type item and I was getting dressed for the day. It was a few minutes before seven," Burgess said later. "I had my back to her and she made a statement about wanting to have her husband killed and would I do it, or would I know somebody that would kill her husband."

Thinking Kim was joking, Burgess turned around to look at her and made an off-the-cuff comment.

"'Why would you want to kill your husband?'" Burgess asked. "'You work in the operating room, why don't you just give him some curare and put him to sleep.' I was kind of joking. When I turned around and I looked at her, I could tell she wasn't joking. She just said she had to get it done."

The next day Burgess asked Kim why she was so angry and why she wanted to kill her husband. Kim didn't want to discuss it, but she told Burgess not to discuss it with Jennifer Gowen, or anyone else. Burgess told Kim she should just forget about her plan. He also told Kim she shouldn't resign from the hospital if she was having problems at home. He figured she probably needed some stability in her life. Burgess told police that Kim probably solicited his help because she knew he never had much money and he was always complaining about living in a trailer that was twenty years old. Kim knew he was always looking for ways to make extra money.

Burgess didn't tell anyone about that conversation until Thursday, February 19, after reading an article about Steve's death in the *Washington Post*. Then he told two of his supervisors and a couple of doctors about Kim's strange request.

After interviewing Burgess, the police asked him if he would be willing to make a telephone call to Kimberly at home and let police tape the call. Burgess agreed. In order to tape a telephone call between two people in Maryland, only one person needs to consent to the taping.

Later that day Gamble and several other state troopers met Burgess at the state police barracks in College Park, Maryland, where they recorded three conversations between Burgess and Kim. During the calls police wrote out questions for Burgess to ask Kim to try and get her to say she killed Steve. Burgess made the first call at 9:14 P.M.:

Kim (K)-Hello.
Burgess (B)-Hey, Kim.
K-May I ask who's calling?
B-Ken Burgess.
K-Hi.
B-Hey, dear how are ya?
K-I've been better.
B-I'll bet. How's everything? You doin' okay?
K-Um, right now, just numb.
B-I bet, I bet.
K-Yea, um . . .
B-How's your daughter?

K-She's okay, I was just tucking her in. Can you call back in like five minutes and I can talk to you? I'd really like to?

B-Sure, dear, no problem.

K-Okay. Thanks.

B-Bye-Bye.

K-Bye.

Burgess called Kim back several minutes later at 9:22 P.M. This call lasted until 9:35 P.M.

Kim (K)-Hello.

Burgess (B)-Hey, dear.

K-Hey.

B-How are ya?

K-Well.

B-Deep subject.

(Kim laughs.)

B-How's your daughter?

K-Um, doing very well, considering.

B-Good, good.

K-She's doing appropriately.

B-You doing all right?

K-Well, huh, um.

B-How surprising.

K-Hm?

B-Surprised?

K-Are you surprised?

B-Yea.

K-That you called?

B-No, I mean when I pick up the paper when I walked into work the other day and, you know. Everybody has the paper and talking, saying, 'my gosh, did you hear what happened to Kim's husband?' So . . .

K-I can't even . . . this is someone else's life.

B-I'll bet. I mean I was thinking about a week or two ago about giving you a call and seeing how the agency was and stuff was doing.

K-I've been working pretty exclusively at Suburban.

B-Are ya? I've been busy here. I just didn't get a chance . . .

K-Well, I thought about you too, to tell ya, how in demand, you know, we are. You know, ah, Janet has been working pretty much at Fairfax exclusively . . . and, um.

B-Yea, I was offered a job but I turned it down about two weeks ago.

K-How much were they giving you an hour?

B-It wasn't much more an hour, about a buck or so more, but it was three-twelves. Would have been nice but with Steven (his son) home, I just couldn't do the twelve-hour shift.

K-Right.

B-So, can I, what the hell happened?

K-Um, well . . .

B-You okay?

K-Well, no. I mean I've been crying for days and I don't have any more . . . It's like I'm numb.

B-Did you go home for a while?

K-Hm?

B-Did you go home for a while?

K-I had to go home to bury him.

B-Uh huh. I didn't know if that happened yet, or . . .

K-Yea, and um, Valentine's weekend Steve, okay, oh, let's get back on track.

B-You don't have to go into it.

K-I do. I mean because I know that you, you'll tell people at work. They need to know.

B-I'd like that. Jill called me.

K-Did she?

B-Yea. Long distance and at that point I was, just couldn't talk.

K-Um. And now I can so I'll tell you a little bit, just to, some of the details. Um, I told Steve in January that he had to change or had to leave.

B-Hm.

K-We started counseling together.

B-Uh huh.

K-And, um, separately.

B-Right.

K-As well.

B-Ah huh.

K-And um, as a surprise he booked a, not telling me where we were going, or what we were doing, to Harbourtowne, on the Eastern shore. I didn't even know what we were doing . . . pack a bag and we were going to stay the night.

B-Ah huh.

K-It turns out that we were going to a murder-mystery dinner theater. But part of our counseling had been, well, it's sort of personal, but like . . .

B-Right, I read that part, that was in the (*Washington*) *Post*.

K-What was?

B-That you all were going down to that murder mystery thing.

K-Oh, right. We had talked, agreed that we wouldn't . . . there would be no pressure in that direction.

B-Ah huh.

K-Because that's one of the issues we were dealing with.

B-What? Remember back before you left, you came to me?

K-Uh huh.

B-Right before you left.

K-Um huh.

B-You wanted to know if I knew anybody that would take him out.

K-Oh, I was just kidding. I mean, you know, I was just . . .

B-I mean that scared the hello out of me 'cause then I picked up the paper and the other day and I was, like what the hell happened.

K-Um huh.

B-But I just ah, you know, I just . . . It scared me a little bit because you know I'm concerned about you.

K-Ah huh. Well don't worry. I mean you know sometimes you say things just to vent.

B-Uh huh.

K-But you know that you would never, ever, actually have the guts to do anything like that.

B-You doing okay?

K-Huh?

B-But you're doing okay?

K-Well, so do you want to hear the rest of my story?

B-I sure do.

K-Anyway we went to this thing, and, um, Steve's counselor put him on some psych meds and doubled the dose and then doubled the dose again.

B-Damn.

K-And he drank a lot that night.

B-Ah huh.

K-A lot, and, um, I guess, I don't know [he got kind of] groppy [Note: gropey] and you know.

B-Ah huh.

K-Man like.

B-I can sympathize. Go ahead.

K-Um huh, and so I just said I have to leave and I left. And um, I knew we were on the Eastern shore and my brother lives on the Eastern shore and my very good friend and her husband live there. So I got in my car and proceeded to get my, I mean just, all I wanted to do was find Route 50 and it's like the world's hardest thing to find. And at 11 o'clock at night no gas stations, no 7-11's, no pedestrians, anything. And I got really severely lost, although I did find Easton once and um . . . but the directions were obviously bogus or I'm really retarded. I don't know, probably both, 'cause I was really upset.

B-Was he American that gave you directions?

K-Women.

B-Oh, see there you go.

K-So, I just got to this point that I was so tired, 'cause I had also had, you know, like two glasses of champagne with dinner, a big dinner. So I go, okay, how much worse is this than anything we've been through.

B-Ah huh.

K-Should I just go back there and he'll probably be sleeping anyway. Well, I went back, which was another adventure because I got lost three times, trying to do that, and um, I couldn't find where I [left] the key, and I went around to the back because we had like a villa that faced the water.

B-Ah huh.

K-And I opened up the sliding glass door, which

wasn't locked. Well, I had actually hung clothes out there to dry. Don't ask. Anyway.

B-Okay.

(Kim laughs.)

B-A little dipping of the skinny?

(Kim laughs and then continues on with her story.)

K-And um, a huge amount of smoke came out, like black, dense heat, so that when I pulled the curtain back and it was just ridiculous all the smoke and I started to scream and there was no light, and there was no noise, and not a light, no nothing. You know it was just so dense, so I ran around to the front of the building, 'cause they're grouped in fours.

B-Ah huh.

K-And I started knocking on everyone's door and no one was, I mean the parking lot was full and no one's answering. So I went to the next group of fours and starting knocking. I was just like running from door to door and whoever answers, you know, I was screaming like an idiot. I think, well, I have to get back in the car and I have to drive back to the main lodge, 'cause it's the only thing that's going to work. I get into the car and I'm, like, I got a car phone. So I call 911, at the same time I was driving back to the lodge and I was like simultaneously talking to the man on 911 and at the same time running into the lobby and screaming. And, um, then everybody in the lobby just bolted and was going to do whatever it was they needed to do. But I was standing there by myself, going, oh Jesus what do I do, what do I do. So, I knew that I was going to hyperventilate and there was no way I could drive, so I sorta just like ran back to the villa, but I didn't even get to it because like the policeman and this woman tackled me and, um, shoved me in the back of the police car and took me away because I guess they had pulled Steve out by that point and it looked pretty bad.

B-Um, well what do the cops think?

K-They think it was a horrible accident, so far.

B-Have they talked to anybody? I mean if they come and talk to me what the hell do you want me to say?

K-I can't believe you're worried about this?

B-You scared me back when you were . . . that's why I came to you the second day about it, you know. You really kinda scared me about it. I mean you know how much I think, I care about you.

K-Um huh.

B-It's just, ah, I hate to see something . . .

K-I thought we were both flippant.

B-Yea, well I figured we both are most of the time.

K-Yea, because I mean, you said, you said . . .

B-Sorry, my car phone.

K-Huh?

B-Sorry, go ahead. I'm on my cordless.

K-Oh.

B-Walking around. I can't sit still.

K-I thought we were just, I mean really considered that this to be like a, a joke.

B-Yea.

K-Because, you said, seriously, I mean, what you said, "Why would you do anything like that when you have all this curare."

B-Right. I remember the conversation.

K-Yea.

B-So, well you know you can get a hold of me if you need anything. You know that.

K-Right and . . .

B-I want you to take care of yourself, that's all, that's why I called. You had me worried.

K-Well, you know.

B-You really had me worried. It's scary. You know, we started there together. I could come to you about anything when I was there. You kept me out of trouble 90% of the time. Now I don't have anybody to keep me out of trouble.

K-Absolutely and that's how I am. I mean if I'd give someone my friendship, I give it.

B-Is Jenny and them okay? I mean is she there for you?

K-No.

B-No?

K-No.

B-What's wrong with her?

K-Just stuff.

B-You sure? I mean you okay?

K-Oh yea. I mean of all the things that are happening that's way low on my priority list.

B-You had a problem before?

K-They had to put me on like a 24-hour watch because I wanted to kill myself after it happened.

B-Oh Jesus.

K-I mean . . .

B-You should have called, baby. You know there's people out there that care about you.

K-Oh my God and my house was full of them.

B-No lie. I mean there's no lack of support, and . . . You know you can call if there's a problem.

K-I mean, please, don't worry about that.

B-It just scared me. I mean you don't pick up the

paper often and see something like that. And you know how I didn't want them coming around, asking. So let me give you my pager number sweetheart, so . . .

K-I have it.

B-You do?

K-It's the one you gave me all along. The same one I've always, put it in . . .

B-It's the same one. Page me if you need anything. It's a lot easier to page me than call me at the house, 'cause I've been pulling about five nights a week call. So . . .

K-You're still a money-making machine.

B-Ah well, I'm not sleeping that much, but you know . . .

K-Why is that?

B-Gotta work. Ain't nobody else left, so we got like five travel techs, so . . .

K-That they're paying?

B-Yea.

K-Huge money?

B-Well, I'm glad we talked dear.

K-Have they given you a raise yet?

B-No.

K-Are we done talking? Is this what you're telling me?

(Inaudible)

K-I wanna talk more.

B-Can't I call you tomorrow?

K-No.

B-Won't you be home?

K-No.

B-No? Where you going?

K-Huh?

B-I said, "You won't be home tomorrow?"

K-No. I have like five thousand . . . It's the first day that I've been home. I just got home tonight.

B-Is it really?

K-I mean I have been traveling, doing funeral-type horrible things.

B-Right. At the same time this happened Jim passed . . .

K-Huh?

B-Jim, my father-in-law passed away.

K-Now, listen to me.

B-Yea.

K-You know me.

B-Yea.

K-Please.

B-Talk to me, Kim.

K-Please do not think that I am capable of this. If the people that know me best think that I am, then it would be worse to me than anything. Besides the actual loss, which is probably the worse thing that has ever happened to me in my life, I was at the funeral and we all . . . The thing's that hardest for me, I mean besides the fact that now, I'm by myself, you know. I really wish I could have just said goodbye, that's all. I mean . . .

B-I know. I know he had done something bad when we talked in November, because you wouldn't say what he had done.

K-Right.

B-So, you know.

K-It's . . . It was just some stuff. But we were getting through it. I mean then, but I don't know what's worse, I don't know. You know it's things have been totally crappy or totally great, which makes it worse.

B-Right. Well, babe, I'm not cutting you off but

I gotta go take care of Steve, he's had a bad toothache and I want to get some sleep. I got to get in tomorrow morning bright and early. But let me call you tomorrow evening, if I can. Okay? Can I do that? Would it bother you? That way you would have somebody to talk to.

K-Okay.

B-Okay. You take care of that daughter. She needs you right now.

K-Yes, she does, she really does.

B-You got my pager, page me if you need me for anything.

K-Okay.

B-All right.

K-Okay.

B-I appreciate it, dear.

K-No, thanks for calling.

B-Take care.

K-Okay.

B-Bye-bye.

K-Bye-bye.

When this call ended, police decided to wrap it up for the night. But at about 11:15 P.M. that night Kim paged Burgess, who immediately contacted police. Police then asked him to make another call to Kim, which they would also tape. Burgess called Kim back at approximately 11:57 P.M. That call lasted about fifteen minutes.

Kim (K)-Hello.

Burgess (B)-Kim?

K-Yes.

B-Kenny.

K-Hi.

B-What's wrong?

K-Oh.

B-I had to take Steve up to the (inaudible) he's got a bad toothache.

K-Umm.

B-Just walked in and Johnny came out and said you had called. Gave a call right back. So what's wrong?

K-I just was a little unsettled by our phone call because I thought if you were worried about me then you might have more time to listen and then I thought, oh God, you know me better than to think any of that stuff.

B-You sure sounded serious that day, that's for sure. That's what had me so worried.

K-Ummm, not any more than you were, you know when we were talking about our various sundry marital problems and you told me you know. You had good advice that day.

B-I told you, you could stay there and pull your resignation.

(Kim laughs.)

K-I'm serious you did, you had good advice that day and can I think that you really think that? I mean the only (inaudible) nothing's gonna . . .

B-Did you ever tell anybody else about us talking that day?

K-No, my God, no. Never.

B-Okay. Big concern.

K-Huh?

B-I said that was a big concern.

K-Oh my God, I would never mention it to anybody because that's how . . . Well after I thought of it until you, until I heard you're . . . I mean myself. I, I, I mean I thought we were kidding. I mean I thought, we both, I mean we were kidding. But apparently only one-half of us, you know we're always saying stuff like that, you and I know.

B-Well, I thought you were serious. It scared the shit out of me. That's why I came to you the next day, you know, about pulling your resignation and staying there and you know. You didn't say what had prompted you to be so upset.

K-Oh yea, well, they just . . . Yea, yea. Those two unconnected incidences.

B-Why did you offer the money?

K-Huh?

B-I said, why did you offer me money?

K-Why did I?

B-Yea, ah . . .

K-I really was just kidding. But I thought, I mean for, if you were a scary individual I wouldn't have said anything to you, but you're not.

B-I'm not real intimidating.

K-You know, you're my friend, Ken. I can say anything to you. That's all. So I think the only thing that could be better . . . is if you really think that. I was desperately seeking him (inaudible). I probably could find some (inaudible). You're just a little fuzzy, you're not shady.

B-Thanks.

K-You know what I mean.

B-I know, yea. I mean I went through it, but I'd never, I'd never do anything. I mean, you know, I'd never do anything crazy like that, that's for doggone sure.

K-I know, I wouldn't want you to. How is your wife? Is she still . . . ?

B-She's doing fine. She's at her mom's and there's no big deal. The kids are doing great.

K-Yea, all of them?

B-Yep, doing great. Yep.

K-That's wonderful. It's another thing that upset me. I thought that I can't believe Ken called me and he's concerned about me and he had to limit our conversation to five minutes.

B-Yea, Steve's been doing . . . About ten, twelve years ago he got hit by a car.

K-Um huh.

B-And it knocked his teeth, at least on the front, so occasionally he gets these real bad canker sores 'cause, I don't know if it's an overbite or what it is. But really hurts on the inside of his jaw and it had just gotten real, real sore over the last couple of days. So Tylenol wasn't touching it so when I, that's what's been going on with him so I had to run him up and tomorrow I've taken off work and I'm gonna have to run him up to the dentist. And a good friend of mine is a dentist in Arlington. I coached ball with him for a long time.

K-Umm.

B-He takes care of Steve, but he's just gotta get, he usually gives him some ointment to put on and I guess that it numbs it up 'cause, you know, him being handicapped, he just picks at them and, you know, he doesn't know to leave them alone.

K-Right.

B-And it just makes it worse.

K-Oh, that sounds horrible.

B-You doing all right now that you know, he's, I mean do you feel relieved, I mean do you feel concerned?

K-I was feeling unsettled before I thought (inaudible) that you called.

B-I called to see how you were doing. I mean I was going to call last week, but, um, I was going to call last week to see how you were doing before I just, about everything, just called this evening 'cause I was sitting around the house and I said, well, you know, give you a call before the first of the week. You know, you know I don't have anybody to talk to at work.

K-You know one thing that you said about the guy in (inaudible) . . .

B-Why did you call me tonight? Back, just for the conversation?

K-Yep, I was just, I was like had this feeling like and I thought, why am I upset and I thought, because if Ken didn't even want to hear my whole story and he's worried about the police talking to him, he must really think that I am a criminal. And I thought, Jesus Christ, I can't stand that. So that's when I called you back.

B-I just, I just . . . The fact that you had done, you know, something happened. I mean, some of the papers are saying it's under mysterious circumstances and, you know, that it could be murder and I mean . . . It's enough to get you, you know and then, you and I talked about it and I didn't know if you had talked to anybody else about it or (inaudible). That's it, I mean so don't . . . The only thing that's going to bring any grief your way is if your, you know, I guess say, Kim and I talked about that. That could bring some grief your way, you know, in the form of questions. I sure don't want no grief my way, you know that.

K-And grief my way.

B-I sure don't want that.

K-I'll be a wretch [*sic*] whatever happens.

B-How's the press?

K-Oh, oh, that thing sucks.

B-Does it?

K-I've been chased from the funeral home to the grave site. People Magazine won't leave me alone.

B-Oh, gosh.

K-My life's a nightmare, but because, it's because we went to that stupid play.

B-(inaudible) Hard Copy chased ya? That's, that's incredible.

K-Who the hell? Who the hell?

B-Have you talked to the police? I mean, the police believe you, don't they? They haven't bothered you anymore, or . . .

K-Well they did until yesterday, but . . .

B-They did what? I'm sorry.

K-They bothered me until yesterday, but . . .

B-Oh, did they really?

K-And um, I was talking to the trooper, the first person I called . . .

B-And they believe you, don't they?

K-Yea.

B-They do?

K-Yea.

B-You gotta good story? I mean sounds like what happened sounds believable, you know, what you're saying. I know I listened to you.

K-What the trooper said was every time I read something about this I wonder how they know more about my case than I do.

B-Well, you know how the press is.

K-Oh yea, blood suckers.

B-You gonna be alright?

K–I'm glad you called me back.

B–Can I help you?

K–No.

B–Sure?

K–No, that's okay, I was just.

B–Can I help you with your story? I mean do you need any help, ah, you know, explaining everything?

K–You know what, if they want to convict me for something like this, then they can just go right ahead and do it, if they can, but I mean (inaudible) at this point, I gotta take care of Sarah, that's all.

B–She's doing all right? I mean she's staying strong?

K–She's, she's amazing.

B–So what's wrong with your parents?

K–They're here.

B–Oh, are they there?

K–My mom is here. She's over in Sarah's bedroom. She's, they really have not been leaving me alone because they are worried about me.

B–I don't blame them. I can understand that.

K–About what I will do because I'm just distraught. But I appreciate your calling both times.

B–You know that I would have called earlier but I didn't know what to do, or, you know, just didn't know what was going on.

K–You got yourself all worked up.

B–Well, if you needed me to help out anyway, you know, I mean . . .

K–Um huh.

B–If there are any questions—they don't believe you or something, give me a call. I mean, you know, I could back you up anyway [*sic*] I possibly can.

K–(Inaudible)

B-Just between you and I, you know.

K-Huh huh.

B-I'll back you up anyway [*sic*] I, you know, I can back up your story. You know what I'm saying?

K-That's sweet.

B-If the police, you know, I mean, you know what I'm saying. If you need any help. If the police call, or you know, there is a question in the story, you know, give me a holler.

K-Okay.

B-Maybe we can work something out.

K-God, I hope that never, nothing comes to this, but umm, obviously you're not on call tonight, right?

B-No, Chris is on tonight, but I gotta work all day tomorrow.

K-Okay. Well, tell Holy Cross, I said hi.

B-I will. I'm exhausted. I worked until four this morning.

K-You poor thing.

B-Just (inaudible).

K-I don't sleep worrying so . . .

B-I can't believe it, that's amazing, Hard Copy. I can't imagine what you are going through, between the police and Hard Copy and . . .

K-The police are nothing. It's the press because the woman that writes these, these plays.

B-Right.

K-Like the one we went to. She sold her story.

B-Ah, Jesus.

K-She sold her story to all these people, like isn't it a coincidence that a man died and now I have the part for my next mystery and she just sensationalized it all (inaudible).

B-That's incredible.

K-Anyway.

B-I'll tell ya, I, I mean what I said. I can help you out, if I have to on your story, but I couldn't tell them that you wanted . . . I wouldn't say anything about our conversation. You know what I'm saying, I wouldn't.

K-Well, I, I . . .

B-So don't worry about that.

K-Okay, I mean I certainly don't.

B-Well get some sleep, dear. If you need anything give me a page again, you know that.

K-Oh, okay.

B-All right, I'm on call tomorrow night, but if you need me tomorrow night or you need me to talk or something, page me. Give me a little while to get right back to you.

K-Thank you.

B-All right.

K-Take care of yourself.

B-You, too, dear.

K-Okay.

B-Bye-bye.

K-Night.

"When Kim called Ken Burgess back, we knew we had her," Gamble said. "I just wish we could have gotten her over the phone. If they kept playing phone tag, we were going to have Burgess say, 'I won't go to [the] police if you give me some of the insurance money.' But it never developed into that. But she says at [the] end of [the] phone call, 'Remember that advice you gave me, that was really good advice.' She was talking about the succinylcholine. Based on that phone call, we believed that Kim had injected Steve with curare or succinylcholine."

The state police then talked again to David Fowler, the medical examiner, who said he was going to do a series of tests to check for the presence of succinyl-choline. Fowler also shipped off some tissue to the FBI, but neither the medical examiner nor the FBI was able to find any traces of the drug in Steve's blood or tissue samples.

"That's because the ME said the body metabolizes it so quickly that it's very difficult to find and also we didn't even have an injection site," Gamble said. "When the ME testified at trial, he said that the only way to find an injection site would have been to skin Steve at autopsy to see the subcutaneous injection site, which he didn't do. Even after death it's very difficult to find. There's no technology to find it yet. And we never found the syringe and we never could prove that Kimberly stole the drug because it's a noncontrolled substance. Ken Burgess told us there's no way to track the succinylcholine. It's not a drug you can abuse—if you abuse it, you're going to die. But, as a surgical technician, she had access to the crash cart, where the drug is kept."

Chapter 9

At 7:00 A.M., on February 23, Corporal Elzey met with his superior to review the three search-and-seizure warrants Elzey was preparing for Kim, her car (a 1995 Dodge Stratus), and her house on Belle Ami Drive in Laurel.

Shortly after going over the warrants, Elzey had them signed by a judge, who also agreed to seal them.

Around 4:20 that afternoon Elzey and Sergeant Alt met with Kimberly at the Easton Barracks. Elzey gave Kim her husband's wedding band and then asked her if she still wanted to go out to Harbourtowne. She said she did.

It was just about 5:30 P.M. when Elzey, Alt, and Kim arrived at Harbourtowne. The first thing they did was go into room 506 so Kim could see where Steve died. Kim seemed calm and not at all affected by what she saw.

Elzey asked her if she wanted to go to another room to talk about the events surrounding Steve's death. She said yes, so she went with Elzey and Alt to room 606, where she again told them her story.

Kim said she and Steve went to Harbourtowne

over the Valentine's Day weekend to try and work on their marriage. She said they arrived at Harbourtowne around 3:00 P.M. on Saturday, February 14, and checked into room 506. Kim said Steve drank a bottle of champagne before they went to dinner and the murder-mystery play. During dinner she said Steve drank beer and wine. In fact, he was drinking heavily throughout the evening, she said. After the play was over, Kim said, they bought beer at the bar and brought it back to their room.

In addition, Steve had taken cold medicine and Xanax before dinner, she said. She also told police that Steve regularly chewed tobacco and smoked when he drank alcohol. But she said she didn't remember Steve buying any cigarettes or cigars to take on the trip, nor did she purchase any.

Kim said the couple watched the end of *Tommy Boy* on television and then the news came on. Kim told Elzey that she cut out the February 14 listings from *TV Guide*, which indicated that *Tommy Boy* was on TV that night.

Kim said she and Steve began arguing when he attempted to pressure her to have sex; she refused because her therapist had advised her not to use sex as a tool to help the marriage. Kim told police that Steve had agreed that they wouldn't have sex that weekend.

Kim and Steve argued for about ten minutes when she decided she wanted to get away from him. So a little after 11:00 P.M. she grabbed her purse and car keys and left the room, planning to go to the Millers' house in Easton. However, she got lost. She said she tried to get directions to Easton from several people, but she was unsuccessful.

When she finally got back to Harbourtowne a little

after 1:00 A.M., she realized she had forgotten her electronic key card. She walked around to the back of the building so she could enter through the sliding glass doors, which she remembered she had left open.

When she opened the door, she was hit with thick smoke. She ran around to the front of the building and started banging on the doors of the other rooms in the 500 complex to get help, but failed. Then she jumped in her car and drove to the main building. When she got there, she ran into the lobby, asking for help because her room was on fire. At the same time she was calling 911 on her cell phone, she said.

During the interview Sergeant Alt asked Kimberly if she was having an affair. She said she wasn't. Alt then asked her if she knew a U.S. Marine named Brad Winkler. Kim appeared shocked, but she didn't say a word. Alt and Elzey told her they knew about her affair with Winkler. Kim bowed her head, then looked up and acknowledged the affair.

Kim explained that she started seeing Winkler several months earlier. She said she met him through her friend Jennifer Moore, who married Winkler's cousin, Sean Gowen. She admitted she was having sex with Winkler, but said she never planned to leave Steve for him. She said Steve did not know about the affair.

Elzey asked Kim to tell him again how much alcohol Steve drank the night before he died. Kim said he was drinking heavily. Elzey then confronted her with the results of the medical examiner's toxicology report, which indicated Steve had a blood alcohol level of 0.00.

Kim appeared stunned and said it didn't make sense.

"Why don't you explain to me, if Steve consumed so much alcohol, why didn't it register?" Elzey asked.

"I don't understand. I don't understand," Kim said, visibly shaken.

Next Elzey confronted Kimberly with the medical examiner's report indicating there was no carbon monoxide or soot found in Steve's body.

Again Kim appeared stunned.

"I don't understand," she repeated.

Kim lowered her head and then looked up.

"How can that be?" she asked, crying.

"Please tell me the whole truth about what happened that night," Elzey said.

Kim bent over, put her head in her hands, and continued crying. Still crying, she got up, sat in another chair, and put her face in her hands.

"If I tell you what happened, can I go home tonight and see my daughter?" she asked.

Sergeant Alt told Kim if she told them the truth, she wouldn't be able to see her daughter. Finally Kim said she wanted to tell the police what happened, but she wanted her lawyer with her. Elzey and Alt then ended the interview and read Kimberly her Miranda rights.

"Kim was almost ready to confess, but Karen Alt screwed up," Gamble said.

"Kim says to Karen, 'If I tell you the truth, will you let me go see my daughter?' Karen tells her, 'You know if you tell us the truth, you won't be able to see your daughter.' What she should have said—and one of the reasons we now have a homicide unit—is 'Absolutely, we'll take you right now,' and then jump in the car and she's in custody and you have her weeping all the way there and you have her confession," Gamble said.

"I think she wanted to confess," Gamble said. "I think

Alt needed to be a little more swift on her feet and say, 'Absolutely—you'll be able to see your daughter.'"

After the interview was concluded, Kim left Harbourtowne and went to the Millers' house for dinner.

"We had made plans that Kim would come down to our house on Monday, after she met with the police, who had called her and said they wanted to take her down to the hotel so they could explain to her what happened and how Steve died," Maureen said. "She was meeting them at the Easton Barracks at ten A.M., and was supposed to come back to our house when she was done and stay for dinner."

When 6:00 P.M. rolled around and the Millers still hadn't heard from Kim, Maureen called the Easton Barracks of the state police to find out what was going on. A trooper told her that Kim was still at Harbourtowne with two troopers, but he didn't know when they would be finished and he couldn't interrupt them.

While the Millers waited, Kim's mother, who was in Laurel taking care of Sarah, was calling Maureen, also trying to find out when Kim would be home.

Finally, around 7:30 in the evening, Kim came strolling through the door.

"What the hell is going on?" Maureen asked.

"They think I killed him," Kim said.

Maureen couldn't believe what she was hearing.

"That's where I've been all day long," Kim said. "They've been interrogating me. They've been trying to make me say I killed him—that I was a battered wife and Steve beat me, so I killed him. They told me I might as well come clean and confess because they know that I killed him. They said all my friends had come forward and they had buckets of evidence against me."

Not knowing quite what to say or do, Maureen tried to calm Kim down.

"What would give them the idea that you were abused?" Maureen asked. "Steve never hit you, did he?'"

"Never. He would never, never hit me," Kim responded.

"Then why would they say that?" Maureen wanted to know.

"Because they're trying to get me to confess," she said. "They're trying to get me to say I killed him."

"Kim, you need to call a lawyer. This is going too far," said Maureen, who, at this point, still thought Kim was being falsely accused.

But Mike knew something just wasn't right. He'd suspected Kimberly was involved in Steve's death from the beginning. And now he was more convinced than ever.

After rambling for a while longer, Kim told Maureen she was tired and didn't want to talk anymore. She said she wanted to lie down.

"I told her to go to sleep, but told her in the morning we were going to sit down and talk about what was going on, because I didn't like what she was saying. And I told her again she had to contact a lawyer," Maureen said.

Kim agreed, so Maureen moved her daughter into the master bedroom and put Kim in her daughter's bed. Once Kim was settled, Maureen called Kim's mother, Lois, and told her Kim was going to spend the night. While Maureen was speaking with Lois, there was a knock on the Millers' front door.

Taking the portable phone with her, Maureen went to the door. She was surprised to see the Maryland State Police standing there. The troopers said they needed to talk to Kim Hricko because they needed to serve her with a search warrant.

"I told Lois I needed to go because the police were at the door and they have a search warrant, and I have to go wake up Kim," Maureen said.

At that very moment Lois started screaming hysterically into the phone.

"The police are here, the police are here!" she shouted. "There are four police cars and they're knocking on the door."

"Well, open the door," Maureen said, exasperated.

"I'm going to have a heart attack. I'm going to have a nervous breakdown," Lois said frantically.

"Lois, open the door for them," Maureen said, forcefully.

Maureen later found out that the state police had timed their arrivals to the minute, so they could execute both search warrants at the same time.

"There are four policemen here and they want to come in and search the house," Lois said again.

Maureen told her she had to let them in if they had a search warrant.

"I'll call you back," Maureen said, trying to get off the phone so she could deal with the troopers in her own home. "I'm really pissed because now I know I'm being lied to by Kim."

At the Hrickos' house Lois had just prayed with Sarah and tucked her in bed when the police knocked at the door to serve the search-and-seizure warrant.

"There were a number of police and I asked them to let me call my prayer partner," Lois said. "They made [us] sit for four hours—they dumped everything out. I was so upset. We were scared, so Sarah and

I just sat there and read the Bible. There was a police-man sitting with us because we weren't allowed to move. They were there a number of hours. When they left, Matt took me to the emergency room because I have high blood pressure."

Some of the items police confiscated at the Hrickos' home included letters to Kim from Steve, two pamphlets about life insurance, a white box containing sympathy cards, the cremation certificate for Steve's body, miscellaneous papers and business cards, a letter to Steve from Kim, a Bell Atlantic Mobile phone bill, a checkbook register, and articles printed from the Internet pertaining to divorce and custody.

During the search of the Hrickos' house, police also found two life-insurance policies on Steve, totaling $450,000, which they believed Steve never signed.

"We believe that Kim signed them," Gamble said.

As part of the investigation Gamble learned that on December 8, 1997, Steve allegedly filled out a benefits enrollment card increasing his life insurance through work to twice his normal salary. As part of its benefits package, Patuxent Greens provided its employees with a term policy that would pay out one year's salary to an employee's beneficiary. The accidental death benefit of Steve's new policy was $200,000, twice his annual salary.

Police learned that Kim took out a $250,000 life insurance policy on Steve in November 1996. As the owner and primary beneficiary of the policy—Sarah was the contingent beneficiary—Kim was making the quarterly payments of $114.08. Kim's mother said the payouts from the life insurance policies have been put in a trust for Sarah.

* * *

After ending the call with Lois, Maureen went into the master bedroom and woke Kim up, telling her that the police were there to serve her with a search warrant.

"You need to get up out of bed right now," Maureen told her.

So Kim got up and sauntered down the hall like she didn't have a care in the world.

"And she's mad—she's nasty mad and throws the keys at the cops because the search warrant is for her car," Maureen recalled. "And I'm thinking, for somebody who's supposed to be innocent, she's not helping herself very much."

The trooper took Kim's keys and went outside to search her car.

Angry, Maureen turned to Kim and said, "You need to come clean right now."

"I will," Kim responded. "I'll tell you everything, but I don't want to be down there while they're doing this. Just let me go take a bath."

"So once again, stupid me says, 'Okay, I'll go run the bathwater for you. You go in there and I'll get a glass of wine for you. They'll serve the search warrant, but then you're coming out and you're telling me what's going on,'" Maureen said.

Maureen then went to the bathroom and started running a bath for Kim. Meanwhile, the state police were unloading Christmas gifts from the back of Kim's car and bringing them into the Miller house. Apparently Kim had a number of undelivered Christmas gifts that she was supposed to give to kids in the CASA program, but they were still in the back of her car.

While Kim was in the bathroom, Maureen went in to check on her.

"She was just sitting on the edge of the toilet and

I told her to get undressed and get in the bathtub," Maureen said. "Then I went and turned off the water and left."

Maureen went into her dining room, where the police were opening and searching the Christmas gifts.

"My dining room is filled with these gifts and the police are going through them, when one of the police officers starts running off at the mouth, saying that Kim is a horrible, evil person and they're going to put her away for a very long time and that she murdered Steve," Maureen said. "He was really angry."

Maureen asked him why he thought Kim killed Steve, but he wouldn't tell her anything because they still suspected she helped Kim kill her husband.

At that point Mike, who was in the room also, turned around and started yelling at Maureen.

"I told you," Mike said. "It's time for you to back away. You need to let her go."

"I can't let her go, she's my friend, and until somebody tells me what's going on here, I'm not going to do that," Maureen told Mike. "I would never be able to live it down if they're wrong—that I turned my back on her when she needed me the most."

The troopers told the Millers that some people had come forward with information and they were going to put her away.

"They said maybe not tomorrow, or next week, or even a month from then, but they were going to get her," Maureen remembered.

Upset and confused, Maureen went into the bathroom and saw that Kim wasn't taking her bath. In fact, she was sitting on the toilet fully clothed.

"You can't take a bath unless you take your clothes off," Maureen said.

"I didn't kill him," Kim said.

"She's talking and she's slurring her words. And I knew she had taken something. At this point she's teetering on the toilet, like she's going to fall off," Maureen said.

"Oh, my God, what did you take?" Maureen screamed as she searched the bathroom.

Soon Maureen found an empty bottle of pills that had Xanax written on it. Frantic, Maureen told Mike to call an ambulance. Mike, however, was furious that Kim would try to commit suicide with his kids in the house.

The ambulance arrived and took Kim to the Easton Memorial Hospital. Maureen followed in her own car. On the way she received a call from Mike, who told her when he was cleaning up the bathroom, he found razor blades on the edge of the bathtub.

"Apparently Kim staged it to make it look like she was going to get in the bathtub, slit her wrists, and kill herself, because it turned out that the medication she had actually taken was not Xanax, according to the toxicology report," Maureen said. "Kim put something else in the Xanax bottle and that's what she took."

The nurse at the hospital told Maureen that Kim would be fine. In fact, the nurse said that Kim would have been worse off taking a bottle of aspirin.

While she was waiting for Kim, Maureen, who was three months pregnant, started to feel really ill. The nurses took her blood pressure and found that it was sky-high. So they asked her to stay in the emergency room until they determined she was okay. In the meantime emergency room personnel were pumping Kim's stomach.

When they were finished, Maureen went to talk to Kim.

"You're a stupid idiot, Kim," Maureen said. "Why are you doing this? You're innocent."

At least that's what Maureen wanted to believe.

In hindsight, though, there were a lot of things that indicated that Kim was guilty of murdering her husband. However, Maureen still wasn't totally convinced that Kim had killed Steve.

"I needed to know for sure because I didn't want to make a mistake," Maureen explained. "This was a person who was at a point of desperation."

Although she helped Kim, Maureen was starting to get a bit annoyed. She wanted Kim's family to step up to the plate and make some decisions about her welfare.

What Maureen wanted and what she got were two different things.

"Kim's mother was absolutely no help whatsoever," Maureen recalled. "She was hysterical at everything and she would call these people over and they would start prayer chains. And I'm like, 'Do you all understand what's going on here.' It was almost like if they prayed, everything would go away. They just had no sense of reality."

Finally Maureen left the hospital, telling Kim she'd be back to check on her the next day.

When she got back to the hospital the next day, Maureen helped Kim out with some insurance issues and also called an attorney friend, Harry Walsh, to ask him to represent Kim.

Walsh agreed, but he said he'd need a $10,000 retainer. Kim agreed and Walsh said he'd come by the hospital at 2:00 P.M.

"We dealt with a couple of the insurance issues, but in the meantime she's trying to get her family to give her ten thousand dollars for the retainer fee, but they wouldn't give it to her," Maureen said. "She even called the Hrickos and asked them for it and was mad because they wouldn't give it to her. She wanted to know why the Hrickos wouldn't give her the retainer, because they had tons of money."

Kim soon started panicking because she didn't have the money for the retainer and didn't know how she was going to get it. She tried to call her father and he said no. Then she called her grandfather and he wouldn't give her any money, either. Maureen just couldn't understand why Kim's family wouldn't help her.

"Kim was talking nasty about the Hrickos because they wouldn't give her any money," Maureen said. "And then she told me that Jenny Gowen was the one who was telling the police stuff. She said Jenny was lying and she wanted me to call Jenny and find out what she was saying, but I said I wasn't calling her, and if she wanted to know what Jenny said, then she should call her. I told her I wasn't getting involved."

Kim actually had told four of her friends what she planned to do to Steve. There was Norma Walz, Teri Armstrong, Jenny Gowen, and Rachel McCoy, although Rachel was the only one who knew Kim's entire plan to kill Steve. The others only knew bits and pieces of the plan.

"I still don't know how much Jenny and Teri knew," Maureen said. "I think Jenny and Teri knew less than Rachel, and I think Norma knew very little."

Even though Kim pressed Maureen to call Jenny, she refused.

Kim continued to turn to Maureen for help, because now that the police were onto her, no one else—not even her family—would help her.

"There was only me," Maureen said. "Stupid me."

Overwhelmed, Kim started crying really, really hard. And Maureen started to feel sorry for her again.

"This was the first time I had seen her cry hysterically since Steve died," Maureen said. "But I don't think she was crying for Steve. I think she was crying for herself."

And, again, Maureen wanted to help her.

"Here she was in a hospital on suicide watch with a nurse in her room around the clock," Maureen said. "I said, 'Kim, I wish there was something I could do, I really do,' and then she leaned forward and whispered something to me. And to this day I cannot say exactly what she said, but I think she said, 'I killed Steve.'"

"I said, 'What did you say?'" Maureen recalled.

But before Kim could respond, state police officers Joe Gamble and Keith Elzey arrived to serve Kim with a warrant to search her purse, and she immediately clammed up. Maureen's head was spinning, because she wasn't quite sure what Kim had said.

"I don't know if I was making myself hear what I thought she said, or if she actually said she killed Steve," Maureen said.

When the police were finished searching Kim's purse—items they seized included one of Brad Winkler's business cards and a piece of paper with Ken Burgess's name, home, and work telephone numbers on it—Maureen walked out with them and followed them to the elevator.

"You guys have to come clean with me and tell me what's going on," Maureen said. "That's when I found out they suspected me."

Gamble and Elzey told Maureen they couldn't tell her anything about the investigation because she was a suspect.

"What do you mean I'm a suspect?" Maureen asked.

"We haven't quite figured out if you're involved in this, but we have enough evidence to arrest Kim for Steve's murder," one of the officers said. "We're just not sure when we're going to do it—it could be tomorrow, it could be next week, it could be next month, but we will be arresting her. And if you didn't have anything to do with this, you may want to back off."

Maureen told the troopers she didn't have anything to do with Steve's death. She begged them to tell her what was going on, but they again refused. By now, Maureen was convinced that Kim was guilty and that the police had the evidence to prove it.

"And I'm thinking she did it, after hearing what I just heard, her behavior, the *Playboy* being too obvious, what Rachel had said; I'm like, 'Oh, my God,'" Maureen said.

When she walked back into Kim's room, Harry Walsh was right behind her.

Walsh showed up, even though he knew that Kim didn't have the $10,000 retainer, because he also knew this was a high-profile case. In fact, that's why Maureen called him—she believed he would be blinded by the limelight.

Maureen went home so Walsh could interview Kim in private. When she called Kim later, she asked her what she was talking about earlier. Maureen wanted to find out if Kim really did admit to murdering Steve, but Kim said Walsh instructed her not to say anything to anyone.

"I'm like, 'Okay, how are you feeling? Is the insurance taken care of?' We had a normal conversation and that was it," Maureen said.

However, later that day Maureen got a call from an employee of Easton Memorial Hospital to tell her

Kim was going to be transferred to the Upper Shore Community Health Center, a state mental-health facility. The employee told Maureen that there was a problem with Kim's health insurance. It seemed because Kim's insurance was through Steve, and because Steve was dead, she technically didn't have insurance.

"So they were trying to get all that straightened out and to ultimately get her into a mental hospital because she was on suicide watch," Maureen said. "But they said that the other hospital couldn't admit her for longer than three days, so I said go ahead and send her up there."

Chapter 10

While Kim was dealing with attorneys and insurance, Corporal Keith Elzey was laying out the case against Kim in a warrant for her arrest. It had only been about a week since Steve's death, but the state police felt they had enough information to arrest Kim for killing Steve and setting fire to room 506 to cover up his murder.

In the charging document Elzey said on Sunday, February 15, 1998, at approximately 1:35 A.M., Trooper First Class Clay Hartness responded to Harbourtowne to investigate an unattended death in room 506. Also present at the scene were members of the St. Michaels Fire Department and other law enforcement personnel.

Elzey said the preliminary investigation revealed that there had been a fire in room 506 and that concerned citizens had removed Steve's burned body from the room and placed it outside on the rear deck before the fire department or law enforcement arrived at the resort. Stephen Hricko was pronounced dead at the scene by a forensic examiner. A subsequent search of the room turned up a package of cigars with one cigar missing from the pack. The missing cigar was not found during the search.

Elzey said when he responded to Harbourtowne he learned that Steve and his wife, Kimberly Michelle Hricko, had arrived at the resort on February 14 and checked into room 506. During questioning by police Kim said that she and Steve were at the resort to attend a murder-mystery play that was being presented on Valentine's Day. Kim told police that Steve had been drinking heavily during the evening and at the end of the play they purchased some alcoholic beverages from the bar at the resort to take back to their room. A short time later, Steve pressured Kim to have sex with him. The couple argued because she said no. Kim left the room at approximately 11:00 P.M. in order to avoid a nasty scene.

Kimberly tried to drive to a friend's house in Easton, but got lost for a couple of hours and subsequently returned to Harbourtowne shortly after 1:00 A.M. on February 15. She tried to enter room 506 through the rear sliding glass door, but was met by thick smoke. Unable to see what was happening in the room, she went to the hotel lobby to get help. The concerned citizens who responded to the Hrickos' room found Steve inside on the floor and pulled his badly burned body out onto the rear deck.

Kim subsequently told Elzey that she and Steve had been having marital problems and they were both seeing separate marriage counselors. Kim also told Elzey that Steve chewed tobacco and smoked when he was drinking. However, Kim said she didn't think Steve brought any cigars or cigarettes with him to Harbourtowne, nor did she buy or bring any smoking materials to the resort for him. After interviewing several people who had known Steve for several years,

Elzey said he learned that no one, except Kim, had ever known him to smoke.

Elzey said Steve's body was removed from the scene and taken to the state medical examiner's office in Baltimore. After performing an autopsy, Dr. David Fowler, the medical examiner, told Elzey that there was no carbon monoxide found in Steve's blood, nor was there any evidence of soot or burns in Steve's trachea or any related injuries to his lungs. That meant that Steve was either not breathing or dead before the fire started, Fowler told Elzey. The medical examiner also said that Steve's blood alcohol content was 0.00 percent, which meant that there was no alcohol found in his blood. At that point Fowler told Elzey he was waiting for the results of more tests to determine the exact cause of Steve's death.

Elzey said on Tuesday, February 17, two days after Steve's death, he spoke with one of Kim's friends, Rachel McCoy, who said that about three weeks before Steve died, Kim told her that she planned to kill him. According to McCoy, Kimberly planned to inject Steve with a drug that would paralyze him and stop his breathing. Kim said because she was a surgical technologist she had easy access to the drug. She said because the drug wasn't classified as a controlled substance she could get it at work without being noticed. Interviews with medical personnel at the hospital where Kim had worked confirmed that she wouldn't have had any trouble obtaining these types of drugs without being noticed.

Then she was going to set the curtains on fire with a cigar or candle, making it look like Steve died in a fire in their town house. McCoy tried to talk Kim out of her horrific plan by telling her it would look suspicious if she used a cigar because Steve didn't smoke. Kim countered that the fire wouldn't look suspicious because she had purchased a smoker's life insurance policy on Steve, so everyone would think that he really did smoke.

In the arrest warrant Elzey said that Sergeant Karen Alt, of the Maryland State Police Bureau of Drug and Criminal Enforcement Unit, had also interviewed several of Kim's other friends. In those interviews Alt learned that Kim was having an affair with a younger man and wanted out of her marriage and even had asked Steve for a divorce, but she didn't think he would agree to divorce her. She also said that Steve would be better off dead and that she would kill him immediately if she thought she could get away with it. Kim advised her friends that Steve would probably just kill himself if she told him about her affair. The problem, though, was that she wouldn't be able to collect on his life insurance if he committed suicide.

One of Kim's friends told Alt that Kim had taken out a $250,000 life insurance policy on Steve. A check by Maryland State Police corporal David Sharp, of the insurance fraud unit, revealed that Kim took the policy out in November 1996.

Elzey said that on February 22 Corporal Joseph Gamble, of the Maryland State Police, met with one of Kim's former coworkers, who had contacted police after he learned of Steve Hricko's death. Ken Burgess, the coworker, disclosed that about six weeks before Steve's death, Kim had approached him and asked him to kill her husband for either $5,000 or $50,000— but later said it was $50,000. She also asked Burgess if he knew anyone who would kill Steve for money; Burgess declined to take Kim up on her offer.

Elzey said on Sunday evening, February 22, Gamble monitored a conversation between Burgess and Kim.

During that conversation Kim acknowledged that she talked to Burgess about having Steve killed. Elzey said he questioned Kim the next day about Steve's death and the fire in room 506 at Harbourtowne. During the interview Elzey presented Kim with the results of the investigation to that point. He said Kim then said if she told him what really happened, would she have to go immediately to jail? Kim never told Elzey what really happened and the interview was ended, he said in the arrest warrant.

"It took us a week to put this case together," Gamble said. "First off, we have a fire death, that's all we have to start with. Then the next day we have the autopsy. On Sunday afternoon the investigators find out there are problems and they start doing some research. But Steve's gone. Kimberly had the body cremated and his sisters are all screaming that there's something wrong."

Not only were Steve's sisters crying foul, so was Mike Miller.

"Mike told us Steve didn't smoke—he chewed tobacco," Gamble said. "He said Steve was often offered cigars at dinners, but he didn't smoke them—although he sometimes took them for Mike. So all these people are calling us saying Steve didn't smoke—even though Kim said he was smoking."

By now the state police knew there was a major problem, but they couldn't tell anyone.

"We're stringing Kim along the whole week," Gamble said. "People from all over are coming to the barracks asking about the case and we're telling everyone, including the press, that it's just a normal death investigation with some weird circumstances. Even *Hard Copy* was calling and telling us they were from the family in order to get information."

Gamble had a theory about how Kimberly killed her husband.

"The guy who dragged Steve out said he was sitting at the foot of the bed and his pants were down," Gamble said. "I think what she did is she killed him, and she staged it to look as if he was masturbating—she pulled his pants down and had the *Playboy* book open to look like he's had all the pleasure that he wanted and then he's puffing on the cigar. I think she's so bizarre that she actually set this thing up."

Gamble believed Kimberly got Steve in a compromising position—either they were having sex, or she was performing oral sex on him.

"He's lying in bed and he's thinking it's all great and she's got all this stuff ready—she goes into the bathroom and she's got this needle ready and tells him, 'Just lay back, honey, I'll take care of you,' and he feels a pinch. 'Oh, what's that?' he says, and she says, 'Oh, I'm sorry,'" Gamble said. "Even if he sits up, all she has to do is avoid him for a couple seconds—and he's gone. The doctor says you're conscious and it's like somebody's suffocating you. You're conscious—you can see, you can hear; your muscles are going, but your brain is still working."

Gamble continued, "The medical examiner thought Steve would be incapacitated within one minute. He thought Kimberly could inject him and he would be totally out in thirty seconds. He'd be conscious, awake, alert; his brain would be functioning, he would know what's going on, but he wouldn't be able to move."

On Tuesday, February 24, Kim was transferred to the Upper Shore Community Health Center, and at

10:30 P.M. she called Maureen and told her the police had arrived and they were arresting her for Steve's death.

"They're saying I murdered Steve," Kim told Maureen. "I told her to call her lawyer and I hung up. That was the last time she and I spoke," Maureen said. "Well, after she had been arrested, everything came out in the paper about the succinylcholine and her affair. And when I heard about the affair, I knew immediately who it was. I knew it was Brad. Then I talked to Jenny Gowen and Jenny confirmed it was Brad, and all the pieces fell into place, and I was like, 'God, how stupid was I?' I fell for everything hook, line and sinker."

In the months leading up to Kim's trial, she and Maureen never spoke. In fact, it wasn't until a week before the trial that Maureen even started talking to Kim's other girlfriends, including Rachel and Norma.

"When we all started talking, then we started piecing the puzzle together," Maureen said. "When I was at Kim's that first day after Steve died and I called Rachel, and Rachel called another friend, and then Rachel called Kim—that's when Rachel knew Kim had killed Steve. And then the next day Rachel called the police and told them everything."

When the women started piecing everything together, they realized Kim had totally screwed them over.

At approximately 4:00 A.M., on February 25, Kimberly was taken before a Talbot County Court commissioner and then was incarcerated without bail at the Talbot County Detention Center in Easton, where she was placed on suicide watch.

At a bail review hearing later that afternoon, Talbot County deputy state's attorney Marie Hill asked that Kimberly continue to be held without bail because of the nature of the charges and because she had no ties to the area. District Court judge William H. Adkins III granted Hill's request. Adkins also granted a motion filed by Kim's lawyer, Harry Walsh, asking that Kim be transferred to the Clifton T. Perkins Hospital Center, the state's maximum-security psychiatric facility in Jessup, for a psychiatric evaluation to determine her competency to stand trial. She was moved to Perkins that afternoon.

That same day Elzey contacted the Maryland Underwater Recovery Team and asked the team to go to Harbourtowne and search the Miles River directly behind room 506, as well as a nearby pier, for a hypodermic needle or anything else related to Steve's murder. The dive team conducted the underwater search on Thursday morning, but they came up empty.

Chapter 11

When police searched the Hrickos' house on February 23, 1998, they discovered a journal that Steve had written in the weeks before he died. Steve's writings painted a picture of a man desperate to do whatever it took to make his marriage work—a man worried about his wife's feelings, even as she was seeing another man and planning his murder.

In an early morning journal entry on January 21, 1998, Steve said he felt terrible, like he was going to die, even though he felt hopeful the previous day. Steve also said he felt like he had ruined his life as well as Kim and Sarah's lives and he was afraid Kim was going to leave him as soon as he got his depression under control.

"I feel she doesn't understand how deeply I love her—I mean real love. I am afraid I won't get the chance to make the marriage right," Steve said, adding that all his fears stemmed from his depression.

Steve said he finally understood the pain he had caused Kim and said he never wanted to make anyone feel like he did again. However, even though he said he had changed and enjoyed talking now, Kim didn't seem to be ready to trust him and try to get to know the new Steve—a sensitive, caring, affectionate man with an inner strength. Steve said he would never stop working, praying and fighting for Kim's love.

Later that day Steve said he felt better because Kim told him she loved him. He said he was even able to eat some cereal.

"I just talked to Kim and she said I love you. She may [have] just said that to make me feel better. I don't care. I never thought three words could cause such overwhelming joy," he said. "I love her so much. Thank you, God."

When Kim called Steve again that day and told him she loved him, he was beyond ecstatic. Just hearing his wife's voice made all Steve's problems disappear. He was so happy he wanted to run through the neighborhood yelling and screaming that Kim loved him. Steve said he was finally able to feel again and he knew that he loved Kim and Sarah more than he could say. He hoped that Kim would give him another chance to show her and their friends that he was more "than a quiet, big jerk."

But Steve's good mood was shattered when Sarah told him that Kim wanted her to watch a show on divorce. Despite this setback, Steve said he was determined to keep working hard so Kim would love him again. Waiting for Kim to come home from work, Steve said that he felt so much better when she was with him.

In a January 27 journal entry, Steve said he and Kim hadn't made love in almost a month. Steve said he wanted to hold and kiss his wife, but not in a sexual manner. He just wanted to feel her body against his. However he knew that he couldn't push her into any type of a relationship. He just had to wait and believe that someday she would love him again.

Steve said he felt like two different people—the guy he was before and the guy he was now and he hated that other person. Steve believed that the other Steve ruined his life as a husband and a father and he was sure the new Steve would be a good husband and he prayed Kim would understand. However, Steve was afraid he had already thrown away his chance at a happy life.

In his journal Steve wrote that he really needed some kind of affection from Kim—a hug when he didn't expect it, or the touch of her hand. He said that although he thought he was getting stronger, he now felt weak and he hated feeling that way. Even though his doctor told him to forgive himself, he couldn't do it, especially since he had caused so much damage to everyone else.

Although Steve didn't expect Kimberly to tell him she loved him, he was very upset that he felt like he couldn't say those words to her. To survive, Steve said he needed to feel love, caring and tenderness from Kim.

"I will love Kim forever and don't care if we would never have sex again. I would trade sex for a night of holding each other and talking in a minute," Steve said.

Steve was in a lot of pain and said he had no one to turn to. But even though he felt empty, he knew he had to stay strong for Sarah. Even if Kim didn't love him, Sarah did and he didn't want to hurt her.

Steve said that although the counselor he and Kim were seeing told him he had to learn to love himself, it was difficult to do especially since he had hurt the two people he loved most in the world—Kim and

Sarah. He said he didn't understand how he could have acted in a way that truly hurt his wife and young daughter. He was having a hard time dealing with the fact that he had hurt them so much. Maybe if he understood why he acted the way he did, then he could begin to forgive himself. Steve said he wanted to tell Kim that he was sorry and that he loved her so much and wanted to make everything right between them.

Steve said he had a good day at work, especially since Kim called him there around 1:00 P.M. In the past, Steve had treated Kim as an inconvenience, but now just hearing her voice was special to him.

In his journal Steve admitted that he had many questions but no answers. And Kim, the person he'd always looked to for love and support, wasn't there for him.

"It's funny how people take things for granted and then it's too late," Steve said. "If anything, I have learned that I won't take the people in my life for granted ever again."

Steve said he feared losing Kim. Even though he now understood what love meant, he couldn't share it with Kim because of what he had done to her in the past. He also said he knew before he could make the other people in his life happy, he had to be happy himself. Recently he felt happy, and he wanted to continue to feel that way, he said. Steve prayed that Kim could understand his depression and forgive him so they could start fresh. He hoped time would heal all wounds, but he was afraid that the counselor and Kim would tell him the marriage was over and he needed to move on. If that happened, Steve said he would be devastated.

All Steve wanted was to make Kim happy. He wanted to be able to talk to her and hear her laugh. At this point in his life he needed affection and tenderness, but not sex. In the past sex was the only way he could express his love for Kim, but now all he wanted was to tell her how much he loved her. He wanted to feel all the emotions he had kept locked up inside, but he knew Kim was not ready yet. So he decided to be patient and continue to believe that she still loved him.

"God I hope these pills kick in. The doctor said they won't solve my problems but maybe I will be able to deal with them better," he said.

Steve said he was trying to take one day at time—something he said was easy because he really didn't think that he had a future. He lived for the day when Kim would tell him she loved him before he said it to her. He also dreamed of the day when she would ask him to go out with her and her friends. Holding on to those dreams helped Steve survive each day.

In his journal entry for January 29, Steve said he and Kim had been to see their counselor, but Kim spent most of the time alone with her. While he waited for Kim's session to end he sat in the waiting room worrying about what they were saying to each other. He was frightened that Kim and the counselor would decide that he and Kim should end their marriage.

Although Kim told him not to worry about the future, he couldn't help thinking that she was going to meet someone else. He understood that a lot of men would be attracted to her because she was such a good person—something he didn't think he was. Steve said he knew no one could love him until he loved himself, but most of the time he hated himself. He hoped that someday he would be able to like himself. But at this point, fear and confusion were ruling his life.

"Last night Kim told me she was proud of me and

she loves me. That meant the world to me," Steve said. "But I am confused [because] she almost never says it anymore. Sex is non-existent anymore [*sic*]. That will take time and I am willing to wait."

On February 1, Steve said he recently tried to make love to Kim, even though he knew she wasn't ready yet. Now he felt weak and helpless and very guilty. Kim told him it turned her off that he was so needy. But he couldn't help it. All the feelings he had kept bottled up over the years were now bursting out of him. The problem was that Kim couldn't return his feelings. But he said he was willing to wait even though he wasn't sure about his future with Kim. But he wouldn't blame Kim if she decided to leave him. He said if he didn't believe that he was a loving person with a lot to offer Kim and Sarah, he'd just leave them.

Steve said he hurt so badly he didn't know how much longer he could make it. He knew that Kim needed someone who was strong and it was taking every bit of strength he had just to go on. He said he wouldn't blame her if she left him that day because of all the pain he caused her. But if she gave him time, he knew she would love him again.

Steve knew he had to back off and give Kim some space, but he said it was difficult, especially since he thought of her constantly. He said he used to think of himself as a big, strong man, but now he knew he was a coward for bottling up his feelings. He said he was so confused he didn't know how to act anymore. All he was sure of was his love and passion for his family.

Although Steve was scared, he was still trying to be strong. But it was hard. His sorrow was overwhelming and he couldn't control it. He tried not to feel guilty about the past, but he just couldn't help it. Knowing he had hurt Kim, the most wonderful woman in the

A young Stephen Hricko. *(Court file photo)*

Kimberly and Stephen Hricko in happier times.
(Court file photo)

Stephen Hricko died in room 506 in this cottage at Harbourtowne Resort. *(Photo courtesy of* The Baltimore Sun*)*

This is what the Hrickos' room would have looked like before the fire. *(Court file photo)*

The Hrickos' room after the fire. *(Court file photo)*

The wood stove with doors open in the Hrickos' room after the fire.
(Court file photo)

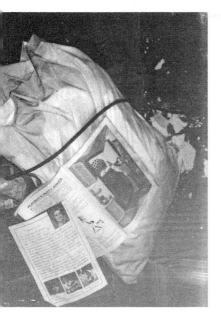

The *Playboy* magazine and pillow found in the Hrickos' room after the fire.
(Court file photo)

The package of cigars and other items found in the Hrickos' room.
(Court file photo)

The burned bed with the scorched headboard, as well as items on the bedside table in the Hrickos' room. *(Court file photo)*

Items found on the bedside table in the Hrickos' room after the fire. *(Court file photo)*

The burned bed in the Hrickos' room. *(Court file photo)*

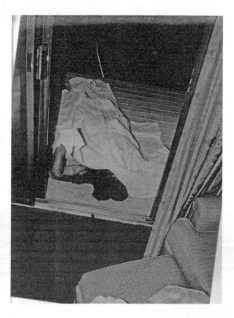

Stephen Hricko's
burned arm.
(Court file photo)

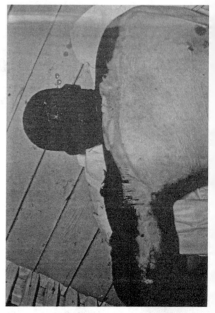

The back of Stephen
Hricko's burned body.
(Court file photo)

Stephen Hricko's
burned body.
(Court file photos)

The first page of Stephen Hricko's autopsy report listing the cause of death as probable poisoning and the manner of death as homicide. *(Court file photo)*

Deputy Fire Marshal Mike Mulligan *(left)* and Deputy Fire
Marshal Joe Flanagan *(right)*.
(Photo courtesy of Mike Mulligan)

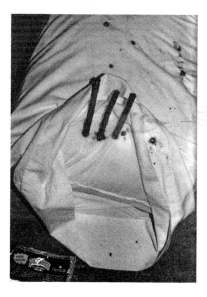

Mike Mulligan's attempts
to light a pillow on fire
with three cigars.
(Court file photo)

State Police Sergeant Joseph Gamble.
(Photo courtesy of Sergeant Gamble)

William Brennan, Kim's defense attorney.
(Photo courtesy of Leslie Billman)

Harry Trainor Jr., Kim's defense attorney.
(Photo courtesy Leslie Billman)

Prosecutor Robert Dean.
(Photo courtesy of Bob Dean)

Kimberly Hricko is helped out of a corrections van on the way to her sentencing hearing on March 19, 1999.
(Photo courtesy of Associated Press)

world, was eating him up. All he wanted was to be happy and make Kim happy as well.

Steve prayed that Kim believed him when he told her wanting to go to bed with her wasn't sexual. He just wanted to hold her body against him. He wanted to touch her and smell her body. In the past, Steve said he used sex just for personal pleasure, but now he wanted to share that with Kim so she could understand the deep emotional bond he felt for her. Steve promised to be patient and work hard forever because he knew he had a lot to offer people, especially Kim and Sarah. He knew he was special and he prayed that Kim would soon realize this fact. But even though he loved her deeply, he knew he couldn't push his love on her.

"I fear that months away she still won't love me and now that I can express and show my feelings I need someone there to share them with me," Steve said. "She says she loves me and I believe her—she needs time. If she only knew what her calling me or holding my hand meant to me. There are no words to express my feelings."

On February 9, less than a week before he was murdered, Steve wrote in his journal that life at home was improving and he was looking forward to Valentine's weekend at Harbourtowne with Kim. He said he was worried about Kim because she had bronchitis as well as blood in her rectum. He said he was very frightened because blood in the rectum can be a symptom of cancer. As far as Steve was concerned Kim's health came first and all he wanted was for her to be healthy.

Kim called Steve twice at work on February 9 and told him she loved him before he told her. This made him very happy. Steve said he had a hard time concentrating on work when all he cared about was his family.

Steve said he and Kim had not made love yet, and even though he wanted to, he said he would wait as long as it took because he loved her so much. For the first time, Steve said he knew what it was like to really be in love.

In his February 12 journal entry, Steve said Kim came home around 9:30 P.M. and accused him of trying to send her a message by locking the door and turning off the lights. But Steve said he did those things because he had gone to bed. Kim was in a bad mood when she got home and didn't even say hello to him. He was upset and didn't feel like he deserved to be treated so badly. Steve said he wanted the marriage to succeed but he refused to put up with this kind of treatment—the same kind of treatment she put up with from him.

"I eventually will need more from her. This weekend will tell me a lot about her feelings. We haven't had sex for two months and I have been very patient but at some point she must let me be close to her," Steve said.

During their investigation police also found some letters Steve had written to Kim showing how much he loved her and how much he wanted to make her happy. But all the time Steve was professing his love for Kim, she was professing her love for Brad Winkler.

In one letter Steve professed his undying love for Kim and told her he hoped she would always be his wife. He told her that, whether she believed it or not, she was the sexiest woman in the world to him—as beautiful on the inside as she was on the outside. He said he noticed that she was working on improving her appearance and that it intimidated him because he was so flabby and out of shape. He told Kim that he knew that any guy in the world would love to be with her and he worried that someone would take her away from him. He said he had to fight with himself all the time so he wouldn't be jealous and he could believe that she loved him as much as he loved her. Steve said no matter what happened in the future, he would always love her and stay faithful to that love.

In another letter Steve told Kim he was working hard to change so he could be the kind of husband she had always wanted. Steve told Kim it hurt so much to see her cry, especially knowing he couldn't erase the pain he'd caused her. But remembering it would help him in the future, he said. Steve said he knew he was pressuring Kim way too much, but he wanted her to understand that he was a special person with a lot to offer. He said he was beginning to forgive himself for hurting her, but he would never forget that fact. Remembering would help him become a better person.

Steve told Kim he would back off and let her discover her own feelings and not try to force his feelings on her. He said he believed that someday she would see that she had a strong husband who was capable of expressing all his feelings to her.

"I'm learning each day but I realize I've been expecting too much," he said. "Never feel you have to say I love you or call me at work."

Steve told Kim he would be there when she needed him and he just wanted her to be herself because he had fallen in love with that woman. He asked Kim to tell her therapist how special she was and that he now understood how lonely he made her feel and that he would do anything he could to make her happy again. He promised Kim he would always be there for her.

Steve said if he and Kim worked together they could have a great marriage, but he admitted it would take a long time. He said he knew he couldn't erase the past but he could slowly build a better future.

In another letter Steve talked about how wonderful their relationship used to be. And he told Kim not to be afraid to trust him and love him again. Steve wrote this letter after a telephone conversation with Kim.

He told her he wanted her to know that hearing her voice made him feel wonderful. He said his eyes had been opened, his mind had cleared and his heart had grown. He said that for some reason he had been remembering the night they first met at Maureen and Mike's house. The minute he saw her he was struck by her beauty and after just a few minutes he felt comfortable with her and knew they were going to have something special. He was drawn to her because he sensed she was kind, sensitive, caring and affectionate. He said by the time he talked to her the next day his heart belonged to her.

Steve reminisced about their wedding and how he had to fight to keep from crying as Kimberly walked down the aisle. He told Kim she was the most incredible looking bride there ever was or ever would be. Steve talked about sitting in bed watching television with Kim when she was pregnant and he told her he remembered all the love and strength she had shown him over the years. He said he always knew he had the greatest, most beautiful wife in the world, but his depression clouded his mind and prevented him from doing all the things he wanted to do now. But he said he knew he was going to make it because she made him want to be a better man. He said now he wanted her to draw on his strength rather than him drawing on her strength.

Steve told Kim not to be afraid because she could trust him and count on him again. And although it would take time, he would do everything in his power to be the man she thought she was marrying.

"I love you with such passion and it is a great feeling. You wrote you were afraid that your feelings for me won't return or maybe that they will," he said. "I believe they are still there but I built such a wall around them it is almost impossible for you to open up to me again. I understand that after all these years it is difficult to put yourself in a vulnerable position where I could possibly hurt you again."

Steve said although he and Kim made a commitment to each other and promised to always stay together, he wouldn't blame her if she wanted to leave him. But he wanted her to know that her husband was a special man—an intelligent, sensitive, caring and affectionate man who loved her very much. He told her not to be afraid to fall in love with him again because he would always be there for her.

The word "wife" meant so much more to him now, he said. Kim had been his lover and best friend. He said their marriage meant everything to him and he believed it was worth it to fight to make it work. If only Kim would give him a chance, they would have the marriage and family that they both had always wanted. Steve told Kim he knew that he had hurt her, but asked her to take a leap of faith and believe and trust that the love they once shared could come back stronger than ever.

"I'm sorry if this has upset you or made you feel smothered. I just can't contain my feelings for you anymore. I have nine years built up in me. Please don't be afraid to open your heart to me. I won't disappoint you ever again. I love you very much," Steve said, adding that if they worked together they could accomplish anything.

In yet another letter, Steve told Kim she was the most beautiful woman in the world, inside and out. He asked her to have faith in him, stand by him and give their marriage one more chance. Not quite what Kim had in mind.

Steve said although he had kept his emotions bottled up his entire life, he just couldn't contain them any longer. He said he was even dehydrated from crying so much and now he understood the saying, "crying an ocean of tears."

Steve said he now knew true happiness was not how green a fairway was, but seeing his wife and child smile at him, knowing they were happy and proud he was part of their lives.

He explained that he couldn't let Sarah grow up believing it was okay for a man to make her feel the way he had made Kim feel. Although he knew it was impossible for him to change thirty-five years overnight, he was taking the first step to becoming the man he had always wanted to be. Steve told Kim he needed her help to change his ways.

"Love is something that is felt and is difficult to put into words. When I look at you I see the most beautiful person I have ever seen, inside and out. Your strength inspires me to become a better person. This can only come from inside of me but I need your support and love for me to succeed," he said.

Steve told Kim although she had been faithful to the vows they made on their wedding day, he had not. He said he had received all the "better," while Kim had received all the "worse." But if Kim had faith in him, trusted him and loved him, he would make their marriage work.

While writing the letter Steve told Kim he had thrown up three times—the result of all his pent-up feelings coming out.

In order to have a complete life with his wife and daughter, Steve said he knew he had to love himself first and he was trying to do just that. Loving Kim and Sarah was the easy part. He said he loved them more than life itself and finally realized just what that meant to him.

"Please stand by me one more time and give our marriage one more chance to succeed. I will fight to improve myself as a husband, father and person," Steve said. "I love you."

While Steve was pouring his heart in his journal and his letters to Kim, she was doing some writing of her own. Unlike Steve, however, who promised to be a better husband and father, Kim didn't talk about the changes she would make to improve the relationship. Instead she focused on the changes Steve needed to make.

Kim wanted Steve to:

1. Be considerate of her feelings and of Sarah's feelings. She didn't want Steve to be mean anymore.
2. Develop friends and be comfortable socially. She wanted Steve to actually enjoy going out.
3. Give affection freely without fear of humiliation or rejection.
4. Develop shared interests and friends.
5. Promote a better relationship with Sarah.
6. Share all household and day-to-day duties without constant prompting.

7. Maintain his own existence—to fend for himself.
8. Watch less television and to do more mean-
   ingful activities with the family.

Kim did take some responsibility for the way Steve
acted throughout the marriage in a note she wrote
before he died. Kim explained that, for Sarah's sake,
for her family to appear normal, she made it easier
for Steve to remain withdrawn and "hermit-like."
Kim didn't want to be someone "who bitches all the
time . . . to change an unchangeable person."

Chapter 12

On March 3 Corporal Joe Gamble talked to Dr. Timothy Wex, chief anesthesiologist at Holy Cross Hospital in Silver Spring, Maryland, who, in the course of his duties, interacted with surgical technologists, including Kimberly and Ken Burgess.

The purpose of the interview was to corroborate Burgess's statements to police that after he learned of Stephen Hricko's death he told Wex that Kimberly had asked him to kill Steve for her. Gamble also wanted to ask Wex about the hospital's policy for storing various drugs in the operating room.

Wex told Gamble he learned about Steve's death sometime around February 16 when he heard other operating-room personnel talking about a newspaper article reporting the incident. Gamble said Wex might have mixed up the date because the *Washington Post* didn't report the story until February 19.

One evening, shortly after Steve's death, while they were in the locker room changing their clothes, Burgess told Wex that Kim had approached him a few days before she resigned in December 1997 and asked him if he knew anybody who would kill her husband for $50,000. Wex told Burgess to call the police and tell them what he knew, which he did.

Gamble then asked Wex about curare and succinylcholine, the two drugs that Kimberly may have used to kill Steve. Wex said both the drugs were present in the operating room and neither was controlled. The doctor explained that narcotics were dispensed by a system that only allowed a user to access the drugs by entering a personal identification number. That system provided a way for institutions to track the different narcotics. However, there was no such system in place for curare or succinylcholine, Wex said.

The reason those drugs weren't tracked was because they couldn't be abused. And for good reason—anyone who attempted to abuse curare or succinylcholine would die.

Gamble asked Wex if there was any way to determine whether Kimberly took either of the drugs from the operating room. Wex said it would be impossible to account for every dose of the drugs in question. According to Wex, if a doctor had a technologist draw a dose of either curare or succinylcholine and then didn't use it, it would just be thrown into the trash.

"Based on your information and experience, do you think Kimberly could steal the drugs in question from the hospital?" Gamble asked Wex.

"It is absolutely possible," he replied.

Wex said that anyone working in the operating room could steal one dose or multiple doses of the drugs because they were not kept under lock and key. Instead, they were kept on a cart, where they were available for immediate use during surgery. Wex added that there was ample opportunity for the surgical technologists, who prepared the room for surgery, to steal the drugs.

Gamble also asked Wex how the drugs were administered. Wex said they were either administered intravenously or intramuscularly. Wex added that during her career as a surgicial technologist, Kimberly would have seen the drugs used many times.

That same day Gamble also spoke with Dr. William Keefe, another anesthesiologist at Holy Cross Hospital. Again Gamble wanted to corroborate Burgess's statement that after learning of Steve's death, he also talked to Keefe about his conversation with Kimberly. Keefe said Burgess told him that Kim asked him if he would kill Steve for $50,000, or if he knew somebody who would do it for her. Like Wex, Keefe advised Burgess to contact police and tell them about that conversation.

Then Gamble asked Keefe the same questions he asked Wex about curare and succinylcholine. Keefe provided the same information as Wex about the availability of the drugs in the operating room. Keefe said the drugs were kept in the top drawer of the anesthesiologists' cart in the operating room. He said there was no accountability for the drugs and it would be nearly impossible to find out if a few vials were stolen during the time Kim worked at Holy Cross.

On March 3 Gamble interviewed Helen Basaman, an assistant nurse manager for the operating room at Holy Cross Hospital. Basaman supervised the surgical technologists, including Burgess and Kimberly.

Basaman said that Burgess also told her about his conversation with Kim. Basaman said Burgess approached her on February 19, the day the *Washington Post* reported on Steve's death. Burgess told Basaman that Kimberly asked him if he could find a hit man to get rid of her husband for $50,000. Basaman recalled that Burgess said he believed Kimberly was serious about having her husband killed. Basaman told Burgess to do what was right and advised him to call the state police.

Basaman told Gamble that Kimberly Hricko was a smart and energetic employee. She said Kim never discussed any personal issues with her. Through this interview Gamble also learned that a former coworker, Marcia Carroll, visited Kim at Perkins after her arrest.

During Gamble's March 18 interview with Carroll, an operating-room nurse at Holy Cross Hospital, she told him that she had visited Kimberly at Perkins three times since she had been arrested. Carroll said she went to see Kimberly to offer spiritual and emotional support, even though the two had not been particularly close outside of work. She told Gamble she started visiting Kim because of her religious beliefs.

During her first visit Carroll told Kim she didn't want to know anything about the case, because she didn't want to become a witness. So Kimberly didn't talk to Carroll about her relationship with Steve or his death. Their conversations were limited to religion and concern for Kim's daughter.

Gamble also spoke with other employees of Holy Cross Hospital. Through these interviews police learned that coworkers and supervisors considered Kim a knowledgeable surgical technologist who enjoyed a good reputation. In fact, the supervisors wanted to hire Kimberly to work at the hospital full-time. During her time at Holy Cross, Kim actually worked for First Assist Inc., a temporary medical-staffing agency.

On Monday, March 23, Gamble spoke with Sean Petrone, the golf professional at Patuxent Greens Country Club, where Steve worked as the course superintendent. Petrone, who first met Steve at Patuxent Greens, worked with him for approximately three years. The two were friends until Steve's death.

Petrone said Steve told him about the problems in his marriage and said he was going to counseling to become a better husband and father. Petrone said he didn't know that Kim was having an affair.

A couple of weeks before Steve died, Kimberly called Petrone and asked him to take Steve out for the evening to have a "guy night," because she would be going out with her girlfriends. Petrone said it was either on a Thursday or Friday night that he, Steve, and Jeff McMackin, who was then the assistant superintendent at the golf course, went to the Green Turtle Pub in Laurel.

Petrone told Gamble that Steve didn't drink much alcohol that evening. In fact, contrary to what Kim wanted everyone to believe, Steve wasn't much of a drinker, nor did he ever smoke. Petrone said he remembered socializing with Steve on four or five separate occasions and never saw him smoke.

Although Steve did chew tobacco, Petrone said he hated cigarette and cigar smoke. Petrone recalled several instances that Steve talked to him about his aversion to cigarette and cigar smoke. Another Patuxent employee, who worked with Steve for about a year, said he had never seen Steve smoke, although he did chew tobacco.

The next day Gamble interviewed McMackin, who was promoted to course superintendent at Patuxent after Steve's death. McMackin, who had worked as Steve's assistant for two years, told police he and Steve were close friends.

McMackin said Steve also told him about his marital problems and that he was in counseling because he wanted to improve his relationship with Kim. Mc-Mackin said he didn't know that Kim was having an affair and he didn't believe that Steve knew about it, either, or he would have mentioned it.

According to McMackin, before Steve planned the Valentine's Day weekend getaway to Harbourtowne, he checked with Kim to make sure she wanted to go, despite the fact that McMackin said it would be better to surprise her. Steve felt that given the problems in their marriage, surprising Kim wouldn't be such a good idea. Steve later told McMackin that Kimberly was looking forward to going on the minivacation.

Before Steve and Kim left for Harbourtowne, Steve called McMackin and asked if he would feed the Hrickos' cat and dog over the weekend, which he did. That was the last time McMackin ever spoke to Steve.

When asked about Steve's alcohol and tobacco use, McMackin told Gamble that Steve was not a big drinker.

"I've seen Steve drink a couple of beers in a social setting, but never knew him to drink to intoxication," McMackin said. "And Steve never smoked anything, but he did chew tobacco."

McMackin recalled once when he and Steve attended a conference hosted by a company that manufactured and sold golf-course maintenance equipment. After the conference the representatives of the company treated McMackin and Steve to an expensive dinner at an upscale restaurant. After they finished eating, the representatives passed a cigar box around the table and encouraged McMackin and Steve to have a complimentary cigar. McMackin said the cigars were high quality and expensive.

Everyone at the table took a cigar, except Steve.

When McMackin lit up his cigar, Steve turned to him and said, "How can you do that to yourself?"

McMackin told Gamble that Steve wouldn't even let anyone smoke in his office. Gamble then showed McMackin a package of Backwoods cigars, identical to the pack found in the Hrickos' room at Harbourtowne, and asked if he had ever seen Steve with that brand of cigars. McMackin said, "No. Steve did not smoke. Never, ever."

Near the end of March, State Trooper Jack McCauley interviewed two of Steve's coworkers at Patuxent Greens Country Club about Steve's habits. Steve's immediate supervisor, Dana Kessler (pseudonym), who had known him for three years, told McCauley she had never seen Steve smoke anything in all the time she knew him. In fact, she recalled that Steve wouldn't even allow her to smoke in the golf cart when they were riding together because the smoke really irritated him.

Kessler said about a month before he died, Steve asked her for some time off because he was having problems with his wife and needed to see a counselor. Steve told Kessler how Kim was his whole life. Shortly before Valentine's Day Steve told his boss that things were better in his marriage. Kessler said she knew Steve had planned something special for Kim for Valentine's Day, but she didn't know what it was.

After Steve's funeral Kim called Kessler to get the address of one of Steve's coworkers. Kessler asked Kim how her daughter was doing and Kim said a trust fund had been set up for Sarah and that they had collected on Steve's life insurance. Kim said Sarah didn't have to worry about money.

McCauley also talked to Mitch Bergman (pseudonym), a mechanic at Patuxent Greens, about Steve. Bergman, who started working at the club in November 1997, met Steve in September of that year when he interviewed for the mechanic's position. Bergman said he saw Steve every day at work and never saw him smoke. Bergman, who was a smoker, said Steve made him smoke outside because he couldn't stand the smell of it.

Bergman told police that Steve said he was having marital problems and that he was working too many hours and not spending enough time at home with his family.

A former Patuxent Greens mechanic, Don Sanderson (pseudonym), who oddly enough lived on Kimberly Drive in Stevensville, Maryland, told police he had worked for Steve for two years and three months, until September 19, 1997, when he left to take a position at another golf course. Sanderson said he and Steve had become good friends and they had similar views about family life. Sanderson said Steve often spoke highly of Kim and Sarah. He said he was shocked to learn that Kim was seeing another man. Sanderson said he last spoke to Steve on January 14, 1998. During their conversation Steve said he was working too many hours and it was affecting his relationship with Kim. Steve said he had set up an appointment with a counselor to try and get his marriage back on track. Sanderson said he didn't know what kind of problems the couple was having.

Gamble asked Sanderson whether Steve smoked, drank heavily, or liked to look at pornography. Sanderson said not only did Steve not smoke, but smoke made him physically ill. Sanderson recalled the night he and Steve attended a retirement party for a coworker. During the party most of the men were smoking cigars and he and Steve talked about how cigar smoke made them sick. Sanderson said he saw Steve drink a beer or two on a couple of occasions, but he had never seen Steve drunk, nor had he ever seen Steve look at pornography of any kind. In fact, Sanderson said, Steve wouldn't allow pornography to be displayed in his shop.

Gamble also interviewed several of the Hrickos' neighbors to find out if any of them had ever heard the Hrickos arguing. None of them had.

During their investigation, the state police, with help from the medical examiner, eliminated every other cause of death and put a circumstantial case together; so when the case went to trial, they would be able to lead the jury into believing Kim killed her husband.

"We subpoenaed all his medical files and we knew we were going to have the doctor testify in court that Steve was healthy," Gamble said. "Then we started trying to attack the story she gave police that night, including that he brought a pack of cigars with him."

The pack of smokes taken from room 506 was a package of Backwoods Mild 'n Natural cigars. The package was light brown with red and white lettering and had a white $2.49 price tag printed on it in blue ink.

"I was assigned to locate the store that the cigars were purchased from," Gamble said.

So on March 20, Gamble visited approximately twenty-five liquor and convenience stores in Prince George's County in the Laurel area, where the Hrickos lived. Approximately one-quarter of the stores sold the Backwoods cigars, but most of them did not use price tags. Although some stores did use price tags, they weren't the right size. Gamble then checked Astors Liquors in the Laurel Shopping Center, which was located about three miles from the Hrickos' house on Belle Ami Drive.

"I had the package of Backwood cigars with me with the pricing label of two dollars forty-nine cents— back then, people weren't using barcodes, so the sticker was unique," Gamble said. "I found this pack sitting on a shelf with a higher price on the tag, but I also found one that had two price stickers on it— one higher than the other. I peeled the first one back, which was two ninety-nine, and there is my two forty-nine, plus tax, sticker. The price had gone up in the two weeks since Hricko died."

Gamble then talked with Peggy Delis, the owner of the store, and asked her if those particular Backwoods cigars had previously been priced at $2.49. After checking her records Delis said the price had been raised from $2.49 to $2.99 sometime during the week of March 15.

Delis showed Gamble a Monarch Marking tag maker model 1115 that her employees used to price items in the store. Delis showed Gamble that the pricing gun could be set to produce the identical $2.49+tax sticker that was on the package of cigars taken from the Hrickos' room at Harbourtowne.

"I bought the package of cigars with the two ninety-nine price tag overlapping the two forty-nine price tag and told the manager that I wanted [the] pricing gun, which I then took back to the state police crime lab, along with some pricing stickers," Gamble said. "The state police forged-documents person looked at the gun and determined it produced the sticker on the package of Backwoods cigars found in the Hrickos' room at Harbourtowne."

Delis also told Gamble that although Astors Liquors was equipped with a video-surveillance camera, the store did not have any surveillance tapes for the days before Steve's death. However, Delis said Gamble could show pictures of Steve and Kimberly to her employees to see if they could remember if either of them had purchased the cigars.

"I had put together a photo spread with Kim and five other pictures of similar-looking people with reddish hair or a reddish tint to their hair, and I did the same for Stephen, and I showed them to each of the clerks at Astors Liquors, but no one knew them," Gamble said.

But luck was on Gamble's side. There was one more Astors employee he hadn't yet interviewed—Doris Grave Coles, who was the cashier on duty Friday, February 13—Kim didn't work that day—and Thursday night, February 12. Gamble went back to the liquor store on March 24 to interview her.

When Gamble showed her the photo lineup, Coles immediately pointed to Kim's picture and said she recognized her, but she could not pick out Steve from the photos Gamble showed her. Coles told Gamble that Kimberly came into the store and bought cigarettes, a pack of cigars, and beer. Gamble asked her if she remembered what kind of cigars Kim purchased. Coles went to the rack and removed a package of Backwoods smokes—the packs come in two colors, dark brown and light brown—but she picked up the wrong-color package. Instead of picking up the light brown package, which was the color of the package found in the Hrickos' room, she picked up the dark brown pack.

"She said those were the cigars Kimberly bought," Gamble said.

Gamble then asked Coles why she remembered Kimberly?

"I asked her for some ID and then I asked her where she got her hair colored," Coles said. "And when I said I liked her hair color and where did she get it colored, she turned into a bitch and told me that her hair was a natural color. She grabbed the driver's license out of my hand and said she didn't dye her hair."

Coles later testified to that in court. Her testimony was important because initially Kimberly said she didn't know Steve had those cigars. In fact, Kimberly said the cigars were on the table at home and she didn't even know Steve packed them.

Gamble later received the report from the Maryland State Police Crime Lab that concluded: "The marketing tag marker used to prepare the known price tag samples and the marketing price tag marker used to prepare the questioned price tag stamp are one and the same tag marker." The examiner also concluded that the ink used on both price tags was the same.

On Wednesday, April 1, Mike Miller called Corporal Keith Elzey at the Easton Barracks to tell him he had found a hypodermic syringe on the Harbourtowne golf course. Elzey then drove to the golf course and met Mike in the maintenance shop to recover the syringe. Mike told Elzey that one of the employees found the syringe in a ditch on Deep Water Point Road, which is located next to the golf course's fifth hole, and is about a mile from room 506. The employee found the syringe on Tuesday, March 31, while he was looking for a golf ball. He then threw it in a trash can at the shop for safety reasons. When the employee told Mike about it, Mike immediately retrieved it from the trash can and placed it in a plastic Baggie.

Mike said Steve used the road where the syringe was found as an alternate route into Harbourtowne because it was the road the maintenance shop was on.

"I told the police officer the road they found the syringe on would have been the road Steve drove into on Valentine's Day," Mike said. "It's not the main entrance, it's the road the maintenance building is on. The syringe was found right off the edge of the road—a little farther past the maintenance building. And anytime Steve came to visit me, that's the way he would drive into the golf course and he would drive to the hotel that way. So if he came in that way during the day, then I would think that would be her way to go back out. And maybe she would have tossed the syringe out the window there."

Elzey sent the syringe to the Maryland State Police Crime Lab to be tested for the presence of succinylcholine or curare. The tests did not turn up any trace of the drugs.

While the police were working the case, Deputy Fire Marshal Mike Mulligan continued his investigation into the fatal fire at Harbourtowne. He spent much of his time trying to get the medical examiner's report to find out the cause of Steve's death.

"I was trying to get the ME's report, but because of the way the case went down with Paul [Schlotterbeck] calling me in there to do the canine investigation, and then giving me the origin-and-cause investigation, it was a little complicated as to who was the primary officer because Paul got the original call," Mulligan said. "Whenever you have a fatal fire, one of the most valuable, if not *the* most valuable piece of information you have, is the medical examiner's report. What you're looking for is evidence of soot in the airways, because that indicates that the person was breathing at the time of the fire. You're also looking for the level of carbon monoxide in the blood, because that indicates how long the person was breathing in that environment."

Mulligan was anxious to get the ME's report, but the state police were holding it back, and he wanted to know why.

"We weren't cooperating," he said. "We were conducting two separate investigations from the time they interviewed Kim. My feeling was that they had the same feeling Paul did—that this was not on the up-and-up—there was something suspicious here and they went full-bore trying to prove it."

But Mulligan felt that because Steve's death involved arson as well as homicide—and the expertise of the police was not in fire investigation—the police should have been more willing to work with his agency.

"So they went to good old-fashioned police work and they did a good job. I'm not criticizing them for that," Mulligan said. "But I recall calling over to the barracks trying to find out if the ME's report was back yet so I could get a copy of it. If the state police weren't involved in it, I would have had it within forty-eight hours. But this went on for a week-and-a-half and I don't know if I had it yet by the time I did the burn test with the cigars."

In terms of the investigation Mulligan said he started out trying to prove a negative.

"First you read your burn patterns and you try to find your point of origin and you're trying to eliminate ignition sources," he said. "So in the middle of that room, you could very quickly eliminate electricity, heating, and air-conditioning. The woodstove was a little bit of a problem. And because of the cigars, there was a suspicion that the fire could have been started by accidental smoking."

In order to prove or disprove that theory, Mulligan went to some resources in his department to learn about what materials could be ignited by a cigarette ash.

Mulligan learned that cotton, for example, could ignite with a cigarette, but, most likely, polyester wouldn't burn. But his research hit a snag. Mulligan said he was looking for information relating to cigar ash, but soon he discovered there had never been any testing pertaining to cigars.

The only thing he could do was conduct his own tests. So Mulligan went to a local Rite Aid drugstore and bought a pack of Backwoods. He then obtained from Harbourtowne the same type of pillowcases and pillows that were in the Hrickos' room when Steve died. Mulligan took the materials to the Salisbury fire company's burn tower, where the company does its training.

"The idea was to give me a place to set fires without any influence from the wind and the weather to try to duplicate the same environment where the fire took place inside the room," Mulligan said. "And Jake Kinhart came down and helped me photograph it."

First Mulligan placed one cigar on top of the pillows and pillowcase, but it burned out. He continued relighting cigars and putting them on the pillowcase—still nothing. Next he took the pillowcase off and folded the pillow up and did everything he could to get the cigar to ignite the pillow.

"I guess this went on for about an hour-and-a-half

until I got nauseous—I'm a cigar smoker, but those were cheap cigars," Mulligan said. "We tested the pillow and the pillowcase at this time. Then when prosecutor Bob Dean got involved, he said he'd like to have some tests done on the bedspread and the victim's coat, which was in the pile of stuff around the point of origin."

Mulligan said he conducted those tests at a later date, but still he couldn't get the cigar to light any of the materials on fire.

"Everybody was suspicious of this fire—sometimes there are inarticulate [*sic*] feelings you get at a fire scene," he said. "In Baltimore City they used to say you get a hinky feeling—something's not right here. It's a combination of your past experience and reading a fire scene, but when you looked at that scene with the *Playboy* magazine and the type of individual you're dealing with, it didn't quite fit," he said.

Chapter 13

As part of their investigation police also spoke with Brad Winkler about his relationship with Kimberly.

Winkler first met Kim and Stephen Hricko on October 31, 1996, during a Halloween party at the Silver Spring, Maryland, home of his cousin Sean Gowen. Winkler only spoke with them once that evening, for about two minutes, and didn't see them again for the rest of the night.

Winkler didn't see Kim again until sometime around November 22, 1997, at the bachelorette party for Sean's fiancée, Jennifer Moore. At the time Winkler was living with his aunt in Silver Spring. Jenny and Kim had gone there to invite Winkler to Jenny's party. The trio first went to Jenny's house because she had to drop something off for her husband. Later that evening the group went to Time Out, a bar in Easton, to continue the party. Maureen Miller, who had had a previous engagement, met them at the bar. At closing time Winkler, Moore, and Kim went back to Maureen's and spent the night there before heading home the next day.

He spent Thanksgiving at the Hrickos', then saw

Kim again at a brunch for the Moore-Gowen wedding party on November 28.

"There we started to show interest in one another for the first time," Winkler said. "We just flirted with one another. Later that night during a party for my relatives and my cousin's relatives at my aunt's house, we flirted a little more."

The next day, the day of the wedding, Winkler didn't see Kim until he arrived at the reception. But the pair didn't get much of a chance to talk because Stephen and Kim's brother, Matt, were also there. In fact, Steve and Matt sat at the same table with Winkler and his sister-in-law while Kim sat at the bridal table.

On December 1 Winkler ran into Kim at his aunt's house. That's when their relationship started to kick into high gear. The couple talked for nearly two hours, mostly about Kim's relationship with Steve. Kim wanted to know if Winkler thought she was doing enough to make her marriage work. Winkler said yes and no.

"I told her that in my relationship with my ex-wife, I gave it a lot of time and tries. Even when I didn't think and even knew there was nothing left," Winkler said. "I just tried, so that I would know, down the road, I gave it my all and that there would never be a question in the back of mind, what if."

Even though Kim told Winkler she understood, he continued to tell her about what he went through in his marriage. He stressed counseling as a way to improve her marriage, but he reminded her it was a two-way street and both she and Steve had to be willing to give it their all. Kim explained that she had been to counseling, but Steve always seemed to have a reason for not going. The conversation was cut short when Winkler's parents showed up at his aunt's house. Kim left shortly after they arrived but later that night she called Brad's aunt to see if she needed help taking care of Sean and Jenny's daughter, Sharon (pseudonym). Winkler and his aunt, Sean's mother, were taking care of Sharon while the Gowens were on their honeymoon.

Kim met Winkler at his aunt's house the following day so she could show him where to pick Sharon up from the babysitter's. During the two weeks the Gowens were away, Winkler was busy with work and school and taking care of Sharon, so he and Kim really didn't get to spend much time together. In fact, they only saw each other for an hour or two every day.

"Our seeing each other usually consisted of just hanging out while I fed Sharon, or played with her, or prepared her for a nap. I always picked Sharon up and met Kim at the Gowens' town house," Winkler said.

When they were together, Winkler did most of the talking, particularly about what he wanted for the future. Winkler told Kimberly about his close relationship with his family and when he thought he might be ready to have a family of his own. Kim loved to hear Winkler talk about himself. She especially loved it when he told stories about how he put the needs of everyone in his life ahead of his own, and how he was so humble about it.

The first time Winkler and Kim were intimate was on December 5. It was a Friday night and Kim stopped by to see Winkler after a Christmas party at Holy Cross Hospital. After that, they didn't see much of each other until the next Wednesday, December 10, when they spent seven hours together, much of the time having sex. For the next several days they saw quite a bit of each other, having sex or just talking.

Then they didn't see much of each other until December 22—although they did keep in touch by telephone—when Kim dropped by to give Winkler a Christmas card.

When Winkler went home to Charlotte, North Carolina, to spend Christmas with his family, Kim called him there and they talked for about five minutes. Winkler stayed in North Carolina until New Year's Eve. He got back to his aunt's house about 6:00 P.M. that evening and hung out there all night watching movies.

Except for spending about thirty minutes together in the parking lot of a Laurel shopping mall, Winkler didn't see Kim again until January 14, 1998. That day they spent their time having sex. After that meeting the two saw each other once or twice a week for about an hour or an hour-and-a-half. Winkler, it seemed, was busy with work and school and didn't have much time for socializing.

"Since we only saw each other on the average of once a week, it was no big deal," he said. "I never saw her on a weekend again, once my cousins returned from their honeymoon."

Winkler said Jenny put a lot of pressure on the pair to end their relationship. He said he would discuss his feelings about the situation with both Jenny and Kim.

"They both understood that I was in no way, form, or fashion ready to take on marriage to anyone or a committed relationship with my schedule and the things I wanted to do—my career comes first," Winkler said. "Their concern for me was not to get hurt. My concern for them was to stop worrying about me."

Winkler said because he and Kim were together for such short periods they spent most of that time in bed. When they did find time to talk, they mostly engaged in small talk. They never really discussed Kim's relationship with Steve.

However, Winkler said he did know the couple was in counseling. And he said Kim had asked him if he thought she should divorce Steve, but he always tried to steer her away from having that conversation.

"I didn't think she had given it her all yet," he said. "Even so, she could never make up her mind about divorce or working things out."

Winkler said Kim told him that she did try to make her marriage work, but that Steve was no help. Winkler, though, told Kim that Steve had taken a big step by agreeing to go into counseling.

"[Kim] said he gets on her nerves following her around the house all day. She said she couldn't handle a one-eighty-degree turnaround, like everything in the past had not happened," Winkler said. "I didn't know about their past or much about Mr. Hricko other than the fact things were not good between them."

Kim told Winkler that for the past six or seven years, she had to do everything around the house by herself, including raising Sarah. And Steve always ignored her whenever she tried to get his attention or initiated lovemaking, Kim told Winkler.

"I don't know, nor did I know, much about their lives, so I could only go on what she told me," Winkler said. "I had become [Kim's] happy place, where she could come and slip away from reality or her problems."

Winkler believed his relationship with Kim was one of convenience for both of them. He never went out of his way to see Kim, he said.

"I never had to alter my schedule to make time for Mrs. Hricko," he said. "For her, I can't really say, but

I think it was a convenience as well. We didn't see each other every day and the days we did it was for maybe thirty minutes to an hour before she had to leave to pick up Sarah, or make dinner, or had a doctor's appointment. As messed up as the circumstances were for both of us meeting the way we did, the relationship was not a burden and was convenient for both of us."

Winkler said there were times when he told Kim he couldn't see her, because he wanted to go out with his friends, and she never had a problem with it. In fact, she encouraged it, he said. She even told him to let her know if the situation became too much for him to handle. It never did, he said, because he didn't have to change his lifestyle in order to be with Kim.

The last time Kim made that statement to Winkler was February 2.

"It was important because that prior weekend my cousin Mrs. Jennifer Moore Gowen and I talked about my relationship with [Kim]," Winkler said. "In that conversation I had stated that the relationship was almost all physical now and that I [didn't] feel like she could work things out, or attempt to, as long as I was in the picture."

Not only that, but Brad said he knew what he was doing was wrong and he wasn't usually the type of person to do something that was so wrong. He decided the relationship needed to end because it just wasn't good for him anymore.

So Winkler mustered up the courage to tell Kim it was over. That was on February 6, the last time Winkler and Kim had sex together. Problem was, when they were together, he chickened out.

"Basically I was enjoying things and I did care for Mrs. Hricko," he said.

Winkler saw Kim for the last time on Wednesday, February 11, just four days before Steve's death. The pair spent about thirty minutes together talking about Winkler's new job and the fact that he'd probably have less free time to see Kim than he previously had.

"Mrs. Hricko knew this when I interviewed for the job, so it was no big surprise," he said. "I knew I needed to let things end until I was ready and she decided what direction she was going in. Plus, I needed to start focusing on school."

Kim called Winkler the next day and they talked a little about his job and the fact that he was going to North Carolina for the weekend. Kim told Brad she needed to give him something before he left, but Brad said he wouldn't be home until after work on Friday. After exchanging several pager messages on Friday, Winkler told Kim he was going out with some coworkers after work and wouldn't be home until later that evening. Kimberly then told him she had left a gift for him on his door. Winkler said he was pretty drunk when he finally got home, but he remembered taking the gift off the door.

"I went in, took it up to my room, and I went straight up to bed," he said. "When I woke up the next morning, I really forgot all about it. I didn't pay much attention to it. I think I looked at it and I might have dumped the bag out. Then I went to Charlotte. It wasn't until when I got back from Charlotte that I actually read the note and realized what it was."

Winkler said his cousin Sean Gowen telephoned him in Charlotte on Sunday night, February 15, to tell him that Steve had died. All Sean knew was that Steve had burned to death.

"I didn't really believe him at first and was really

shocked and thought he was joking around," Winkler said. "And he was calm, and said, 'Brad, no, I'm serious.' Then he told me the generic story that Mrs. Hricko had told everyone. I didn't believe the story right off. It sounded very fishy."

When Winkler returned from North Carolina on Monday, February 16, he went straight to the Gowens' town house, where he met Sergeant Karen Alt and another state trooper. The troopers questioned Winkler about his relationship with Kim. They asked him if she had ever told him that she was going to kill Steve, or that she was going to get someone else to kill him for her. Winkler said Kim never talked that much to him about Steve, and she certainly never talked to him about murdering Steve.

The troopers also asked Winkler if he and Kim ever talked about a future together. Winkler told them yes and no.

"It was weird because it never was a direct question from Mrs. Hricko," he said. "Instead, she asked how I felt about children whose parents were divorced and their parents getting into other relationships or possible marriage. My response was just about how two people have to do a lot of communicating for it to work for the child or children."

Winkler also said Kim might ask him about his future, but never directly about marriage.

"From what Mrs. Hricko had told me, she could never make up her mind whether or not to stay in or get out of the marriage. Plus, just hearing me talk . . . she knew and was well aware that I was in no position to take on a family. Not just financially, but that there were a lot of things careerwise I could not do with a family that I wanted and am going to do," Winkler said. "So at a minimum she knew it would be three years before I was ready, regardless of our situation. I had been married already. I know what I missed out on and what I need to do before I take on that commitment for the rest of my life again," he said. "We both knew the whole situation with us was a messed-up one and that there was too much that needed to happen before even thinking about the future—as in marriage. We, or I should speak for me, were just enjoying the time we were having. It was convenient."

Winkler didn't hear from Kim again until February 24 when she paged him, leaving only her home telephone number on his pager. Winkler didn't call Kim back. Instead, he called Sergeant Alt to let her know Kim was trying to contact him.

Nearly a week later, Winkler received a note from Kim, who was in the Clifton T. Perkins Hospital Center. In the note Kim told Brad she hoped he wouldn't get hurt and that she knew he'd be okay.

Later in the investigation Winkler gave police a number of cards and notes Kim gave to him during their relationship. It seemed that while Steve was professing his love for Kim and promising he'd change for her, Kim was professing her love for Winkler.

In one of her notes Kim told Brad that she wanted to be with him night and day and that she wanted to experience all of him. She said she could only dream of the day when they could be together. She told Brad he was a wonderful man who was full of the best kind of love and she wanted to make him happy for the rest of his life.

In a note she gave Winkler before he went to North Carolina in December to visit his parents Kim told him she already missed him. She said she was thinking of being in his arms and kissing his neck. She told him he was important to her and that she wanted to have many years to learn about all of him. She told him to savor the time with his family and hurry back to her.

In a note Kim enclosed in the gift bag she gave Winkler for Valentine's Day she told Brad that she was proud of the job he was doing in the service. She said she missed him and loved him very much.

Chapter 14

On June 4, 1998, a Talbot County grand jury indicted Kimberly Michelle Hricko on first-degree murder charges for the murder of her husband, Stephen Michael Hricko. She was also indicted on charges of first-degree arson and attempted first-degree arson. The indictment was handed up less than a week before Kimberly was set to appear in district court for a preliminary hearing on the charges.

Because of the indictment the state avoided the preliminary hearing, at which time Scott Patterson, the state's attorney for Talbot County, would have had to present enough evidence to convince a district court judge that there was probable cause to send the case to the circuit court for trial.

"We call a special session of the grand jury for all our murder cases in the county and what we put in our charging documents is the least amount of facts we need to get probable cause for the murder," said Joe Gamble. "Just enough to get the person charged, and once we go to the grand jury, we tell them anything they want to hear. They can ask questions, but no information is released to the press."

At a preliminary hearing police officers would have taken the stand and testified to the evidence they had in the case, Gamble explained. The defense attorney wouldn't have been able to put any witnesses on, but he would have been able to cross-examine the prosecution witnesses, he said. Then the district court judge would have determined if there was probable cause or not to send the case to the Maryland Circuit Court.

"We don't like to do that in murder cases because the grand jury is secret, and we tell the grand jury what we would have told the district court judge," Gamble said. "So the grand jury indicted her and an indictment from the grand jury automatically goes to circuit court."

The reason the prosecution called the grand jury was to avoid the preliminary hearing and not give Kimberly's lawyers the opportunity to cross-examine the police, he said.

"They'll cross-examine the police officers in a hearing," Gamble said. "They'll want more evidence [immediately]. We have to turn everything over in discovery anyway, but discovery doesn't come for months and it gives us time to write our reports and get our evidence processed. And we didn't want the defense attorneys to question Joe Gamble on the stand and cross-examine me because they're going to cross-examine me at trial. And at trial I won't have to remember if at the preliminary hearing I said Kim was wearing a blue shirt or a pink shirt, because they'll bring out a transcript and say you said XYZ at the preliminary hearing."

One of the witnesses who testified before the grand jury was David Scott Widener, also an inmate at the Clifton T. Perkins Hospital Center, who claimed he had a close relationship with Kimberly while they were in that facility.

Widener, who testified against Kim in return for a lighter sentence on several bank robbery charges, told the grand jury that he and Kim were best friends at Perkins.

According to Widener, he and Kim were together all day, every day, in the hospital's dayroom from 5:45 A.M. until 9:00 P.M. During that time, Widener said, he and Kim and another inmate talked about freedom and the crimes that brought them to Perkins. At some point, Widener said, he and Kim started talking about Steve's death.

"It was like two days after she came there that we first started talking about it," Widener told the grand jury. "Somebody asked her what her charge was and she was directing the answer towards [*sic*] me. She had been charged with killing Stephen Hricko. She didn't admit it then, but she had just stated that she had been charged with Stephen Hricko's murder. And I said, 'I know.' And she asked me how I knew and I told her it was pretty obvious. 'You've been all over the news and newspapers. I know. I know what you're charged with.'"

Widener said although Kim didn't admit to killing Steve during that conversation, she did confess to him at another time.

He said Kim confessed to killing Steve one night when they were watching the television show *Dharma and Greg* in a special room that was off-limits to most inmates. While they were there, Kim started talking to Widener about the fire marshal's report.

"And she said, 'I killed him, you know. I killed Steve . . . but they are not going to be able to prove

it because they don't have forensic evidence,'"
Widener testified.

Widener said Kim told him she used the drug succinylcholine to kill him.

"She told me when she was being questioned . . .
by the state police, she said, they set the stuff on the
counter in vials, the drug, and she said right then she
wanted a lawyer. And she said what she used was succinylcholine," Widener said.

Kim then laughed and asked Widener if he was
planning on selling her out to get his sentence reduced. Widener said that's when the light went off
and he decided to do just that. So he excused himself and went to the bathroom, where he wrote the
name of the drug down on a napkin before he could
forget it. He then went back into the television room
and continued talking with Kim as if nothing had
happened.

Widener said the next day he called his public de-
fender to tell him about Kim's confession. And then
he began keeping a journal of everything Kim said
about Steve's death. He gave those notes to police the
day before he appeared before the grand jury.

Widener testified that Kim said the heat from the
fire in room 506 melted the television and that the
smoke in the room was very thick.

"She was talking about how she thought the fire . . .
may have burned the alcohol and drug out of [Steve's]
system," Widener said. "I didn't think that was possible,
but I went along with it. Anyway, she was hoping the fire
caused a lack of the forensic evidence they needed."

Widener said Kim told him she injected Steve with
succinylcholine, which she got at the hospital where
she worked, and then got rid of the syringe. She said
there was a needle found in a ditch in a surrounding

neighborhood, but it had heroin on it when it was tested, according to Widener. Kim told Widener she lit a pillow on fire with a cigar. And she said that one of the fire marshals tried to light one of the pillows on fire with a cigar, but couldn't.

"And I told her that's probably because most pillows are fire-retardant," Widener told the grand jury. "She said, 'Well, the one he had wasn't. I didn't have any problems—it lit right up with the cigar.'"

Kim also told him that a guy she worked with at the hospital knew about her plan and also knew that she had taken the drug, Widener said.

"She also said she was seeing somebody, a younger man that was twenty-two. She didn't say his name [and] I didn't get into that. I didn't think that was too important," Widener testified.

Widener said Kim told him that Steve didn't smoke, although he chewed tobacco. She explained that when she and Steve were looking to take out an additional life insurance policy on him, they learned that a smoker's policy was more expensive than a policy for a nonsmoker. She said the mandatory blood tests Steve had done indicated that he had nicotine in his blood, so they had to take out a smoker's policy. Kim told Widener because of the nicotine in his blood she would have the proof she needed to say that he smoked, even though he only chewed tobacco. Widener said Kim told him Steve wasn't smoking a cigar the night he died.

Kim also told Widener that after reading an article about the case in *People* magazine, a woman from Dallas, Georgia, called Kim's real estate agent to tell her that she had worked at a golf course and that the chemicals used on the course had made her ill. Widener said the Georgia woman called the real estate agent because she was the only person who had said anything nice about Kim in the *People* article.

"[Kim] planned on using that as some kind of defense, [claiming] that it would cause cardiac arrest," Widener testified.

"Did she ever tell you why she killed her husband?" Patterson asked.

"Yes, she said that they weren't getting along the last month and that she was seeing somebody, a twenty-two-year-old. She said he was about my age," Widener testified. "She said . . . [Steve] would stay up at night. He was making her sick. When she would wake up, she would see him staring at her—sitting in the bed staring at her. And all she could think about, these are her words, 'All [I] could think about was how [I] could get rid of him.' She asked him for a divorce and he didn't want to divorce her. And all she could think of was how she could get out of it."

Despite Widener's grand jury testimony, state's attorney Robert Dean, who eventually took over the case from Patterson, decided not to call him at trial because he didn't think Widener could help his case.

"I figured I had a strong case without him," said Dean, who even went to visit Widener in a Maryland prison. "Widener testified in front of the grand jury and that's why I went out to talk to him to see what kind of a witness he'd make. But based on my experience you only call a jailhouse snitch, which is what he was, if you really are desperate. Another reason I didn't call him was because he wanted a deal and I wouldn't give him one."

Even though Dean thought part of Widener's testimony to the grand jury might be true, he really didn't want the convict to be part of his trial team.

"And as I sized him up and his motivation—I

couldn't see Kim cozying up to him for any reason and I thought the defense attorneys would have a field day with him, even if he was telling the truth. So I said no way was I going to put that guy on the stand," Dean said.

However, Dean did have Widener brought to court every day as a sort of insurance policy in the event other witnesses, such as Rachel McCoy, didn't testify the way Dean expected them to testify.

"Better safe than sorry," he said.

About ten days after Kimberly was indicted on charges she murdered Steve, Talbot County Circuit Court judge William Adkins asked officials at Perkins why Kimberly was still being held at that facility. The judge gave them a week to provide him with a report explaining why she was still there.

When Kim was arrested in February, Adkins sent her there for an evaluation to see if she was competent to stand trial. At that time the hospital's psychiatrists determined she was competent to stand trial. Adkins now ordered her to be held without bond at the Talbot County Detention Center. However, he ruled that she could stay at Perkins but would have to be sent immediately to the detention center as soon as she was released from the hospital.

A week later, Talbot County Circuit Court judge William S. Horne ruled that Kimberly would stay at Perkins until doctors there determined her condition had stabilized.

In a letter to Judge Horne, as well as in a hearing, Dr. Stephen Rojcewicz, a Perkins psychiatrist, said that Kimberly suffered from a "recurrent major depressive disorder." He said she required inpatient care and treatment because of symptoms that included suicidal thoughts and urges, depressed mood, insomnia, and mood swings.

"These symptoms, and her recent increase in fragility and suicidal ideation, which is precipitated by court developments, such as her formal indictment for first-degree murder and the indication that the state will be seeking the death penalty, lead the hospital to its conclusion that she presents a danger to herself," Rojcewicz said. "Mrs. Hricko remains on a maximum-security unit of the hospital. It was the hospital's intention to return her to the detention center once her condition stabilized and the presence of suicidal ideation diminished, or could be appropriately addressed by the detention center."

Kim was ultimately transferred to the Talbot County Detention Center about a month or so before her trial began in January 1999.

In July, Kim's attorney, Harry Walsh, filed a motion to have the charges against Kim dropped because a witness might have lied to the grand jury. At the time Walsh did not name the witness, but one of Kim's friends said he was referring to David Scott Widener.

Walsh said he had received information that the witness might have given perjured testimony in order to receive a lighter sentence on bank robbery charges in another Maryland county. In a letter written to Kim's attorney, another inmate, who was Widener's roommate at Perkins, claimed Widener was testifying in order to get his original thirty-year sentence reduced to eight years.

"David repeatedly said, 'That bitch is going to fry,'" his roommate wrote. "He also said to me that the reason he's doing this to Kimberly is that he doesn't know her—he just met her and he doesn't have to see her again when he gets out. He also said she's a girl and what's she gonna do to him. Other reasons he gave for doing so is that he has two twin sons and their mother to get home to and he said he has a newborn daughter to get home to—the daughter has a separate mother than the twin boys of David. And the last reason he gave was that he missed having sex with his children's [mothers]."

Widener's roommate believed that Widener gleaned whatever information he had from newspaper reports. In addition, he said some of Kim's court papers, as well as the charging documents, were stolen when she and Widener were assigned to the same ward at Perkins. The roommate implied that Widener stole them and that's how he knew so much about Kim's case.

Walsh believed that Widener's testimony had a lot to do with the indictment against Kimberly. In his motion to dismiss the charges against Kim, Walsh made it clear that Talbot County state's attorney Scott Patterson wasn't involved in any deal with Widener. He also said if the witness lied to the grand jury, Patterson wasn't aware of it.

Patterson said he would investigate the allegation, but insisted there was enough evidence without Widener's testimony for the grand jury to indict Kim on charges of murder and arson.

The motion was ultimately denied.

Shortly after Walsh filed the motion to dismiss the charges, he withdrew as Kimberly's lawyer. He gave no reason for his withdrawal except to say it was in Kim's best interest. Kim, however, said once she was indicted, Walsh panicked and started calling her several times a day at Perkins pressuring her to plead guilty, and say she was insane at the time she killed Steve.

Walsh told Kim that if she did plead guilty he could probably get her a sentence of only five years. Kim said he also wrote to her telling her that he didn't have the time or the staff to represent her at trial.

Not knowing what to do, Kim asked a close friend for advice. The friend said she should not plead guilty to killing Steve if she didn't do it. Looking back, however, the friend said, "If he could have gotten her off with just five years, she'd be out now."

When Kim's new lawyers, Harry Trainor and William Brennan, came on board, Judge Horne postponed until January 1999 Kim's trial, which was slated to begin in October, to give them more time to prepare her defense.

"Bill and I, we were involved in a capital case—the first federal capital case ever tried in Maryland, the Anthony Jones case in Baltimore," Trainor said. "At some point, just as that trial was ending, we got a call from someone who was trying to help Kim and he asked us if we would get involved with the case. It had already got a little notoriety, I think. We agreed to do it as long as we could do it together, because Bill and I were in separate law firms then. We met with Kim and worked out the arrangements. We always found her quite pleasant to deal with," he said.

In an order signed on October 27, 1998, Judge Horne took the Talbot County prosecutor's office off the case. The order came in response to a request from Trainor asking that Patterson not be allowed to prosecute Kim's case because Henry Dove, one of Patterson's assistants, was involved in the murder-mystery dinner-theater production at Harbourtowne and had sat at the table with Kim and Steve.

Patterson agreed with Trainor's motion and said it was better to assign a special prosecutor to handle

Kim's case. Patterson tapped Montgomery County prosecutor Robert Dean to take over the case as a special assistant state's attorney for Talbot County. At that time Dean, who had been a prosecutor in Montgomery County for twenty-one years, was in the process of changing jobs to become a prosecutor in Prince George's County.

"Patterson decided to bring in another prosecutor because his office was such a small office, and one of his trial prosecutors was a key witness in the case, so Scott called me and asked me if, in the interim, I'd be interested in taking this case, and I told him I'd be glad to," Dean said. "So in October 1998 he had me appointed a special prosecutor for the case and sent me the file and I got working on it."

Although technically Dean was acting state's attorney for Montgomery County until January 4, 1999, he was able to conduct the investigation and the interviews because he was still a sworn state's attorney. Dean worked the case from October to November. He made numerous telephone calls, went through the police reports, went out to Easton a number of times, and did what any prosecutor would do—he totally immersed himself in the case.

"I went out to the crime scene and met with Joe Gamble and Keith Elzey and familiarized myself with the case as much as I could," Dean said. "I also spent a lot of time with Deputy Fire Marshal Mulligan. But I didn't interview some people until right before the trial in January because I knew what they were going to say and I didn't need to spend a lot of time with them. In November and December I did spend a lot of time with some people as I was working the case up and before I shifted my headquarters over to

Easton, which I did for a few weeks in January during the trial."

By the time Dean got involved, Mulligan had completed his investigation and went over it with the new prosecutor. Dean was pleased with Mulligan's work and told him he had made his case that the fire in the Hricko room was set.

"You've made your point—you looked at your burn patterns, you determined your point of origin, and you eliminated all your possible sources of ignition—but you haven't eliminated the possibility that it was a set fire," Dean told Mulligan.

In part, Mulligan's conclusion was based on the medical examiner's report that found that Steve wasn't breathing at the time the fire was set because there was no soot or ash in his airways and because there was no carbon monoxide in his blood.

"But Dean asked me if I could prove my case without bringing in the medical examiner's report," Mulligan said. "I told him I would never try to do that because you would never make your determination of whether a fire was accidental, or set or undetermined, unless you had the medical examiner's report."

Dean, however, insisted that Mulligan get on the stand and make his case that the fire was incendiary without using the ME's report, because he wanted that information to come in to the jury from the doctor.

"When I look back on my time on the stand, Brennan was attacking my expert opinion that this fire was a set fire. He was saying it was an accidental fire and that it could have been started by the wood-burning stove—by accidental burning," Mulligan said. "I kept looking to Mr. Dean because it was like trying to fight a fight with one hand tied behind your back. I had the information that there was no soot in the airway and the carbon monoxide level was normal. That meant the victim didn't start this fire. It wasn't started by smoking. Although Judge Horne recognized me as an expert in fire investigation, he wouldn't allow me to put my opinion in—in order to get your opinion you can only testify to facts, but if you're qualified as an expert witness, you're allowed to put your opinion in. Brennan accepted me as an expert, but they still wouldn't let my opinion in. I kept looking to Mr. Dean to let me say what was in the medical examiner's report, but he didn't."

Dr. David Fowler, the medical examiner, testified after Mulligan and he told the jurors that there was no soot in Steve's lungs or carbon monoxide in his blood, which meant he was dead or not breathing when the fire was set.

"Looking at the whole case, Dean probably did the right thing because Kimberly was convicted and he won his case," Mulligan said.

In the months and weeks before Kim's trial, Dean also met with Rachel McCoy a couple of times in Baltimore. And he also met with Jennifer Gowen. He went to the liquor store in Laurel to talk to witnesses, and he went to the Hrickos' house, which wasn't very far from the liquor store.

"I talked to the medical examiner extensively and I spent a lot of time working on the case," Dean said. "There was no one who testified that I didn't spend time with before the trial talking to them."

It wasn't until December that police also met with Kim's childhood friend Rachelle St. Phard, who thought it was odd that they hadn't contacted her before that time.

"In December the police talked to me, but Kim's

friends never talked to me because they thought I was so close to Kim that I would never say anything against her, even if I knew anything," Rachelle said.

Rachelle said she believed police waited until December to get in touch with her because they made a mistake.

"I think when they heard about me, they thought I was Rachel McCoy," she said. "What finally brought them to me was a card I had written to [Kim] after she told me she wanted to get divorced. I said, 'Whatever you need I'll help, you just let me know.' I meant I'd help her financially, but the police thought I was going to help her murder her husband. I wanted her to be happy. I was going to tell her to move here, live with us for a while until she got on her feet. But I truly think all along police thought that card was from Rachel McCoy because it was just signed Rachelle. I don't know that they put two and two together. But at the same time, the other women had to have mentioned me to them. Her lawyers knew I existed."

Although Rachelle initially questioned Kim's involvement in Steve's death, she ultimately concluded that it just wasn't possible for Kim to have killed her husband.

"Was there ever a time where there was doubt? Certainly there was a question about whether she did it," Rachelle said. "But I believe Kim, and I don't believe she'd do this to the father of her child. I didn't know a whole lot about the relationship. She told me in recent times that she loved him. She doesn't strike me as a person who would be capable of that. She really is a kind person—all the things she was involved in, the child advocacy issues—murdering your husband doesn't go along with advocating for children. I can't grasp that."

Rachelle said she didn't find out about Kim's affair with Brad Winkler until just before Kim's trial, and she didn't believe Kim murdered Steve to be with Brad.

"I was certainly disappointed that she did that," Rachelle said. "I think if she wanted out, she should have just gotten out rather than abusing their marital vows. I think that Brad probably went a long way in making Kim feel good; because for a long time in Kim's life, she didn't feel good. But I really don't think she killed Steve."

Chapter 15

With Kimberly's trial set to start January 11, 1999, her lawyers filed motions to keep certain statements she made to police, as well as the statements of other potential witnesses, out of court.

Defense lawyer William Brennan argued that the statements Kim made to police at Harbourtowne just after Steve died were not made voluntarily because she was under extreme emotional distress. And Brennan said the statements she made to Sergeant Alt and Corporal Elzey on February 23 were not admissible under the Supreme Court's Miranda ruling. According to Brennan, if Kim was in police custody when she was being questioned on February 23, then she should have been read her constitutional rights. Police, however, said she was always free to leave at any time, and ultimately she did leave.

But on Wednesday, December 2, 1998, Judge Horne ruled that Kim was not in custody on either February 15 or February 23 and the statements she made to police at those times were made voluntarily. That meant those officers could testify about what she said to them in court. However, Horne ruled to exclude testimony about Kim's suicide attempt because it would be prejudicial to her case.

Horne also ruled that the Astors Liquors clerk Doris Grave Coles, who identified Kim from a photo that Corporal Gamble showed her, would be allowed to testify that Kim purchased a package of Backwoods cigars at the store a day or two before Valentine's Day, 1998.

In motions filed at the end of December, Kim's lawyers asked Judge Horne to allow jurors to travel to Harbourtowne at some point during the trial to see the room where Steve died. The defense argued that photographs and a video of the room didn't adequately represent the site. The judge denied this motion, saying viewing the room was unnecessary and would just waste time.

Kim's attorneys also asked Horne to exclude information about the hypodermic syringe found at Harbourtowne, as well as one found at the Hrickos' Laurel home. The defense team argued that there was no evidence connecting any needle to Steve's death. In fact, Kim's attorneys said because there was no evidence Steve was injected with poison, allowing jurors to hear about the needle would cause them to speculate that there was a connection between the needle and Steve's death. Judge Horne agreed with defense lawyers that the needles were not relevant to the charges against Kimberly and granted the defense motion to exclude testimony about the needles at trial.

In addition, defense lawyers asked Horne to exclude testimony about the behavior of Bear, the K-9 dog that accompanied Deputy Fire Marshal Mike Mulligan to the scene of the fire at Harbourtowne. Even though Bear's actions signaled the presence of an accelerant at the fire scene, his findings could not be verified by scientific means, Kim's lawyers said. Horne also granted this motion.

Kim's trial began on Monday, January 11, 1999. After spending the first day of trial questioning potential jurors, prosecution and defense attorneys finally selected a jury consisting of nine men and three women, as well as four alternates—three women and one man. After the jurors were seated, Judge Horne told them they would be working long hours each day in order to wrap up testimony from the eighty-three potential witnesses by the end of the week.

The next day prosecutor Robert Dean gave his opening statement to the jury.

"Last year, at a beautiful and pleasant location known as Harbourtowne here in Talbot County, a resort located just outside of St. Michaels, tragedy struck. A young man, Stephen Hricko, married and the father of one, came to Harbourtowne with his wife for a Valentine's Day weekend. And as this trial will show, his wife, the defendant in this case, planned and successfully arranged to have her husband of nine years murdered and to [have him] die here in Talbot County on the Miles River."

Dean told the jury that over the next week they would be dealing with the entire spectrum of human emotions—hate, love, betrayal, loyalty, and greed. But, he said, the hardest of all the emotions to deal with was the torment Kim's friends felt knowing that they had to do the right thing and provide police with the information necessary to solve Steve's murder—information that could send their friend to jail for the rest of her life.

Dean told the jurors that the evidence would show that Kimberly wanted nothing more than to get rid of her husband. He said through witness testimony they would learn that the Hrickos' marriage started to fall apart in the fall of 1997 and that Kim told her friends how unhappy she was with Steve. She told them that Steve was boring, that he didn't do his share of the housework, that he was too wrapped up in his job, and that he didn't make her feel good anymore.

"To put it bluntly, the evidence will show that she was sick and tired of her husband," Dean said.

Dean explained that no matter what Steve did to make the marriage work, it didn't do any good. In fact, she complained constantly about him and even asked him for a divorce.

"She even, ladies and gentlemen, went to the extent of telling her friends, or a few of them, that Stephen would be better off dead," Dean said.

Dean told the jury that Kim even asked a coworker at Holy Cross Hospital if he would kill Steve for $50,000 or find someone else who would do it for her. The jurors heard that Kim told other friends that she was thinking of ways to kill Steve. And just two weeks before Steve died, Kimberly told a friend exactly how she was going to murder her husband. Her plan was to steal a drug from the hospital to paralyze Steve and then set a fire to make it look like he died in the blaze.

"Ladies and gentlemen, you will see that the defendant was progressively digging herself into a hole of violence from which she could not escape and which was being created by her own obsession to get out of a marriage, but which she was unwilling to do in a civilized manner," Dean said. "After all, the evidence will show that there was a bit of insurance money to collect with the death of Stephen."

Dean then talked to the jury about Kim's affair with Brad Winkler and how she became increasingly infatuated with him and wanted to spend more and more time with him.

The jury also heard about the Hrickos' trip to Harbourtowne on Valentine's Day weekend 1998. Dean told them about the murder-mystery dinner-theater production the Hrickos attended, where they just happened to be seated at the same table as Henry Dove, an assistant state's attorney for Talbot County. When the play ended around 10:30 P.M. or so, the Hrickos returned to their room.

"Those were Stephen Hricko's last moments alive," Dean said.

Dean then told the jury how Kim left Harbourtowne and came back between 1:15 and 1:30 A.M. to discover her room on fire and then went to the lobby to get help. Then some "brave people," who were there, went to the room, pulled the charred remains of Stephen Hricko out of the room, and tried unsuccessfully to save him. There was no reason for Stephen to die, Dean said. He was healthy. He was strong.

"But what makes your skin crawl is that the autopsy revealed that this man was dead before the fire," Dean told the jurors. "And you will learn in the fire marshal's determination, this fire was set. . . . Not an accident. Not spontaneous. Set. The question will then be, who set the fire? It wasn't Steve. Stephen was dead."

Dean then told the jury that Kim's story about what happened that night was "patently absurd." He said the evidence would show that Steve died just as Kimberly had planned. Steve was murdered by his wife—a wife he so desperately loved, Dean said.

Defense attorney Harry Trainor rose next to give his opening statement.

"On February fifteenth of last year [Kimberly and

Stephen Hricko] were at the Harbourtowne inn,"
he said. "Stephen Hricko tragically died. That's the
part that's undisputed. That's a fact. But what you will
see as this case proceeds is that there is a great deal
of this case that is undisputed."

But there was considerable doubt about the circumstances surrounding Steve's death, as well as what
caused it, he said. If the prosecution wanted the jury
to believe that Steve was poisoned, then it was up to
the prosecution to produce evidence that some toxic
substance was delivered into his body, Trainor told the
jury. If prosecutors couldn't do that, then they were
obligated to rule out every other reasonable explanation for Steve's death. And even though the prosecutor said Steve was a healthy man—he really wasn't,
Trainor said. In fact, shortly before his death he was
referred to a cardiologist by his doctor for a stress EKG
because of some sign of heart trouble, he explained.

Trainor asked jurors to consider whether Steve
committed suicide because he was depressed. Or
maybe the fact that he worked with toxic pesticides
on a regular basis had something to do with his
death, Trainor said.

"These are examples of issues that ought to be examined before one can say fairly and reasonably that
all causes of death other than poisoning have been
ruled out," he said.

Trainor told the jury that because the scientific
evidence didn't point to a cause of death, the medical examiner shouldn't have speculated that Steve was
poisoned. He should have listed Steve's cause of
death as unknown, or undetermined, Trainor said.

"And I submit to you in fairness that if the prosecution is going to call a medical doctor to tell us what
caused Stephen Hricko's death, then that medical

opinion should be based on science and not guess-work, not in a serious criminal case such as this," he said.

Trainor also asked the jurors to examine all the evidence before deciding whether Kimberly actually set the fire, as the prosecution alleged. He then reminded them that every defendant is innocent until proven guilty and told them to use the presumption of innocence as an analytical tool to analyze the testimony in the case.

"If you look at, for example, that fire in room five-oh-six, and you absorb all of the testimony, all of the evidence about the fire and you look at it and you're left with two fairly equal inferences, one that would be supporting guilt and one that would be consistent with innocence; the presumption of innocence is powerful enough that you would have to reject the inference consistent with guilt in favor of the inference that supports innocence," Trainor said. "That's an example of the power of the presumption of innocence."

Trainor then told jury members that the prosecution had to prove its case beyond a reasonable doubt—meaning that through the evidence presented, the prosecution had to prove each element of its case to eliminate any reasonable doubt about that particular element.

"Unless the evidence reaches that level of proof beyond a reasonable doubt, the presumption of innocence standing alone is enough to require a not guilty verdict at the end of the case and send Kimberly Hricko home to her family," he said, adding that it wasn't up to the defense to prove Kim's innocence.

Then, alluding to the statements Kim made to her friends about killing Steve, Trainor told the jurors that while loose talk, inappropriate comments, or conduct before the fact were suspicious, they were not enough to convict a person beyond a reasonable doubt.

"The presumption of innocence is not refuted by suspicions," Trainor said. "The prosecution's case against Kimberly Hricko cannot rise to the level of proof beyond a reasonable doubt without hard evidence to corroborate the suspicions."

Finally Trainor asked the jurors to wait until they heard all the evidence before deciding Kim's guilt or innocence.

"If you will approach your job as jurors in this case in that way, Mr. Brennan and I know that our client, Kimberly Hricko, will have a fair trial," he said. "And I can tell you basically, at this point, fair consideration is all we're asking."

Harbourtowne banquet manager Elaine Phillips and her cousin Philip Parker were among the first witnesses to testify on Tuesday. The pair told the jury about their actions the night Steve died. They also testified about Kim's demeanor when she entered the resort's lobby to report the fire. But their testimony about Kim's behavior wasn't quite the same as their statements to police on February 15, 1998—something the defense team immediately pounced on.

At that time Elaine Phillips told police Kim was "shaking" when she walked into the lobby. But at trial when Dean asked Phillips to describe Kim's demeanor, she said, "She walked in the lobby . . . there was no evidence. I mean, there was nothing that she was upset . . . she was just walking into the lobby. She was very calm. Even when she said, 'There's a fire in my room,' we were more excited . . . and we were all very excited and nervous as to what was happening. And I just remember her just standing very calm and being very calm."

On cross-examination Trainor asked Phillips to read the statement she wrote for police that Valentine's Day weekend.

"If you look at the second page and see if you wrote in your own handwriting on February 15, 1998, at four-thirty A.M., whether Mrs. Hricko was shaking?"

"Uh-hum."

"Did you write that she was shaking?" Trainor asked.

"Yes, yes, I did."

When Philip Parker got on the witness stand, he initially told the jurors that Kim was "agitated or upset about something" when she walked into the Harbourtowne lobby. Later when asked by Dean to describe Kim's behavior, Parker said, "It was actually really calm. . . . She seemed quite calm to me."

When Trainor cross-examined Parker, he called attention to his earlier testimony.

"In response to Mr. Dean's questions, you described the demeanor of Mrs. Hricko when she came into the lobby as calm?"

"Yes, sir."

"But you've also described her as upset and agitated, correct?"

"Yes, sir."

"And isn't it also true that when she came into the lobby, she was screaming?" Trainor asked.

"No, sir, that would not be true," Parker responded.

Trainor then asked Parker to read part of the statement he gave police shortly after he pulled Steve out of room 506.

"Does it say, in your own handwriting, that the young woman ran into the lobby, screaming?"

"Yes, sir," Parker replied.

The defense had scored some points—minor points, maybe, but points nevertheless.

The next witness to testify was Bonnie Parker, Philip's mother and Elaine's aunt. Bonnie told jurors that after learning Steve was dead, she comforted Kimberly and took her upstairs to one of the rooms the Parkers had reserved for the weekend, so she could lie down. She said once in the room she sat Kim down on one of the beds and asked what happened. Kim told her the whole story—the dinner, the argument, leaving, and getting lost. Then, after telling Bonnie how she was trying to find Mike Miller's house in Easton, Kim told her Mike worked at Harbourtowne. As Bonnie asked a police officer if he wanted her to find out who Mike was, Kim rattled off Mike's telephone number. The police officer wrote it down and then called Mike to tell him what had happened, Bonnie said. Bonnie told the jurors that while she was with Kim in the room, Kim kept saying, "Oh, God; oh, God," and started dry heaving, although she never actually vomited.

The rest of the day jurors heard from police and others, including Talbot County assistant state's attorney Henry Dove, Mike Miller, and Father Paul Jennings, the state police chaplain, who testified about the events that occurred before and after Steve's death.

Dove explained that he was part of the murder-mystery dinner-theater show that the Hrickos attended on Valentine's Day in 1998. He said he was playing a detective in the production of *The Bride Who Cried*, and he just happened to be seated at the Hrickos' table. Dove testified about how much alcohol the guests at his table consumed that evening.

"Everybody there ordered at least one drink or beer. One of the couples ordered a bottle of wine, and I think drank the whole bottle of wine before they were through that night. It was not the Hrickos,"

Dove said. "I believe Mr. and Mrs. Hricko each ordered a beer right about the time I sat down, which was about a half hour into the reception time. I think they might have ordered another drink—I'm not sure—later on. It could have been two more, but I'm not nearly as sure about that. And then there was champagne served to everybody at the end of the dinner for the toast."

However, according to the Hrickos' guest check for that night, they only ordered two drinks, a Budweiser and a Wild Goose ale.

Jennings told jurors that Kim was "very calmly upset" after he notified her that Steve was dead. He said her response was not very emotional.

Analysts from the Maryland State Police Crime Laboratory testified that although they recovered three fingerprints from the cover of the *Playboy* in the Hrickos' room, only one was good enough to be compared to Steve and Kim's fingerprints. However, it didn't match prints from either Steve or Kim.

Steve's best friend, Mike Miller, told jurors that he went to Harbourtowne to be with Kim after Steve died.

"I walked into the room where Mr. and Mrs. Parker were. They directed me into the adjoining room. I walked in," Miller said. "Kim was laying on the bed farthest away from me. I had noticed keys on the bed and a cell phone there. She got up, walked over to me and looked up and said thanks for coming. I reached out to give her a hug. She did not respond in any way with a hug or [anything] other than just thanking me for showing up."

Mike said Kim really didn't even talk to him about what had happened that night. She didn't answer any of his questions, he added. He told the jurors that Kim's demeanor was "flat," and devoid of any emotional highs or lows. Mike also said that although Steve chewed Skoal tobacco, he never smoked cigarettes or cigars.

The last witness of the day was Deputy Fire Marshal Mike Mulligan. During his testimony Mulligan told the jurors he believed the fire in the Hrickos' room was a set fire. However, after an objection by the defense team, Judge Horne ordered the jury to disregard Mulligan's opinion about the cause of the fire.

The defense attorneys argued that although Mulligan said he ruled out all natural and accidental causes for the fire, he really didn't eliminate every possible accidental cause, including a lit match. Defense lawyer William Brennan said if Steve had been smoking a cigar, he would have had to light it somehow. And even though Mulligan tried to set a pillow and other items like those found in the room on fire with a lit cigar, he didn't try to light them on fire with a lit match or other ignition source. The judge agreed.

Judge Horne also took issue with Mulligan's testimony regarding the woodstove in the Hrickos' room.

Mulligan testified that even though the doors to the wood-burning stove were open, he eliminated it as the ignition source because it was too far away from what he said was the fire's point of origin. Mulligan told the jurors that there was a store-bought log in the stove that was not made of wood. He said although the log had burned, part of the wrapper, as well as a paper match, remained in the stove. Mulligan said if the log had been made of locust wood, it would have been possible for a spark to have jumped out of the stove and to ignite a fire. But he said he didn't think that was possible in this case, so he eliminated the store-bought log as the ignition source.

"I don't know that we have an exhaustive list from

Mr. Mulligan of all the potential accidental or spontaneous causes of a fire," Horne said. "And finally and most fatally, in my opinion, is the potbellied stove with its two doors open and its ash showing that there had been a log burned therein. It's all well and good to say, 'But those logs can't spark. Hey, they're wrapped in paper and they're designed so they don't produce any spark.' But they also come with a strong warning on the paper, as I recall . . . and I think it cautions you against using an artificial log with any other source of fire because it may cause little mini-explosions, if you will. Did that happen in this case? I don't know. And that's my problem."

So Horne said, "The court finds in this case that there has not been that proper foundation and accordingly without such proper foundation, the testimony of Mr. Mulligan as to the . . . beginning of the fire, incendiary, accidental, or spontaneous will not be introduced into evidence and the jury will be instructed to disregard the opinion. . . ."

Among the witnesses who testified on Wednesday, January 13, was Trooper Keith Elzey. Elzey told the jurors about the version of events leading up to Steve's death that Kim had given him when he first met her. He also described Kim's behavior and physical appearance at that time.

"When you first met Kimberly Hricko, describe for us her demeanor and her physical appearance," Dean said.

"She appeared to me to be somewhat tired. Appeared to be sobbing, not actually crying, but had her head in her hand sobbing a lot," Elzey said. "But I didn't see any tears."

During cross-examination by Harry Trainor, Elzey agreed that Kim appeared to be upset.

"Now, when you first noticed her, her demeanor was that she was crying, is that right?" Trainor asked.

"I didn't see any tears, but she was moaning, yes, sir."

"She was moaning. As a matter of fact, she had a washcloth that she was holding to her face or to her eyes. Is that right?" Trainor asked.

"Yes, sir."

"Good, she appeared to be upset, sobbed and moaned, and had a washcloth in her hand, is that right?"

"Yes, sir."

The jurors also heard about Kim's meeting with Elzey and Sergeant Alt on February 23, 1998.

One of the things Mike Miller's wife, Maureen O'Toole-Miller, told the jury was that she had made most of Steve's funeral arrangements for Kim. She said Kim really didn't care about the specifics of the arrangements.

"She was very noncommittal," Maureen said. "The only thing that she was definite on was that she wanted the body cremated. She was very adamant on that, because she said that's what Steve had said he wanted."

After Maureen testified, Kim's attorneys told the judge they might call her as a witness for the defense, so she wasn't allowed to stay in the courtroom. But she made good use of her time, waiting in the hallway, talking to everyone else who was getting ready to testify.

"I got the behind the scenes of everything before they testified; because once they came out, they couldn't talk about their testimony," Maureen said.

But as the trial progressed and the defense began its case, Maureen remained in the hallway, waiting to be recalled.

"I was getting mad," she said. "So Bob Dean went

to the defense and asked if they were going to call me back to the stand, and they told him they weren't."

In the months leading up to Kim's trial, she and Maureen never spoke. In fact, it wasn't until a week before the trial that Maureen started talking to Kim's other friends.

"It was kind of strange, but during the trial the five girls, me included, had this odd, strange bond because we were all kind of victims, except for Teri Armstrong, who assumed my role after I found out the truth," Maureen said. "She stepped in and started taking care of Kim's business between the time she was arrested and the trial. She was selling some of the Hrickos' stuff for Kim."

Maureen said she and Mike asked Teri if they could have Steve's weights because they wanted to have a weight room, or at least part of the weight room, at the high school in State College, Pennsylvania, rededicated in Steve's memory. But Teri kept telling the Millers that she didn't know where the weights were.

"We told Teri that we'd buy the weights back from whoever she sold them to. We didn't care how much money it would take, we wanted to buy them back," Maureen said. "But she wouldn't give us any information. She was being totally evasive. Well, it turned out she gave the weight set to her husband. And even though she knew what we wanted them for, and that we were willing to pay any amount of money for them, she wouldn't give them to us."

During the trial, in the witness room, Maureen got into a huge fight with Teri over the weights again. Tired and emotionally drained, Maureen confronted Teri about giving the weights to her husband. Once again Maureen explained that the Millers would like to buy the weights back, but Teri said her husband didn't have them.

"Teri, you must think we're really stupid if you think we're going to believe that," Maureen said to Teri. "And we got into a big fight and it started escalating. I accused her of being as bad as Kim, because she was covering up for her, knowing she killed Steve."

"I loved Steve," Teri responded.

"You didn't love Steve. You didn't even know Steve; because if you knew Steve, you wouldn't be defending Kim," Maureen screamed.

"Teri burst into tears. That's the closest thing I ever came to a physical fight," Maureen revealed. "I was about two seconds from jumping across the benches and hurting her, because she kept trying to lie, but Rachel grabbed me and dragged me out of the room and forced me to go downstairs before someone came in to find out what was happening."

Maureen said that's why, during the trial, when they were all waiting to testify, the women were all very closely connected, except for Teri.

"We hated her, but we couldn't cause any problems, because we were afraid she wouldn't testify," Maureen said.

The day Maureen testified against Kim was the same day Brad Winkler testified. At this point Mike had never spoken to Brad, nor did he ever want to.

Mike was angry with Brad because Brad had an affair with a married woman. What Brad did went against Mike's strict Catholic upbringing. As far as Mike was concerned, what Brad did was a sin and he felt Brad was just an unworthy person. Mike didn't want anything to do with Brad because he had betrayed his best friend.

But Mike soon came to understand that Brad was as much a victim as everybody else.

"We had all made plans after everyone had testified that we were going to go get something to eat," Maureen recalled. "So Steve's sisters, Jenny and Julie, were there, Brad, Brad's cousin Jenny, Rachel, Norma, Michael, and me. We went down the street to a restaurant for dinner and Mike told me to sit Brad at the other end of the table because he didn't want to look at him."

Maureen told Mike to lay off Brad, because he was suffering, too. Mike agreed and behaved himself for the entire evening. When the evening was drawing to a close, Brad stood up and said he wanted to say something.

"I am so sorry for what I've done," Brad said, choking up. "I feel so bad and I'll have to live with this for the rest of my life. I feel responsible for what Kim has done and I am so sorry to you and your family. And I just wanted you to know it."

Then Brad started crying and Mike got up, went over and hugged him, and said, "We forgive you."

"It was the most compassionate thing I've ever seen anyone do because I knew how much Mike hated him at that point," Maureen said. "It was just a very touching moment and it just brought all of us closer together."

Kim's friend Ken Burgess took the stand after Maureen finished testifying. Burgess told the jurors that Kim had asked him to kill Steve, or find someone who would do it, for $50,000. In an attempt to discredit Burgess's testimony, defense attorney William Brennan attacked his credibility. Brennan questioned Burgess about his conviction on welfare fraud for lying on an application for welfare benefits in 1985.

"Welfare fraud involved applying for benefits from the state, filling out an application under oath, is that right?" Brennan asked.

"Yes, sir."

"You lied under oath in 1985, isn't that right, Mr. Burgess?"

"I suppose so, sir."

"You lied under oath to get money from the state that you were not entitled to," Brennan said.

"No, sir."

"So you didn't lie to solve financial problems, you lied for the fun of it?"

"I lied to put food on the table for my kids," Burgess responded.

"You're always having financial problems. Okay. And you heard about the death of Ms. Hricko's husband and realized it could be an opportunity for you to make some money and solve your financial problems, isn't that right, Mr. Burgess?" Brennan asked.

"It's entirely wrong," Burgess said.

"All right. At Washington, at Shady Grove Hospital in Rockville, haven't you had conversations with your coworkers over there about contact with tabloid-news organizations about selling your story?"

"No, sir. I have not. I've had conversations at my new job about the situation, but never about selling my story," Burgess responded.

The witness who probably did the most damage to Kim's defense that day was Jennifer Gowen, who said she learned about Kim's affair with Brad Winkler, her husband Sean's cousin, shortly after she returned from her honeymoon in December 1997.

"She told me they were having sex and that she was becoming more and more dissatisfied with her marriage to Steve," Gowen said on direct examination. "She expressed that she was interested in getting a divorce from Steve. Then she became more and more negative in her comments about Steve."

"What negative comments did she tell you?" Dean asked Gowen.

"She told me he repulsed her and that she didn't want to be with him anymore. That she wanted to leave him, to get a divorce," Gowen testified. "She talked a lot about Brad and gave me quite a lot of details about their intimate contact and that she was happy with what was going on with Brad."

Gowen said Kimberly told her Brad treated her the way a woman should be treated and that she could open up more to him than she could with Steve.

"She told me that at one point in those several weeks after I got back from my honeymoon that she had had sex with Steve once and that it made her want to throw up, and that was the one time she'd had it in quite some time," Gowen told the jurors, adding that as December turned into January, Kim's comments about Steve become increasingly negative.

"And as we go into January, what is she now telling you about Steve?" Dean asked.

"She continues in a very negative vein," Gowen replied. "She tells me that she would like to kill him."

"Did she ever talk to you about a way in which she would kill Steve?"

"At one point [in January] she mentioned Sodium Pentothal, which is an anesthetic agent," Gowen said. "We had a discussion about a case history where a woman had injected some children with succinylcholine and that was a muscle-relaxing anesthesia agent and that it would go untraced."

Gowen told the jurors Kim wanted her support even if she killed Steve.

"She mentioned to me that her brother would support her even if she killed someone and she was asking me for support," Gowen said. "She did tell me that if I killed someone, that she would support me."

Gowen said one day shortly before Steve's death, Kimberly told her that if she could kill Steve and get away with it, she'd do it the very next day.

After Kim was arrested, Gowen visited her in jail and said she had a lot of questions for her about Steve's death.

"Did you have any questions to her about money?" Dean asked.

"Kim said, 'I don't care what anyone says, it wasn't for the money,'" Gowen testified.

Brad Winkler also testified on Wednesday, telling jurors about his affair with Kim. Winkler told jurors that Kim never talked to him about wanting to kill Steve. He said he was shocked when his cousin Sean Gowen told him Stephen Hricko was dead.

Kim's friend Norma Walz testified that Kim told her she was falling in love with Brad Winkler and that she was going to ask Steve for a divorce.

"She told me she had asked Steve for a divorce and that he had broken down and cried and begged her for a second chance," Walz said. "She said that she gave him a week to see if he could get into a doctor and at least show that he was trying to turn himself around."

"Did she at any point complain to you about Steve and his actions toward her after that?" Dean asked.

"She made a comment that 'he's smothering me

and following me around the house like a puppy dog,'" Walz responded.

Jurors also heard about the $450,000 worth of life insurance Kim stood to collect when Steve died. And a doctor, who had treated Steve for poison ivy in 1996, testified that Steve also wanted to go on the nicotine patch so he could stop chewing tobacco. The doctor said when Steve filled out a medical history form he indicated that he smoked zero packs of cigarettes per day, but he chewed tobacco and rarely drank alcohol.

Chapter 16

Teri Armstrong, Kim's friend and former neighbor, was the first to testify on Thursday, the fourth day of the trial. Armstrong told the jurors that shortly before Steve died, Kim told her she wanted out of her marriage and that she had even been thinking of different ways to kill him.

"I asked her, 'What would you get out of it?' and she said 'Well, the insurance money,' so her and Sarah can live their life the way they want, the way she wanted to live her life," Armstrong told the jurors.

Armstrong said she stayed at the Hrickos' house on February 13, 1998, the Friday before they left to go to Harbourtowne.

"[Kim] told me that Stephen made plans to go to a resort and to see a play and they weren't leaving until the next day," Armstrong testified. "She was not looking forward to it."

Armstrong told the jury that after Kim was arrested, she told Armstrong she was feeling a lot of remorse about Steve's death.

The next witness was Dr. David Fowler, the deputy chief medical examiner for the state of Maryland.

Fowler testified about his efforts to determine how Steve died.

"The initial case did not seem to be terribly suspicious and so I ran the confirmatory tests and they came back negative for the products of combustion in the bloodstream," he said.

Those products would confirm death in a fire, he said. A normal level of carbon monoxide in a person's blood is between 0 percent and 10 percent, Fowler explained to the jurors. For someone who died in a fire that level would be 50 percent or higher. However, if a young child or an elderly person died in a fire, the carbon monoxide level would be slightly lower— about 30 to 40 percent, he said.

There was no carbon monoxide in Steve Hricko's blood, so he didn't die in the fire, Fowler told jurors.

"In fact, the only conclusion from that particular result is that the individual was dead before the fire actually reached him," Fowler said. "This man did not breathe any of the products of combustion of that fire, i.e., was dead, not breathing, at the time of the fire."

Although Steve's face and upper body were severely burned and charred and there was a lot of soot covering most of the front of his body, there was no soot in his nose, mouth, trachea, windpipe, or lungs, Fowler said.

"If the body was breathing at the time of the fire, would you expect to find soot?" Dean asked.

"Oh, absolutely. In fact, in very large quantities, given the amount of soot on the outside of the body," Fowler told jurors. "And as far as I was concerned, this merely confirmed the result that I had received from the laboratory that the person was not breathing at the time the fire was, in fact, going on."

Fowler said that after further examining Steve's

body, he didn't find any abnormalities in any of his organs or in his brain.

"So I saw at the time I'd finished the autopsy, [there was] no physical reason that I could identify for this man to have died," he told jurors. "But now I'm beginning to wonder whether or not there's a chemical reason. Alcohol, drugs, such as street drugs, or an overdose, a suicide, what else could be going on here? Is there, in fact, a chemical reason for his death?"

At this point Fowler said he voided the death certificate he had signed earlier listing the cause of death as smoke inhalation because it was no longer correct within a medical degree of certainty.

Findings from the toxicology laboratory showed there were therapeutic amounts of a decongestant and an antihistamine found in over-the-counter cold medications, as well as therapeutic amounts of the antidepressant Effexor, Fowler told the jury.

However, the tests indicated there was no alcohol in Steve's bloodstream. The blood alcohol level was 0.00, he said. That result concerned Fowler because he had received information that Steve had been drinking heavily right before he died and because police found a number of partially full, or empty, bottles of alcohol in the Hrickos' room at Harbourtowne. So Fowler asked the lab to test three more samples. All four samples came back negative for alcohol.

Now Fowler's suspicions were heightened even more.

"The evidence that I have now obtained in the way of the cause of death, the alcohol levels, and everything else are totally contrary to the actual scene evidence, nothing is absolute, nothing is fitting together," he told the jury. "I have a person who's allegedly drunk, but he's not drunk. I have a person who allegedly dies because of a fire. He did not die because of the fire. He was dead before the fire. And there is no physical reason for him to have died. I also have no drug levels. I don't have heroin or cocaine or anything else that I can blame it on. I don't have an overdose of medications. I have nothing from the obvious chemical analysis to explain this person's death."

Because Steve was a golf superintendent, Fowler also considered environmental hazards, including insecticides and pesticides. He said he had narrowed those down to a small class of pesticides known as organic phosphates that could kill a person quickly, but would not cause obvious symptoms. However, Fowler said if Stephen Hricko had been exposed to organic phosphates, there would have been an elevated level of pseudocholinesterase in his blood. That wasn't the case, Fowler told the jury.

After ruling out other pesticides, such as rat poison and certain weed killers, Fowler said he began to look at paralyzing agents used by anesthesiologists that were available in operating rooms.

"The two which really concerned me would be the neuromuscular blocking agents or muscle-paralysis agents, which are used during operations or surgical procedures," Fowler testified. "There are two different groups of drugs—one which is based on curare, which is a poison derived from South America, and now they've made multiple different artificial forms of that. That is a long-acting muscle-paralytic agent. It takes several minutes, in fact, to achieve its activity. Completely paralyzes all the muscles when given properly. Lasts for hours and requires an antidote to revive the person and give them their muscle activity back."

Fowler said curare was easy to detect in the bloodstream. It was not present in Steve's blood, he said.

"The other substance which concerned me was succinylcholine," he said. "It's only found in operating rooms. It's a drug which causes very, very rapid paralysis of all skeletal muscles, which involves also the chest muscles (so a person couldn't breathe). . . . It acts within seconds if it's given intravenously and usually will actually begin to wear off within two to four minutes."

Fowler said succinylcholine could also be given intramuscularly with a hypodermic syringe. Fowler said he examined the outside of Steve's body for a small puncture hole, but didn't find one. He said because those needles were so sharp and fine, it was often difficult to detect a puncture hole. Trying to find one on Steve's corpse was even more difficult because he had been severely burned on the upper portion of his body. Fowler said trying to find the needle mark on Steve was worse then trying to find a needle in the proverbial haystack.

Even so, Fowler said he tried to detect the presence of succinylcholine in Steve's body, but he was unable to because it had been broken down and removed by a natural substance that was present in the body. Succinylcholine usually wears off naturally within about four minutes. Fowler said the drug, combined with the heat from the fire, might have hastened rigor mortis in Steve's body.

"And so this is a substance that our body will destroy in about four minutes," Fowler said.

During questioning, Dean directed Fowler's attention to a photograph of Steve's body and asked him to look specifically at the position of Steve's left arm, which was crooked and bent up at the elbow.

"Is that consistent with death by succinylcholine?" Dean asked.

"That is consistent with death," Fowler responded.

Fowler said the position of Steve's arm was the result of rigor mortis, which meant his muscles had stiffened after he died.

"Muscles do not contract [after death]," he said. "They will simply fix in the position in which they were at the time of death. Eventually the body begins to decompose and break down . . . and the person will become floppy again."

In the small muscles, such as the arm muscles, Fowler said, it takes between three and six hours for rigor to set in. Fowler also said fire could accelerate the onset of rigor.

"Would the introduction of a paralyzing agent in any way hasten, or could it in any way hasten, the onset of rigor?" Dean asked the medical examiner.

"In theory, yes, it could," Fowler replied. "In my opinion it would probably push the person into rigor sooner."

Dean asked Fowler if he had an opinion as to Steve's cause of death.

"In my opinion he died of probable poisoning, although we could not confirm the agent," he replied.

"And were you able to reach an opinion to a reasonable degree of forensic and scientific certainty as to the manner of death?" Dean asked.

"Yes."

"What is that, sir?"

"Homicide."

On cross-examination Brennan asked Fowler if he found any evidence that there was a needle puncture in the layer of skin and muscle under Steve's charred skin. Fowler responded that the only way to determine that would have been to skin Steve. But he said he never skinned anyone during an autopsy.

"That would have been a mutilating and . . . an unethical procedure to go to those lengths to do," Fowler said.

When asked by Brennan if Steve could have died in a "flash fire," in which case his carbon monoxide levels might be normal, the medical examiner said no, because the heat would have injured the lining of his mouth, his tongue, and his upper airway. But Fowler said Steve didn't have any of those injuries.

Brennan then questioned Fowler about an EKG, done on Steve on January 15, 1998, exactly a month before he died. Fowler said Steve's doctor had circled "normal" on the summary sheet of the EKG, but also indicated small "q" waves. The presence of a "q" wave in some people is an indication of a myocardial infarction, or heart attack. Fowler said Steve should have been referred for a stress EKG. Brennan said Steve's doctor did refer him to another doctor for the stress test, but Steve didn't keep the appointment.

Fowler said he wouldn't have altered his findings despite the indication of the small "q" waves, because he had personally examined Steve's heart and coronary arteries and they were of normal size and did not have any defects in them.

"And the other thing which is also very important, his heart was of entirely normal weight," Fowler said. "Anybody who has any disease process going on in their heart for any significant period, the heart is certainly going to enlarge to compensate and is going to begin to change."

Marc LeBeau, a forensic chemist and toxicologist for the FBI laboratory, was the next witness for the prosecution. LeBeau testified that the medical examiner's office sent him samples of Stephen Hricko's blood and urine to test for the presence of succinylcholine. He said he didn't detect any succinylcholine in either Steve's blood or urine.

The witness told the jury that succinylcholine was a very dangerous, fast-acting muscle relaxant that not only relaxed the muscles used to move around, such as arms and legs, but it also affected other muscles, such as those needed to breathe. LeBeau said the drug was dangerous if not administered in a hospital setting because it caused the body to suffocate itself. He said typically the drug started working about fifteen to thirty seconds after it was injected intramuscularly. LeBeau said the body rapidly broke down succinylcholine into two compounds, succinic acid and choline, both of which were normally found in the body, even if a person had not been exposed to the drug.

"Within a few minutes you may not be able to detect succinylcholine in a blood specimen," he said, adding a person could test for choline and succinic acid and find them.

To test for the presence of succinylcholine in the samples of Steve's urine and blood, LeBeau used a fairly new technique, known as liquid chromatography, that allowed him to try to look for a chemical based on its molecular weight. Testing Steve's urine was simple. LeBeau said all he had to do was shoot the urine into the instrument and monitor for the presence of succinylcholine. But before putting the blood in the instrument, he had to clean it up first.

"Well, if the succinylcholine breaks down in the body, what were you trying to find in the urine and blood?" Dean asked.

"Well, there have been a number of papers that suggest that really your only chance at finding succinylcholine in a forensic specimen or a postmortem specimen is in the urine. Only about two to five percent of the injected succinylcholine actually gets into the urine without breaking down into succinic acid and choline. Only about two to five percent. So you have a little bit of a chance to find it in the urine versus the blood, [where] it's very rapidly hydrolyzed into those two components."

LeBeau also told the jury that the chance of finding succinylcholine in the urine decreases the longer a person has been dead. He said that was because the enzymes that break the succinylcholine down into succinic acid and choline still exist. He said although there had been some success detecting a small amount of the drug in the urine of living patients, the likelihood of finding it in the urine taken from a dead person was slim.

Steve's sister Jennifer Hricko testified next. Jennifer told the jury that over the years she had never seen her brother with a pipe, cigarette, or cigar in his mouth.

On direct examination Dean asked Jennifer if she ever talked to Kim about her plans for Steve's funeral. Jennifer said on Monday, February 16, she discussed Steve's funeral with Kim while they were at Jennifer's parents' house in State College. The only substantial issue, as far as Kim was concerned, was cremation. She said her plan and desire was to have Steve cremated, Jennifer said. The next day Jennifer also questioned Kim about Steve's funeral arrangements and again Kim said she didn't really care about the arrangements and would leave it up to the Hrickos. The only thing that did matter was that Steve had to be cremated. Later, Jenny, who was living two miles from her parents, picked Kim up at the senior Hrickos' house to take her to talk to the funeral director, because the medical examiner had not yet released Steve's body for cremation.

"When I picked her up at the curb, she appeared to be restless. She was walking up and down, pacing, and in an anxious manner," Jennifer told the jury. "She got in the car. She affirmed that she felt too anxious and shaky to drive herself and that is why she wanted someone to drive her to the funeral home."

Kim explained to Jennifer she had to go to the funeral home to sign some papers that she then had to fax to the medical examiner so he could release Steve's body.

"She was concerned," Jennifer testified. "She didn't quite understand why. She felt she had taken care of all those arrangements prior to coming to Pennsylvania."

Dean also asked Jennifer if she ever talked to Kim about whether she and Steve used the woodstove in their room at Harbourtowne. Jennifer said ever since Steve died, she kept trying to figure out how it happened. She said during the week leading up to Steve's funeral, she kept asking various people questions about what had occurred at Harbourtowne. One of the things she learned was that there was some kind of wood-burning stove in the room and that the hotel supplied a fire log, for each of the guests. So Jenny asked Kim if she and Steve had burned the log, and if so, did they burn it before or after they went to dinner and the show. Kim hesitated for a few seconds and then said it was before they went to the murder-mystery dinner show.

"Now at any time during that week, the week following the death of your brother, did Kim tell you that she was going to go back down to Maryland for a day or so?" Dean asked.

Jennifer testified that Kim pulled her aside on Wednesday to tell her that her friend Rachelle St. Phard, who had driven to Pennsylvania from her home in New Jersey to be with Kim, was driving her back to St. Michaels. Kim was very vague about why she wanted to go back to the place where Steve died. Jennifer was surprised Kim would leave Pennsylvania, because Steve's viewing was the next day. Jennifer said Kim asked her not to tell any of the Hrickos that she and Rachelle were going back to Maryland.

"She goes, 'I really don't want any questions or hassles. I just want to go,'" Jennifer told the jury. "So after they left, I did wait till she left and then I told my family she left."

Astors Liquor clerk Doris Grave Coles told the jury that Kim bought a package of Backwood cigars, the same brand that was found in the Hrickos' room at Harbourtowne, sometime between January and February 1998. And David Sexton, a Maryland State Police forensic document examiner, said the machine that was used to make the price tag that was on the cigars in the Hrickos' room came from Astors Liquor.

Joe Gamble, who had been promoted to sergeant before the trial, testified about his attempts to determine where the cigars found in room 506 were purchased. He explained that he decided to focus his investigation in the area near the Hrickos' home in Laurel. He told the jury he went to approximately twenty-five stores on March 19 and 20, 1998, before going to Astors Liquor and finding a price tag on a package of Backwoods cigars that was identical to the price tag on the pack of cigars found at the fire scene.

The last witness of the day, as well as the prosecution's last witness, was Rachel McCoy, Kim's former best friend. Rachel told the jury that she met Kim in 1986 at the Pennsylvania restaurant where they both worked. She said they quickly became best friends and were even roommates for a time. Rachel told the jury that in the fall of 1997 Kim told her she wasn't happy in her marriage and was looking into getting a divorce. Then in January 1998 Kim told Rachel she was seeing a younger man, insisting, however, that their relationship was just about sex.

"She told me Jenny and Teri were not being very supportive of her in pursuing that relationship and they wanted her more to try to work it out with Steve and concentrate on that, and she didn't appreciate that they didn't support her," Rachel said.

Rachel also told the jury about the night at Kim's house when she talked to Rachel in detail about her plan to kill Steve.

"She was talking about how it would be easier if Steve were dead and she told me she had a plan on how to do it, where she wouldn't get caught," Rachel testified. "She told me that she could get a drug that would paralyze Steve, that would stop his breathing, and then she would set the curtains on fire with a candle or a cigar and that he would die of smoke inhalation in a fire and nobody would know."

Rachel said she tried to poke holes in Kim's plan, but Kim had answers for everything.

"I [asked her] where she was going to get this drug," Rachel said. "She told me that she could get the drug at work very easily—that it was in every hallway or every [operating room]. That they used it for trauma victims to stop their breathing so they could put a tube in their throat to put them on oxygen, so it was right there. She told me the drug wasn't traceable in the blood."

"Did she mention at all how she would give it to him?" Dean asked.

"She would inject it in a muscle."

"Did you try to tell her about the option of divorce?"

"Yup, I said that to her a number of times. 'Why don't you just get a divorce?'" Rachel told the jury. "And she seemed to think that this would be easier."

"Were you close to Kim at this time?" Dean asked.

"I was very close to Kim."

"Did you love her?"

"Yeah."

Several people who were at Kim's trial, including assistant state's attorney Henry Dove, said at one point during Rachel's testimony Kim gave her the finger.

Rachel told the jury that after Kim recounted her horrific plan, she went upstairs. Rachel thought she was going to use the bathroom, but when she didn't come back right away, Rachel went up after her and found her standing in the bedroom staring at her sleeping husband. She then coaxed Kim back downstairs.

"I just tried to calm her down and get her to stop crying and I was telling her that she needed to go to bed and go to sleep," Rachel said. "And just really a few minutes later, she did go upstairs and go to sleep and I waited about twenty more minutes."

However, before Kim went upstairs, Rachel called her neighbors in Baltimore to tell them what Kim was saying about killing Steve.

"I told them what Kim said, and Kim was yelling in the background, 'What, are you going to tell everybody?'" Rachel said. "And I didn't talk to them very long, but I did tell them that—because she was making me nervous with her behavior—if I called them again and hung up the phone, because they have caller ID, I said, 'If I call you again and hang up, I want you to call the police and tell them to come here.'"

But soon after Kim went upstairs, Rachel went home and never had to put her plan into action.

Rachel said she called Kim twice the next day to make sure everyone at the Hrickos' house was okay. Both times Kim told her everything was fine. That was the last time Rachel spoke with Kim until after Steve's, death. Rachel said after she learned the circumstances surrounding Steve's death, she called police to tell them what she knew.

Dean rested his case after Rachel finished testifying. At some point during the day Judge Horne dismissed two jurors, who appeared to be sleeping during testimony, and replaced them with two alternates. That left twelve jurors and two alternates hearing the case.

After the jurors were dismissed and before court adjourned for the day, Bill Brennan moved for a judgment of acquittal of the charges against Kimberly. Brennan argued that premeditated murder required three elements: the killing had to be willful, was a result of deliberation, and was premeditated.

"We feel that the state has failed in its proof to prove that . . . Mrs. Hricko was the one who actually did the killing and . . . they have also failed in its proof on the issue of premeditation," Brennan argued.

Brennan told the judge that from a scientific point of view, the state didn't prove that Steve was murdered. In addition, there was no proof that Kimberly was the person who actually set the fire at Harbourtowne.

"There was no opinion, evidence in this record, Your Honor, to indicate that the fire was incendiary in nature or that it was deliberately set," Brennan said.

"The state has not met its burden, Your Honor, that this was not an accidental fire and/or that my client was the one that set it."

In addition, Brennan said that first-degree arson required that the perpetrator intended to burn down a dwelling, not burn up a body to cover up a crime. And, he said, there was insufficient evidence for the jury to find that she willfully and maliciously intended to burn down the cottage that housed room 506.

Bob Dean said at that stage of the proceedings, the question was whether or not the state had presented evidence that was legally sufficient to allow the jury to make a decision on the charges. Dean said the state had met its burden of proof.

Judge Horne agreed with the prosecutor and denied the defense's motion for acquittal.

Chapter 17

On Friday, the last day of Kim's trial, the first witness called by the defense was Officer First Class Stephen Craig, of the St. Michaels Police Department. Craig said he and two other St. Michaels officers were the first to arrive at Harbourtowne in the early-morning hours of February 15, 1998.

Craig said when they first arrived, they were directed to the back of the building that housed room 506 and told there was a fire in the room. He said he first met Kim as she was walking toward the cottage.

"Was she running toward you?" Harry Trainor asked.

"A speeded walk, yes."

He said he put out his arm to stop her from moving forward and she "sort of" collapsed in his arms. Craig told the jury Kim was "upset." When Trainor pressed him on the issue, he admitted that previously he had said she was "hysterical" and later appeared "despondent."

Next the defense called forensic pathologist Dr. John Adams to the stand to try and refute testimony given by the medical examiner. Adams, who had worked as an assistant state medical examiner in

Maryland from 1962 to 1965, spent twenty-five years as a general pathologist in a Baltimore hospital before starting a private consulting business in 1990.

Adams said after reviewing Stephen Hricko's autopsy records, his opinion was that Steve's cause of death was unknown and the manner of death was undetermined. He said he reached those conclusions because the autopsy and toxicology studies of Steve's body did not establish an exact cause of Steve's death.

"Doctor, now can you give us, sir, the basis for your opinion as to the cause of death and the manner of death, relying on the science and the medicine that you have reviewed in this case?" Trainor asked Adams.

"Sure, the basis for my opinion is this: that a complete autopsy was done, including microscopic study, and no cause of death was found," Adams responded. "A fairly complete toxicology study on various tissues and organs and fluids of the body was done and no cause of death was found as a result of that study as well. So that based upon the science and leaving the circumstances out, it's my opinion that the cause of death was not determined by autopsy and not having the cause of death, it's impossible in this case to know what the manner of death is, i.e., whether it's natural, homicide, suicide, accident, or whatever."

Trainor then asked Adams about deaths due to smoke inhalation.

"In many, if not most, cases of fire deaths, death is caused by inhalation of smoke, which produces a couple of important things," Adams told the jury. "The carbon monoxide in the smoke is absorbed into the blood and that gets attached to the oxygen-carrying molecules in the blood and competes for oxygen, so that you basically wind up with no oxygen in your bloodstream and that's lethal. A second effect in fire deaths, of smoke inhalation is irritation and damage to the airway. Those are the main features in fire deaths where the cause of death is a result of smoke inhalation. Another important factor in many fire deaths is the fact that when you burn plastics, these artificial materials, you commonly get cyanide from it. And, of course, we all know that cyanide is very extremely lethal and so it's common to find lethal levels of cyanide in the blood of people who have died in fires."

Adams said that while the presence of an abnormal level of carbon monoxide or cyanide in the bloodstream and the presence of soot in the airway, in the lungs, or in the upper airway, confirms that the person was alive when the fire was started, the absence of carbon monoxide and the absence of smoke damage or soot in the airway doesn't necessarily prove a person was dead when the fire started.

"There are many recorded examples of both fast fires and some slow fires where neither smoke inhalation with soot nor carbon monoxide or cyanide were found and yet it's known that the person was alive at the time of the fire," Adams testified.

So as far as Adams was concerned, Steve still could have been alive when the fire started.

Adams said it was unlikely that a paralyzing dose of succinylcholine could be given to a physically fit 245-pound man without his cooperation. He also said succinylcholine could be detected in a person's urine after death.

The defense recalled Bonnie Parker to ask her about statements Mike Miller made to her the morning Steve died. Trainor asked Parker if Miller expressed his concerns about the possibility that Steve committed suicide. During his testimony Mike denied saying anything about Steve killing himself.

"What he said was that he could believe that Steve was capable of committing suicide, but that he would never, ever, do it by way of fire because he didn't smoke," Parker told the jury. "And he just had a lot of questions about the manner of Stephen's death by fire."

"But he told you that he could honestly picture him committing suicide?"

"He said something like if he thought that he was going to lose his wife and his daughter, he could get into a depression," Parker said.

"And he specifically mentioned suicide?" Trainor asked.

"That he could see it," she responded.

Under cross-examination Parker said Miller made those statements as he was trying to determine how Steve died.

Before the defense rested its case, the jury also heard from Kim's uncle David Woleslagle and her mother, Lois Wolf.

Woleslagle, an equipment operator for the state of Pennsylvania, testified that he had seen Steve smoke a cigar at a couple of family gatherings. Woleslagle's testimony was in direct contradiction to the testimony of Steve's friends and coworkers, who said they had never seen him smoke cigars or cigarettes.

"During the time that Kim and Stephen Hricko were married and after their daughter, Sarah, was born, did you have occasions to see them during family gatherings?" Trainor asked Woleslagle.

"Yes."

"During any of those gatherings, did you interact or communicate with Stephen Hricko?"

"Yes, I did."

"Were you able to make any observations about any tobacco usage Mr. Hricko did?"

"Yes, I can tell you whenever we had a discussion on an occasion—you can't smoke in my sister's house, so we went outside and he smoked a cigar while we were outside on the side porch of her home discussing various things, sports, golf. We were discussing just all kinds of odds and ends," Woleslagle said.

"On how many occasions did you observe him smoking a cigar?" Trainor asked.

"Twice."

Kim's mother told the jury about Kim's behavior and emotional state in the days after Steve's death.

"She was very, very upset. She was just desolate," Wolf said. "She cried a lot. She was a basket case, she really was. In fact, she was so bad that when we took her back up to the Hrickos,' I had to drive her car. She was in the back comforting Sarah. She couldn't even drive."

After conferring with her attorneys, Kimberly decided not to testify, as was her right. Before resting its case, the defense asked the judge to enter a Judgment of Acquittal, which was denied. Judge Horne then gave jurors the instructions they were to follow during their deliberation before the attorneys gave their closing arguments.

First he reminded the jurors that they had to completely disregard any newspaper, television, or radio reports they might have read, seen, or heard concerning Kim's case. Then he said Kim was innocent of all charges unless they were convinced beyond a reasonable doubt that she was guilty.

"Proof beyond a reasonable doubt requires such proof as would convince you of the truth of a fact to the extent that you would be willing to act upon such belief without reservation in an important matter in your own business or personal affairs," Horne said. "However, if you are not satisfied of the defendant's guilt to that extent, then reasonable doubt exists and the defendant must be found not guilty."

He told them in making their decision they should consider the evidence, which was the testimony from the witness stand, the physical evidence or exhibits that had been admitted into evidence, and stipulations of the attorneys.

"In evaluating the evidence you should consider it in light of your own experiences," he said.

The jurors were told they could not consider the charging document, inadmissible or stricken evidence, and questions or objections of counsel, because they were not evidence. Horne also said the jurors could not draw any conclusions or inferences from his comments or questions as to the merits of the case or his questions of the witnesses. He reminded them that opening and closing statements were not evidence, but only could help them understand the evidence.

"There are two types of evidence, direct and circumstantial," he said. "The law makes no distinction between the weight to be given to either direct or circumstantial evidence. No greater degree of certainty is required of circumstantial evidence than of direct evidence in reaching a decision. You should weigh all evidence, whether direct or circumstantial."

Horne said the jurors couldn't convict Kimberly unless they determined that the evidence, when considered as a whole, established guilt beyond a reasonable doubt. He explained that they should take into account all of the testimony and evidence, as well as the circumstances under which each witness testified. The judge told them to consider a witness's behavior on the stand and the manner in which he or she testified.

He said the jurors should try to determine if the witness was telling the truth, if the witness had the opportunity to see or hear the things he or she testified about, if the witness accurately remembered the events in question, if the witness had an interest in the outcome of the case, if the witness's testimony was consistent, if the witness's testimony was supported or contradicted by other testimony, and if the witness's testimony in court differed from his or her previous statements.

Horne told the jurors they didn't have to believe a witness's testimony—even if that testimony wasn't contradicted.

"You may believe all, part, or none of the testimony of any witness," Horne explained.

The judge also said the jurors didn't have to accept anything an expert witness said on the stand. He said they should consider an expert's opinion in conjunction with all the other evidence that was presented.

"In weighing the opinion of an expert, you should consider the expert's experience, training, and skills, as well as the expert's knowledge of the subject matter about which the expert is expressing an opinion," the judge said.

Horne then reminded the jurors that Kimberly had an absolute, constitutional right not to testify and the fact that she chose not to testify should not be held against her.

In this case the state introduced evidence that Kim made a certain statement to police about the crimes she had been charged with and it was up to the state to prove beyond a reasonable doubt that she made that statement freely and voluntarily, Horne said.

"If you don't find beyond a reasonable doubt that the statement was voluntary, you must disregard it," he said. "The burden is on the state to prove beyond a reasonable doubt that the offense was committed and that the defendant is the person who committed it."

Although the state wasn't required to prove motive, he said the jurors could consider motive or lack of motive as a circumstance in the case.

"Presence of motive may be evidence of guilt," he said. "Absence of motive may suggest innocence."

Next, Horne explained to the jurors that Kim had been charged with first-degree, as well as second-degree, murder.

First-degree murder was the intentional killing of another person with willfulness, deliberation, and premeditation, he said. In order to convict Kimberly of this crime, the jury had to be convinced beyond a reasonable doubt that Kim caused Steve's death and that the killing was willful, deliberate, and premeditated.

Second-degree murder, he said, was the killing of another person with either the intent to kill or the intent to inflict such bodily harm that death would likely result. In order to convict Kim of second-degree murder, the jury had to decide beyond a reasonable doubt that she caused Steve's death and that she engaged in the deadly conduct with the intent to inflict such serious bodily harm that death would likely result.

To convict Kimberly of arson the jury had to be convinced beyond a reasonable doubt that she set fire to room 506 and that she did so willfully and maliciously.

With that, Judge Horne finished his instructions to the jury, and closing arguments began.

Chapter 18

Prosecutor Bob Dean was first to give his closing statement.

"As I indicated to you on Monday, a trial is designed to re-create an event that occurred in the past," he told jurors. "What we have seen this week in this courtroom and what we have brought to you in this courtroom is by every count tragic, heartbreaking. But at the same time, ladies and gentlemen, it's cold-blooded and sinister."

Dean told the jury that just over a year earlier, Kim had set a course of action in motion that eventually would lead to despair, destruction, and death—the death of a young man, her husband, who was so desperately in love with her, and who was the father of their nine-year-old daughter, Sarah.

The evidence was clear, however, that the marriage was over and that Kimberly wanted out. As far as she was concerned, Steve was no longer any fun—he never went out anymore, nor did he help Kim around the house, Dean said. To put it simply, Kim was tired of Steve and she wanted a change. In fact, Steve repulsed Kim, Dean said. He made her sick.

Dean said it was through the testimony of Kim's friends that police and prosecutors were able to reconstruct the journey that she embarked upon in late 1997 and early 1998. A journey, he said, that ultimately led to the tragedy that brought everyone together in the Talbot County Courthouse.

Even though Kim's friends loved her, Dean said, they understood that they had an obligation to tell police what they knew about what Kim was doing, about what she was thinking. Dean told the jury that it must have been pure agony for them to come forward.

Dean then explained to the jury the difference between first-degree murder and second-degree murder. First-degree murder required premeditation; some thought beforehand, he said. It didn't matter whether it was ten minutes or twenty minutes, or longer. What mattered was that the perpetrator planned to kill someone before he actually did it.

"If ever, ladies and gentlemen, there is a situation involving premeditation, it is the situation that we are dealing with in this courtroom today," Dean said.

He told the jury that the arson charge against Kimberly simply meant the burning of a dwelling, such as an apartment, a house, or a hotel room. First-degree murder and arson were the two charges that were before the jury, he said.

Now, Dean said, it was the jury's role to assess the evidence and answer two questions: Was he murdered? And if so, who did it?

"Why did this man die? There's a reason behind everything," Dean told the jury. "How did he die? What caused this guy's death? There's some very basic facts, and from those basic facts we can logically reach a conclusion."

Dean then asked the jurors to take a look at a couple of aspects of the case.

"When did Stephen die?" he asked.

Dean said there was roughly a two-hour window in which Steve could have died—from a little after 11:00 P.M., on Saturday, February 14, to a little after 1:00 A.M., on Sunday, February 15.

"By about one twenty-five A.M., when Philip Parker went in there with Elaine Phillips, who worked there at Harbourtowne, and dragged that poor man out of the room, he was dead," Dean said. "And I suggest to you he'd been dead for some time because rigor had already set in."

Dean said he believed Steve died closer to midnight.

Dean called the jurors' attention to the medical examiner's testimony and reminded them that Steve had no soot, or injuries caused by fire, in his breathing passages or lungs. That meant that Steve wasn't breathing when the fire started. He was dead, Dean said.

"Why was he dead?" Dean asked.

The evidence showed that the only other person in the room that night was Kimberly, he said.

"How did the fire start? Of course, Steve's already dead," Dean said. "Was it electric? Was it spontaneous—it just started? Was it cigar ashes on the pillow or bedspread? I suggest to you the fire marshal tried every which way in the world to get those pillows and the bedspread to light with cigar ashes."

Dean told the jury the fire's point of origin was in the area on the floor by the foot of the bed—where the pillows were, where his head would have been. All that remained after the fibrous filling of the pillows had burned was the brittle brown substance left on the floor, he said.

"But, ladies and gentlemen, how did that pillow

ignite?" he asked. "Wasn't by a cigar ash. It was not by a cigar ash."

But back to Steve, he said. Dr. Fowler did an exhaustive study on Steve's body, but couldn't find any reason for him to be dead, he continued. There was no evidence of trauma, no dangerous substances detected. Fowler did find some cold medicine and antidepressants in Steve's body, but they were within therapeutic levels. Dr. Fowler didn't find any alcohol in Steve's bloodstream and his heart was the normal size and weight, he said. The lungs, the liver, the brain—everything was intact; everything was in order, Dean said.

"This is now where we have to leave the autopsy table and we need to leave the toxicology lab and go out and examine the people that Steve had interaction with," Dean said. "This is where we now must look at the defendant. What was going on in her life that led up to that night in St. Michaels?"

Dean told the jurors that the evidence showed that in her own twisted way Kim developed a motive to kill Steve. And she had the means, the motive, and the opportunity, he said. Her marriage had gone sour, she was getting sick and tired of Steve, and she wanted out. She made that very clear to her closest friends, he said. She even wanted and needed them to understand and support her in her plan to kill her husband.

All the while, Steve was trying desperately to make the marriage work, Dean said. He even wrote about his torment in his journal. But Kim's answer was to complain that now Steve was smothering her, following her around the house and making her sick. She said he disgusted her, Dean told the jury.

Kimberly sought physical and emotional love, Dean said, but in the arms of Brad Winkler, not her husband.

At this point Dean read some of the notes Kim and Brad had sent to each other.

"Now, this is going on, folks, at the same time that Steve is desperately trying to put this marriage back together," Dean said.

Dean said although it was sad to pry, in a murder case it was important to examine closely what was going on in the lives of the people involved. He said even though he didn't take any pleasure in presenting Kim's deep, dark feelings to the jury, he had to do it so she would be held accountable for what she did to her husband.

Why didn't Kim just divorce Steve? Because she convinced herself that murdering Steve was the best way out of her situation. Dean reminded the jury that Kim offered Ken Burgess $50,000 to kill Steve for her and she wasn't joking about it. She also told Teri Armstrong that Steve would be better off dead. And one day she told Jenny Gowen if she could kill Steve and get away with it, she'd do it the very next day.

Kim certainly didn't want to push Steve into committing suicide, because then she wouldn't be able to collect the $450,000 from his two life-insurance policies. Kim told Teri Armstrong that she and Sarah would be able to live the way they wanted to live with that money. Dean reminded the jury that Kim told Jennifer Gowen that she had been thinking of ways to kill Steve without getting caught. Kim told Jenny about succinylcholine and how some people had used it as a murder weapon in the past because it couldn't be traced.

"Late January, just two weeks before that fatal Harbourtowne visit, Kim realized suddenly, ladies and gentlemen, that she could do it. She could do it," Dean said. "And she would do it."

Next, Dean told the jury to step back in time to January 30, 1998, the night in the Hrickos' town house when Kim told Rachel McCoy about her plan to kill Steve. Rachel just stood there listening to Kim, appalled, scared, and confused. Kim told Rachel about a drug that she could easily get at work—a paralyzing drug. She said she was going to inject Steve with the drug and then she was going to set a fire to finish him off. And Rachel was trying to poke holes in Kim's plan, Dean said, but Kim had an answer for everything. She said the drug couldn't be detected in the body, so she could kill Steve and not get caught.

"Imagine the feeling that Rachel McCoy, a decent woman if there ever was one, felt upon hearing her best friend say this," Dean said.

The final piece to the puzzle, Dean said, was how Steve died.

"Why is it there was nothing left in his body to tell us the way he died?" Dean asked the jury. "No bullet, no wound, no deadly chemicals detectable. No illness. No disease."

It was because Kim had access to a drug at her job that could help her commit the perfect murder, he said. It was a deadly, quick-acting drug that left no trace. Kim's motive was to be free of Steve—to be free of the guy who was making her sick. To be free to make Brad happy forever. In the process she would become somewhat wealthy, he said.

Dean said Kim had the perfect opportunity to kill Steve at Harbourtowne. They were alone and away from home. It was late. Kim was the last person to see her husband alive, he said. Dean told the jury Kim created her own bogus alibi about a ninety-minute-to-two-hour odyssey she took from St. Michaels to Easton trying to get to the Millers' house. But she told some people she was going home, while she told others she was just driving around and got lost.

Dean derided Kim's statement that she got lost, saying she had driven to the Millers' a couple months before Steve died and it wasn't hard to find their Elizabeth Street home in Easton.

"She needed to have a reason to be away from that room, quite obviously," Dean said. "She's staging an accident. She's creating her own bogus alibi. She tells everyone he's drunk. He's not. Her plan—create a scene, a drunk husband with cigars. Easy enough to explain. The careless guy had an accident. Problem is, folks, he was dead before the fire started."

Dean said time and again she told her friends basically the same story. She and Steve got into a fight because he wanted to have sex and she didn't. She got angry and left the hotel room. She got lost looking for the Millers' house and ended up driving around for ninety minutes to two hours.

"Of course, she never, she never called, did she?"

Dean asked the jurors to recall the meeting Kim had with the state troopers Keith Elzey and Karen Alt at Harbourtowne on February 23, 1998. She told them the same version of the story that she told police when Steve died, with the exception of a few changes, he said.

"And finally Detective Elzey says, 'Kimberly I want the truth.' And then Kimberly says, 'I want to tell the truth.' Note that Kimberly didn't say she had told the truth," Dean said. "Kimberly said she wants to tell the truth and then she asks the detective, 'If I tell the truth, can I go home to see my daughter? Can you promise me that?' Detective Elzey couldn't do that and the interview was over."

Dean said what was implicit in Kim's exchange

with Elzey was that up until that point she had been lying to everyone.

The prosecutor now shifted his focus to Kim's actions in the weeks after Steve's death. First she made sure his body was cremated, ending any chance of an additional forensic examination. He reminded the jury that when Teri Armstrong visited Kim after her arrest, Kim told Teri that she had remorse for what had happened to Steve. During their conversation Kim told Teri she knew it was Rachel who called the police because she told her exactly what she planned to do to Steve. After her arrest Kim also asked Maureen Miller to call Teri, Rachel, and Jenny Gowen to find out what they said to police. Why did she ask Maureen to call those three people? Because those are the people she told about her plan to kill Steve, Dean said.

"It's a curious request, isn't it? And it speaks volumes," Dean said.

The jurors were reminded that while in custody, Kim told Jenny, "I don't care what anyone says—it wasn't for the money."

"That screams at you, folks," Dean said. "It screams at you."

Dean shifted gears again back to Kim and Steve's relationship.

"The evidence shows clearly, overwhelmingly, disturbingly, that Kim and her husband—from different perspectives, nevertheless—were each kind of living their own hell those last few months leading up to Valentine's Day last year," Dean said.

Steve was desperate to make his marriage work. He was desperately in love with Kim. He was in emotional turmoil. He had ups and downs. The marriage was crumbling. He was taking antidepressants and getting counseling because he wanted the marriage to work, Dean explained, but Steve was on the bad end of a bad marriage. Kim, meanwhile, had her sights set on other things, and those things didn't include saving her marriage. She made it clear she wasn't anxious to go to Harbourtowne that weekend. She had a new star in her life and a new goal. She wanted to be with Brad.

"Her infatuation, I would suggest to you, her obsession, he was everything in her twisted mind. . . . Brad was everything that Steve wasn't," Dean said. "Cared and played with the kids and went out and helped out with the dishes and hung around with the girls. He was a great party guy. Went out all the time. Not her husband."

The evidence showed that in the weeks and months before Steve's murder, Kim was becoming more and more convinced that the only way to get rid of Steve, and have the life she wanted was to kill him, Dean said. Then she could collect the insurance money and live happily ever after with Brad Winker. She was looking forward to making Brad the happiest guy in the world. She was looking forward to over $400,000 in insurance money.

"The case is sad," Dean said. "It really is very sad."

Dean told the jurors that although there was nothing pleasant about dealing with the facts of Kim's case, it was their duty to sit as a jury and to rule and to reach a verdict based on the facts.

"The only way, ladies and gentlemen, we can obtain justice in this case is for you to consider the evidence carefully, objectively, and then to come back and say, 'Kimberly Hricko, you planned the death of your husband. You carried it out. You are guilty of murder in the first degree and you are guilty of arson.' Thank you."

* * *

After a brief recess Kim's attorney Bill Brennan rose to give his closing statement.

Brennan began by talking to the jury about the difference between a church and a courtroom. In a church people deal with the concepts of moral guilt and moral innocence, but in a courtroom people deal with the concepts of legal guilt and legal innocence. And in a church people are governed by the law of God, but in a courtroom they are governed by the laws of man.

"I mention that to you because it's very important for you to consider in the decision you are about to make," Brennan said. "Because the decision that you make . . . is not a moral decision or not an ethical decision. It's not whether you morally approve of Kimberly Hricko. It's not whether or not you ethically approve of her conduct. The issue in this courtroom is whether or not the state of Maryland has proven, beyond a reasonable doubt, legal guilt."

Brennan said he understood that the jurors might not approve of Kim's extramarital affair with Brad. And they would be right if they thought it was morally wrong. But that wasn't the issue before them. The issue before them was whether or not the state of Maryland legally had proven or not proven that Kim was guilty of killing Steve and then setting their room on fire.

"I'd suggest they have not proven the concept of legal guilt on [those] charges," he said.

The jurors were reminded that they had to judge the case without prejudice and not on emotion or sympathy, but on the law, on the facts, and on logic. Brennan also asked them to remember that a defendant was innocent until proven guilty. The defendant didn't have to prove his or her innocence; it was up to the prosecution to prove his or her guilt. And the standard of proof in a criminal trial was "beyond a reasonable doubt," or a doubt founded on reason, not a fanciful doubt or a whimsical doubt, Brennan said.

In his summation Brennan referred to Judge Horne's instructions to the jury to evaluate the credibility of the witnesses. Brennan said jurors should not just determine whether witnesses were telling the truth, but also whether those witnesses were exaggerating or putting a spin on their testimony.

"Many times as people talk, as they think about things, as they tell one another, as they talk about things, they sometimes will say what they think it should be, or what they want it to be, or what they thought it should be, or what they believe it to be, not what it really was," he said.

Brennan recalled the testimony of Elaine Phillips, who said that when Kim went into the lobby of Harbourtowne to report the fire she wasn't shaking, she was calm. But when he was cross-examining Phillips, Harry Trainor showed her the statement she wrote a couple of hours after Kim went into the lobby. In her statement Phillips said Kim was shaking.

"Didn't remember that. Didn't want to remember that," Brennan said. "I'm not saying she's lying about that. Just that she felt, 'Well, I'm a prosecution witness. I shouldn't remember those things.'"

Her cousin Philip Parker did the same thing, Brennan said. When asked by Trainor if Kim ran into the lobby, screaming, Parker said no. She was calm, he said. In his statement written shortly after Steve had died, Parker said she ran into the lobby, screaming, but he didn't remember that when he was on the witness stand.

"Why?" Brennan asked. "Is he lying? No. Has he got it wrong? Has his memory failed him? ... It serves to illustrate the point that oral testimony, what people say, what people hear, how they report things, how they want to report things, how they think they should report things, is inherently unreliable. It does not reach the quality of proof that the judge has talked about."

Brennan made it clear to the jury that Teri Armstrong, Jennifer Gowen, Rachel McCoy, and Norma Walz had plenty of time to talk to each other and compare their stories in the year or so before the start of Kim's trial. How much of that, he wondered, was reflected in their trial testimony. Brennan's point was that the jury shouldn't always trust the oral testimony of a witness.

For example, take the testimony of state Trooper Clay Hartness, who told the jury that Kim was slightly intoxicated when he interviewed her after Steve's death. However, Brennan said, no one else at the scene made the same observation. Not Bonnie Parker, who was in close contact with Kim, and not Father Paul Jennings, who was also very close to her when he delivered the news that Steve had died. Trooper Hartness was the only person who testified that Kim was slightly intoxicated.

"Why does he say that?" Brennan asked the jury. "Again, perceptions, unreliability."

Rather than relying on witnesses' recollections during deliberations, Brennan told the jurors they should, instead, look at the scientific evidence, because those personal recollections were often based on the moral beliefs of the witnesses.

Brennan asked the jurors first to focus on the arson charge against Kimberly. The first issue to think about was how the fire started, because no one really knew how it started. What jurors did know was that by the time people arrived at the Hrickos' room the fire had already burned itself out. And they knew it was a dirty fire, a smelly fire, a very short, intense fire, but it was also an odd fire, because it only burned the bed closest to Steve.

"But how did it start?" Brennan asked. "Can anyone in this courtroom tell us how the fire started? . . . There was no accelerant."

Because no one knew how the fire started, the jury would have to play detective and guess and speculate about how it started.

"You are trying to fill in the blanks on how this fire started," Brennan told the jury. "'Then you've got reasonable doubt."

Brennan said the prosecutor didn't prove the arson count against Kimberly because the state couldn't say how the fire started. He said because there was no expert testimony that the fire was set, and because the jury would have to guess and speculate about its cause, then the law required them to find Kimberly not guilty on the arson charge.

And if the jurors weren't satisfied about how Steve died, then they should find Kim not guilty on the murder charge as well.

"How did he die?" Brennan asked.

Dr. Fowler testified to a reasonable degree of medical certainty that Steve was probably poisoned, but there wasn't a single piece of medical or scientific evidence to show that succinylcholine was ever injected into Steve's body, Brennan said. But Dr. Adams, the forensic pathologist, said the cause of Steve's death was unknown and the manner of death should be classified as undetermined, rather than homicide, he said.

To put doubt in the jurors' minds about the cause of Steve's death, Brennan reminded them that just weeks before he died, Steve didn't keep an appointment with a cardiologist for a stress echo test which had been set up by his physician, and he never called to reschedule.

"Were there heart problems?" Brennan asked.

Steve was also suffering from depression, Brennan said. So even though Steve appeared to be a strong, physically fit, healthy man, he really wasn't.

Next Brennan tried to discredit the testimony of the medical examiner, Dr. Fowler, by telling the jury that Fowler admitted that there had been cases where someone had died in a flash fire, a sudden fire, a fire that just bursts up, and the fire shut down that person's airways so there was no carbon monoxide in the blood, no soot in the airways. However, what Fowler actually had said in his testimony was that even though there was an absence of carbon monoxide in a flash fire, there would still be heat damage to the lining of the mouth, the tongue, and the upper airway. Fowler testified those injuries were not present in Steve's case; therefore, he did not die in a flash fire.

Even though there was no scientific evidence that succinylcholine killed Steve, Brennan asked the jurors to think about how Kim could have injected Steve with the drug.

"Dr. Wex, the anesthesiologist, says it would take two to four minutes to take effect," Brennan said. "Dr. Adams says intramuscularly you need ten cc's of it, which means you'd need [a large needle]. And for a noncooperating person you're only going to get about one cc in. Dr. Fowler [agreed] that even if you use a small needle, you're going to feel it; it's going to hurt."

Brennan said it didn't make sense to think that a physically fit, 6-foot three-inch, 245-pound man, who wasn't drunk, would just let someone stick him with a big needle and not react.

"You're going to pull it out. You're going to struggle. You're going to break the needle off. Something's going to happen," he said. "You're going to sit there willingly while someone takes a few seconds to pump that kind of drug into your body? Does that make sense? No, it makes no sense evidence. There is no scientific evidence that succinylcholine was used. There is no medical evidence that succinylcholine was used. And there is . . . no common sense evidence that succinylcholine was used, because they don't have a delivery vehicle to get it in the body. The only nonsense about succinylcholine comes from the Four Musketeers. And it cannot be backed up by facts, by science, by medicine, or by common sense. The state has not proven, beyond a reasonable doubt, the delivery mechanism. They have not proven, beyond a reasonable doubt, this theory. And that's what it is, a theory."

Brennan then read some of Stephen's journal to the jurors, implying that he was so depressed he could have committed suicide. He reminded the jury that the state had the burden of proving that Kim killed Steve—beyond a reasonable doubt.

"They have a theory, want you to guess, speculate, that a physically fit, six-foot three-inch, two-hundred-forty-five-pound man, unbeknownst to him, got shot full of a deadly drug," Brennan said. "If this were a case where someone's charged with enabling a suicide, it might be one thing. But it's not. It's a murder case. It's not first degree. The law, the science, the evidence, common sense, says that the state of Maryland has not met its burden in a courtroom according to law to convict Kimberly Hricko of murder. Your verdict should be not guilty. Thank you."

Bob Dean had the final word before the jury.

The first thing Dean told the jurors was that he was waiting for Brennan to make some reference to the fact that Kim told her four closest friends that she wanted Steve dead. Brennan did mention her friends, but in a disparaging way, calling them the Four Musketeers, Dean said.

"Now think about that for just a moment and I think you can then appreciate what the defense theory is," Dean said. "The theory is to ignore the fact that their client, Kimberly Hricko, indeed did want Stephen dead. Indeed did have a plan to kill her husband. Indeed did have a motive to kill her husband. Indeed had every reason in the world, in her own twisted mind, to have her husband taken away."

The defense, though, didn't mention any of that to the jury, he said. Dean told the jury that the state's theory of how Kim killed her husband wasn't really just the state's theory—it was really Kim's own plan. The plan she talked about with Rachel McCoy. Dean scoffed at the defense's contention that Kim's friends made up the story that she told them she was going to kill Steve. Why would they do that? The defense implied that it was because they didn't approve of her affair with Brad Winkler, he said. Coming forward to tell police about Kim's plan was probably the most difficult thing they had ever done and it wasn't right for the defense to demean their actions, he said.

As for the testimony of Dr. Adams, Dean said he just wasn't believable. In fact, he was the only person in the courtroom, actually the only person in the city of Easton, who didn't know that succinylcholine disappeared in the body.

"That tells you how much he knows about the subject matter we're dealing with," Dean said. "He doesn't know [anything] about it. There's a lot more to this case as you well know and as he would not acknowledge. I suggest to you his understanding of the case is rather limited. It's as limited as his understanding of the substance used and the plan to kill Steve."

Dean told the members of the jury they needed to focus on the evidence, not what a paid witness came in and said, especially when he really knew nothing about the case.

Next the prosecutor talked briefly about the fire and its point of origin, which was on the floor where Stephen's head was resting on the pillows. Dean said the pillows were set on fire by a flame. And setting Steve on fire was part of Kim's plan.

"And when Kimberly Hricko says, 'I'm going to set him on fire as part of my plan,' you have the answer to the arson," Dean said. "You have the answer to the murder."

The jurors were told to use their common sense as well as all the information from the case during their deliberations. Dean told the jury that Kimberly really didn't have a theory as to how Steve died. All the defense said was that the medical examiner didn't find any succinylcholine in Steve's body, so no one can be sure that's how he was killed.

"Kimberly, the defendant, was on a mission of death," Dean told the jurors. "That woman had ice water running through her veins. Kim nearly, nearly committed the perfect crime. Staging an accident, using the substance that disappears in your body. She knew more about the substance than her expert witness did."

But, he said, Kim's tormented and brave friends knew what was going on and they knew what they had to do.

"You can't just sweep a life under the rug," Dean said. "All that's left of Steve now is his memory and his ashes. Justice and decency demand that the defendant be held accountable."

Dean, like Brennan, read a portion of Steve's diary to the jury: "'I have a lot to offer someone. I eventually will need more from her.' Here's the phrase I want you to remember. 'This weekend will tell me a lot about her feelings.' Well, I guess so, folks," Dean said. "That weekend said an awful lot about her feelings. Truer words were never written."

Finally Dean told the jury members to use common sense as they considered the evidence.

"There's only one verdict that's consistent with the facts. There's only one verdict that's consistent with justice," he said. "The only verdict consistent with justice in this case, ladies and gentlemen, is guilty as charged. Thank you."

Chapter 19

The jury deliberated approximately three hours before reaching guilty verdicts on the arson and murder charges. As the foreman announced the verdicts, Kim remained stoic, showing no emotion. Steve's family and friends, however, hugged each other and cried after the jury was excused.

Jury foreman Curt Hutchinson explained what happened in the jury room.

"We took an initial vote and there were about five people who didn't want to vote at that time—not that they thought she was not guilty—they just said they needed further information," Hutchinson said. "The other people were ready to vote. I took a secret ballot—the five wanted more deliberation and the other folks were leaning toward guilty."

Hutchinson said after the initial vote, the jurors went through the notes they took during trial.

"We talked about it and we got different people's viewpoints, particularly the ones who had questions," he said. "They were looking at motive and going back and looking at the information that was provided by the various witnesses. Over several hours it became very evident to most people on the jury that there really wasn't a lot of doubt that she was guilty."

Hutchinson said one thing that came out during trial that helped the jury reach its verdict was the fact that Kim had ready access to the succinylcholine because she was a surgical technologist.

In addition, testimony by state fire marshal Mike Mulligan also played a part in the jury's decision. Hutchinson said Mulligan spent a lot of time on the stand and basically demonstrated to most people that there was no way the fire had been started by careless smoking, as Kimberly had claimed.

"Steve had burned from the head down to the midchest, and she had said that he had smoked a cigar, but she bought the cigar and he didn't typically smoke, from what I understood," Hutchinson said. "And the fire marshal was unable to get any of the materials to burn, using the cigar, although they smoldered a little bit."

Hutchinson said the jury also believed Mulligan's testimony that an ember from the woodstove couldn't have started the fire. He said the scientific evidence was pretty much overwhelming and the prosecutor did a good job laying out a very succinct case. The facts were there, he said.

"There was so much real evidence against her," Hutchinson said. "I based most of my decisions on the scientific evidence that was presented. I was surprised that I got on the jury, because I told them I was a toxicologist—but I looked at pretty much the scientific evidence and to me it was irrefutable that there was no other way it could have happened."

Hutchinson said he didn't know what the defense could have done differently. They just didn't have a good argument, he said.

"They brought in some witnesses, but their medical guy was just a hired gun, a charlatan, who really didn't help at all. He almost got laughed out of the place. He was so pathetic," Hutchinson said. "He tried to say it could have been this, it could have been that, but it was obvious that those were not really choices."

Hutchinson said the testimony from Kim's friends also played a part in the jury's verdict, but that wasn't the overriding factor.

"It added fuel to the decision that she had motive and she had discussed it and she had the means," Hutchinson said. "To me it was a slam dunk."

After the jury talked long and hard about the trial, Hutchinson took a second vote.

"Once everything got talked out—the sequences, the fire marshal, the medical examiner, seeing the pictures and listening to Kim's friends, all the jurors—except one—believed Kim was guilty," he said. "But once she read all the letters Steve had written to Kim, she, too, agreed to go along with the guilty verdict. It really took her reading the letters that he had sent—that's what finally won her over. It can be exasperating when people don't believe the way you think they should, but in the end it was total commitment to the verdict."

Kim's attorneys were a bit surprised to hear that Hutchinson mainly based his decision on the scientific evidence.

"As we're sitting there in the courtroom and the testimony is coming in, we felt that we were winning on the science and we were winning on the technical aspects of the case," Harry Trainor said. "But what we felt hurt us the most was when her girlfriends came in and testified regarding what they claimed she had said. We felt that's where we sustained a lot of damage in our case. We were damaged by the personal stuff—the testimony from people who knew her. And clearly the access to medications that might have been used was not helpful to us, even though no doctor ever found any point of entry for the succinylcholine—no needle marks or any delivery device, such as a syringe or anything like that. The gamble in a trial is that you don't know how the twelve people you pick are going to interact with each other and who will be the opinion leader and how strong people will hold to their views—that's the riskiest factor in a jury trial."

Judge Horne set Kim's sentencing hearing for Friday, March 19, 1999.

The first person to give a victim's impact statement at Kim's sentencing was Steve's mother, Mary Esther Hricko, who said it was impossible to put into words the effect Steve's death had had on the Hricko family.

"But nothing has been the same," she said. "My husband can't talk about him without crying. I don't sleep. It really has had a rather devastating effect on us."

Mary told the judge that since Steve was murdered, her husband had suffered two devastating illnesses, although she said she didn't believe the illnesses were just the result of an elevated stress level. Steve's mother told the judge that since Steve died, she had only been able to see Sarah a couple of times. She said Sarah was the person who would suffer most from Steve's death.

"To lose your father, who would have protected you, is quite a thing," she said.

Mary Hricko told Judge Horne that her family

didn't want him to show Kim any leniency when he sentenced her.

Jennifer Hricko, one of Steve's three sisters, also spoke at Kim's sentencing. Jennifer, a psychological-services specialist at a state prison in Pennsylvania, reminded the court that many people had been affected by Steve's murder, and none of them deserved it.

"There is no way in the world we deserve this," Jenny said. "Nobody deserves this, no matter what, but we did not deserve this. Sarah, Kim and Steve's daughter, is an intelligent, beautiful child who did not deserve this at all. Her life, whether she knows it or not, to this point, psychologically is ripped apart."

Jenny told the court that no matter how Sarah seemed to be doing on the outside, there was really no way to predict totally how the devastation of her father's death would affect her future.

"I know that people have suffered, perhaps including the perpetrator," Jenny said. "But she needs to now go on and do what she can to help her daughter. And if she doesn't, I will then be assured of the cold nature of this woman. I hope she can find it in her heart, and I think there is a spark in her heart that can come through with this, and face this honestly and with responsibility and help herself and her daughter."

Jenny told the court that although Steve had not been perfect, he was a gentle and good man.

"He was a big, strong man and we all valued him and expected to have him in our lives," Jenny said. "And I just pray that he can find peace where he is."

At the hearing Kim's lawyers submitted letters to the judge from friends and family who asked him to be lenient when he sentenced Kim. Some of the letters sent in on Kim's behalf came from relatives, including her paternal uncle and grandparents. But the Kim they described was a far cry from the Kim who had injected her husband with a drug to paralyze his muscles and then set him on fire.

Kim's paternal grandparents, Anna and Glenn Aungst Sr., asked Judge Horne to show compassion when he sentenced her. They told Horne that they were very close to Kim when she was growing up. Kim had always been a polite, caring, bright, and very religious person, who had never been mean to anyone, the Aungsts said.

They told the judge that Kimberly was a very caring mother to her nine-year-old daughter, and that Sarah was very close to her mother and both mother and daughter really needed one another. They pleaded with the judge to show compassion and find it in his heart to return Kimberly to her family as soon as possible.

Kim's stepmother, Karen Pasquariello, told Judge Horne that throughout the twenty-six or so years she had known her she had always exhibited many wonderful qualities. Kim had always displayed an extreme love for God and for other people, she said in her letter.

Pasquariello said Kim had always shown integrity, kindness, helpfulness, compassion and unselfishness toward others. She said Kim was sympathetic to others who were less fortunate or troubled, and Kim never appeared to be materialistic.

"I have known her to be always focused on spiritual rather than material things. I trusted and believed in Kim. Kim has always extended kindness and respect to me," Pasquariello said.

Kim's aunt, G.R. Matthews, said she had always been a very sweet, unselfish girl, whom she had enjoyed being around. She said when her mother passed away, Kim couldn't take time off from work to be with her. But she did call to offer her condolences and also made arrangements for food to be available after the funeral.

"This was a compassionate act that I shall always remember," Matthews said.

Matthews also said Kim had always demonstrated only positive characteristics in her life and in her interactions with others.

Ronald Aungst, Kim's uncle, also wrote to Judge Horne telling him about Kim's life. He said Kim was a good little girl, happy and loving. He said Kim was a very good student in school and graduated from a private Christian high school in Altoona, Pennsylvania. Kim then attended two private Christian colleges, working her way through school as a waitress. Then she got married and had Sarah. He told Judge Horne that Kim graduated from Penn State University and was a registered nurse and a surgical nurse.

Ronald Aungst explained that Kim had always been caring and concerned about helping sick people. He said Kim's grandmother had had many mental and physical illnesses over the past twenty-five years and Kim had always been there for her in her time of need, caring for her, supporting her and helping her work through those difficult times.

"I know, Judge Horne, that you take into account the kind of life a person has lead when sentencing them and know what's best to help each individual person," he said. "I thank you, Judge Horne, for helping my dear niece, Kimberly, receive the treatment she needs to bring her back to health."

Although not at Kim's sentencing, her mother remembered what her only daughter had been like growing up. She told the judge Kim was born in 1965 and she was four when the divorce from her father, Glenn Aungst, was final. The family lived in California for the first three years of Kim's life—her dad was in the service—then he went to Vietnam and Lois moved back to Hollidaysburg. She said she married her current husband at the end of 1970.

Lois said Kim had gone to Hollidaysburg Junior High School, and then she chose to go to Calvary Baptist Christian Academy. She had been valedictorian of her class in 1983. She had played basketball in high school and had been a cheerleader there, too. Matt, her half-brother, had been born in 1971, Lois said. Kim liked to roller skate and shop and she liked to have sleepovers with friends. She was a good student, always on the honor roll, her mother said. However, although Kim had many friends, she wasn't allowed to date until she was sixteen, she said. Lois said when Kim started dating she had a lot of boyfriends.

"She never caused a problem anywhere she went. She never got a traffic ticket and never had any problem with the law, ever," Lois said.

Lois said her second husband had difficulty accepting Kim, but he was never mean to her.

"He wrote her a letter when she was first arrested saying he should have loved her more," she said.

Kim went to Messiah College where she took classes in communications and was also a cheerleader. However her father wanted her to go to Penn State. He didn't want her at a Christian College so she ended up quitting and without telling Lois. Kim met the Millers at Penn State.

"She sort of walked away from the Lord. But she didn't start living for the Lord until she was inside that prison," Lois said.

At the sentencing hearing Prosecutor Bob Dean told the judge why the state didn't want him to show her any leniency and why Kim should receive a life sentence for the murder conviction and a consecutive sentence for the arson conviction.

Dean said on the outside Steve and Kim seemed to have captured the American dream. They were a young, healthy, successful suburban couple with a beautiful young daughter. They had it all—good jobs, a lovely home, family, friends. But appearances were deceiving, he said.

"I'm not going to try to explain it. And I, quite frankly, think it would be impossible to understand it, but there were storm clouds in the heart of Kimberly Hricko and she kept that hidden for some time and it all poured forth about a year ago. And by doing so, Kimberly Hricko threw away her life as she knew it, and it was a life that many people can only hope for."

Dean said Kim had become a twisted, angry woman full of hate.

"She had two months of virtual infatuation with a younger man," Dean said. "And we saw how she gave her heart to that younger man, Brad Winkler."

Dean said even as the Hrickos were preparing to go on a romantic weekend getaway to Harbourtowne that fateful Valentine's Day weekend, Kim was more interested in making sure she delivered some Valentine's Day presents and a note to Winkler.

"The ironies in this case are compelling," Dean told the court. "She had two-and-a half-months to figure out the course of her life back in late fall 1997 and early 1998. And, as it turns out, I think the evidence tragically shows she had two months to figure out how to get rid of her husband. And, again, why she felt she had to do what she had to do, in the way that she did it, is something I don't think any of us will totally understand."

Dean told the judge that Steve was a decent, hard-working guy, whose young life was now over. And now a ten-year-old child was virtually orphaned because her mother killed her father. He said the Hrickos' family and friends were left wondering if there was anything they could have done to prevent Steve's death.

"There probably wasn't," he said. "Suffice it to say, it's clear that the defendant premeditated this murder for quite some period of time. And she was obviously propelled by a vision of some sort of a better life that she had created in her mind with this new young man and an insurance recovery of well over four hundred thousand dollars."

But only one thing stood in the way of her goal, and that was her husband, Stephen, Dean said. So she eliminated him and nearly got away with it, he said. Kim used her special skills and knowledge and access to highly dangerous substances to get rid of her husband, Dean said. The irony was that as she planned Steve's murder, he thought they were well on the way to fixing what was wrong in their marriage, Dean told the court.

"And that screams out at you when you look at that journal that was presented in evidence about Stephen's feelings, about how he felt and how he hoped. And how she literally abused that trust that weekend," Dean told the judge. "The cold cruelty of this woman defies any further description, Your Honor. She stands convicted of the most serious of all crimes, first-degree, premeditated murder. The legislature here in Maryland has required a life sentence and I suggest that this woman richly deserves that sentence."

Dean said her conviction for arson was a felony that carried with it a sentence of thirty years. Dean asked the judge to impose consecutive, not concurrent, sentences, because she not only subjected her dead or dying husband to the horror of the fire she set, she also endangered other people in the same multiunit cottage.

Next to address the court was Kim's attorney William Brennan. Brennan told the judge that although the legislature mandated that the court must impose a life sentence for a first-degree murder conviction, it also left it to the court's discretion to decide if it should suspend any portion of that sentence. And, he said, the legislature also gave the court the discretion to determine whether or not the arson conviction should run concurrent or consecutive.

"And in looking for aid and guidance in sentencing, the legislature has acknowledged that not all murders are the same and not all persons convicted of murder are the same. [The legislature has acknowledged] that people are different and crimes are different."

Brennan said although some murders were so heinous, so cruel, so beyond the pale, that the murderers, who were evil and vicious, deserved life sentences, Kimberly Hricko was not one of those people.

"In this case, Your Honor, the record is before the court, the presentence investigation and the letters [that] have been sent to the court indicate this person, Kimberly Hricko, Your Honor, does not deserve a life sentence and nothing suspended," Brennan argued.

Brennan told the judge that it was no surprise that some people ended up before the court, because they had led a life of crime, but it was a complete shock in Kimberly's case. He said Kim's supporters still couldn't believe that she killed her husband, because the Kimberly Hricko they knew was a good, honest, decent person. They knew her as a volunteer, a soccer mom, a wonderful person, not as a person who committed a crime, he said.

"And by way of explanation, but not excuse, Your Honor, the presentencing investigation indicates that Ms. Hricko has suffered from depression for over six years," Brennan said. "She was on Zoloft . . . and obviously, we all know, Your Honor, that depression can affect judgment. It can change personality."

Brennan told the judge that although some people didn't deserve leniency when they were sentenced, because they had committed crimes that were so vicious and had always led lives of crime, Kimberly Hricko was not one of those people. Therefore, Brennan asked the judge to impose concurrent, not consecutive, sentences and to suspend a portion of the life sentence.

Kimberly asked the court for leniency as well, but she never admitted she killed her husband.

"Your Honor, on January [15], 1999, the jury returned its verdict and I have no choice at this point but to accept that verdict," Kimberly said. "I understand the grief and pain expressed by the Hricko family. I feel love and compassion for them and I have prayed daily for their peace. I hope they can understand that I share a great deal of the loss and grief for the loss of Stephen. I feel so sorry for all the sorrow and loss they've endured. I also understand the impact that Stephen's death has had on my daughter, Sarah. Her loss is double. She has neither parent now. Your Honor, please look beyond the simple one-dimensional version of me. Please look at my life with an open heart. A life that feels so disparate from all this. Thank you."

Now it was Judge Horne's turn to speak. Horne said he had read all the letters submitted by the defense and the prosecution, as well as the presentencing investigation report and had listened to the attorneys' statements and Kim's statement.

Horne said although the people involved viewed Kim differently, they were all united in one way—in the belief that it was a very sad occasion for everyone, not just one group or the other. Horne said he guessed they were also united in the hope that Kim's sentencing would bring them some degree of closure so that they could all go on with their lives.

And, he said, they were all united in something else—their compassion for Sarah.

"There's no one in here that does not feel great compassion for this little girl," Horne said. "And that's wonderful, but I would urge you to remember that in the years to come that she will continue to need your help and your thoughts and your compassion and your love and your assistance and your support. This won't end for her and she will continue to need all of you."

Horne said that no matter how they felt about Kimberly, they all must make sure Sarah had all the family support that they could provide.

"With respect to Kimberly Hricko and her supporters, I understand Mrs. Hricko that your position throughout this incident has been that you were not guilty of this crime," Horne said. "And you have just acknowledged that you understand, and I hope your supporters understand, that I must proceed today on the basis of the jury's finding that you are guilty. . . . Given that fact, what I am presented with is a planned, premeditated destruction of another human being's life. And a destruction of that life in such a manner that . . . jeopardized the lives of other innocent people, who could easily have perished in the fire that occurred on the evening in question."

Horne told Kimberly her crime was not one of "hot blood," nor a reaction to any stimulus that had just occurred. Instead, he said, it was a deliberate crime that had been planned for a considerable period of time.

"And . . . if you were able to commit such a heinous crime against someone you had once felt so strongly for that you married that person, you had a child by that person, then I would submit that would make you a very dangerous person to everyone else in society, because you would be capable of doing the same thing to anyone else who caused you difficulty or stood in your way or incurred your wrath," Horne told Kimberly.

"You will be incarcerated, and in the reality of the world in which we live, there is every reason to believe that the day will come when you will be released from incarceration," he said.

Therefore, Horne told Kimberly, her life would be divided into three parts—the life she led before she went to jail, the life she would lead in jail, and the life she would lead when she was released from jail.

"And it is the hope of this court that when that occurs, you will be prepared to act right and be the person that all of your supporters know," Horne said. "I hope you will be the fine person that they know and that they expect you to be."

Horne then sentenced Kimberly to state prison for life on the murder charge and sentenced her to thirty years on the arson charge. The sentences were to run concurrently, he said. After explaining Kim's postconviction rights of appeal, court was adjourned.

Chapter 20

One of Kim's strongest supporters, Laurel real estate agent Cathy Rosenberger, was at Kim's sentencing hearing. She wanted to speak on Kim's behalf at the hearing, but Kim's defense attorneys decided against it.

Rosenberger, who put up $40,000 of her own money for Kim's defense, helped Kim after her trial by presenting her postconviction attorneys with information that she and Kim thought would be useful in developing alternative theories to explain Steve's death. And she provided them with her insights into Steve's personality and health. She also supplied this information to Kim's trial lawyers. Although she has stopped contributing money to Kim's postconviction relief efforts, Rosenberger said she still believes in her innocence. Rosenberger said she was the person who asked Kim's family and friends to write letters to Judge Horne on Kim's behalf.

"Kim's attorneys told [Kim and me] it would be beneficial for Kim if all her friends and family wrote letters to Judge Horne describing how they knew her and a story or two about something Kim had done for them," Rosenberger said. "I was instructed by Brennan and Trainor to contact all the people and ask if they would write on Kim's behalf. The lists of names came from Kim, her mother, and friends. I did not have much time, so I wrote to everybody and told them if they had any questions to call me."

Rosenberger wasn't prepared for what happened next.

"Lots of people called to find out how Kim was doing and to say how concerned they were. Before I wrote to them, they didn't really know who to talk to," Rosenberger said. "I talked to [one woman] who had many kind things to say about Kim being a volunteer for children in the courts. Sarah's teacher talked for a very long time. She had been a dinner guest at Kim's and they went shopping together. One time she was sick and Kim sent her a get-well card and called to see if she could bring her some food. One soccer mom told me about how Kim was very involved in Sarah's soccer team. Kim was a coach and also gave an end-of-season party at her house for the kids and coaches."

Rosenberger turned over all the letters she received to Kim's lawyers, but was surprised that they only submitted the best fifty letters to Judge Horne.

"Judge Horne took a recess to read the letters before he gave the sentence," she said. "When he came back from his chambers, he put the binder containing the letters on his bench in front of him. When he started to talk, he put his hand on the binder. He looked as if he was touched by the letters and all the people's lives that have been touched by Kim—from a grade school teacher to ministers. There were four ministers in the courtroom to give support to Kim at the sentencing. Horne made a comment about them. There are not many people in this world who could ask sixty or seventy people to write a kind word about them and how they have touched their lives."

Rosenberger recalled the first time Kim touched her own life. She said it was in 1996 when she rented the Hrickos their town house on Dorset Road in Laurel. However, when Rosenberger took Kim and Sarah out to look at various properties, Steve wasn't with them, she said.

"We found a place and Kim said it would do fine and I asked her if she wanted her husband to see it and she said no, he trusted her judgment," Rosenberger said.

The Hrickos moved into the town house and Rosenberger stopped by during the 1996 Christmas season to visit. That's when she first met Steve. Her first impression of him was that he was not very friendly.

Rosenberger talked with Kim several times after Christmas and stopped by to see her one more time. Eventually in July 1997 the Hrickos were told they had to move by August. So Rosenberger took Kim and Sarah to look at houses—the Hrickos had decided to purchase a home rather than continue to rent.

Steve didn't go with them until they had narrowed the choices down to four. Each time Rosenberger took the Hrickos to look for homes, she would meet them at the town house on Dorset Road. Sometimes Kim came straight from work; because Steve got home first, he was in charge of feeding Sarah.

"He acted like this was hard for him to do," Rosenberger said. "I remember seeing some burned French fries and something else that looked bad on a cookie sheet."

Rosenberger recalled one particular time she picked up the Hrickos to go look at a house. First, however, she had to drop Sarah off at soccer practice. When they arrived, Kim and Sarah got out of the car, leaving Rosenberger alone with Steve for about eight minutes.

"It was a very long eight minutes," she said. "Steve was very unfriendly and I tried to talk to him about golf and where he works. Nothing would loosen him up. He just would not talk. He made me very uncomfortable. If Kim was not so outgoing and friendly, I probably would not have continued to work with them because Steve really made me nervous."

Rosenberger and Kim felt that the pesticides Steve used in his work somehow contributed to his death.

"I have spoken with several people who had the same job Steve had and they all told me that up until recently golf course personnel were very careless about the use of pesticides," Rosenberger said. "I have done research on the Internet and at the National Medical Library of Medicine in Bethesda, Maryland. There are many side effects from using pesticides carelessly for a long period of time."

Rosenberger said at trial Kim's lawyers only touched on Steve's medical history. She said Steve was seeing several doctors for a variety of ailments, including depression, insomnia, back spasms, and bronchitis. One doctor even set up an appointment for Steve to get an EKG, but Steve blew off the appointment.

"That doctor ran one test and saw something that concerned him enough to send Steve for more extensive tests," Rosenberger said. "Since Steve didn't show [up], the tests were not done. What did that doctor see in a physically fit thirty-five-year-old man that concerned him enough to want Steve to get further tests?"

Rosenberger wanted to know why Kim's defense team didn't call Steve's doctor as a witness, especially since Steve was mixing several medications when he died. And, she noted, his depression medication had just been doubled. Steve was taking Xanax, Flexeril, Effexor, and he also took Theraflu shortly before he died, she said. Doing her own investigation, Rosenberger asked three pharmacists their opinions about mixing those particular medications.

"They all said they didn't like the mix, especially topping it off with Theraflu," she said.

Rosenberger said she read a story in the June 1999 edition of *Reader's Digest* about the dangers of mixing drugs prescribed for depression with cold medicines.

"The medical examiner did not test for all these drugs," she said.

Rosenberger also said that Kim's attorney William Brennan read part of Steve's journal at trial and it was obvious that he was severely depressed and had a number of other medical problems. Although Steve looked big and strong, he really was not a well man, she said.

Rosenberger said she had her own theory about what happened in room 506 of the Harbourtowne resort over Valentine's Day weekend, 1998—a theory obviously arrived at with input from Kim. The following is Cathy Rosenberger's theory:

Steve had been planning the weekend for weeks. His best friend, Mike Miller, had suggested that he bring Kim to a special event at the resort. Mike told Steve about the weekend package that consisted of a room rental, champagne, and a murder-mystery play with dinner. Steve reserved one of the cottages on the water, away from the main resort hotel. He wanted everything to be perfect. Their marriage was not healthy and Kim had been threatening to leave him. Other than taking Kim out when they were dating, Steve had not really taken her out to celebrate anything since they got married.

Steve hadn't been feeling well for some time and had been

seeing several doctors. Kim was upset with Steve because he failed to keep an appointment for an EKG that his doctor had ordered. Steve also was under a lot of pressure at work. There had been a major fire in his maintenance shop and equipment shed in the summer of 1997. Steve was in charge of the rebuilding, but the city of Laurel was making it hard for him to get the job done. The shed was dangerously close to a residential neighborhood and the city was concerned about another fire. The shop also held gasoline and chemicals that were flammable.

The new building was months behind schedule. Steve just wanted to quit and move on, as he'd done at several other jobs. But this time Kim insisted they buy a house so Sarah could stay in one school and the family could have a permanent home. For his part Steve wished Kim would have more patience and be more understanding with him, considering all he was going through.

Sarah and Steve became accomplices in the surprise weekend and worked out the details together, including where Sarah would stay while Kim and Steve were away. Steve didn't tell Kim where they were going. (Contrary to Rosenberger's theory, however, Steve's friends and coworkers at Patuxent told police Steve told Kim that they were going to Harbourtowne for the weekend because, given their marital problems, he knew she wouldn't want to be surprised.)

Steve and Kim dropped Sarah off at a friend's house on Valentine's Day, then headed to St. Michaels and Harbourtowne. Once on the road Kim became sleepy and dozed off. She was still feeling the effects of the sigmoidoscopy that she had the previous day.

Eventually they arrived at the resort and checked in. Room 506, which was called a cottage even though it was just a room, was in an area called "The Point." The room consisted of two double beds, a desk, nightstand, TV cabinet, and a woodstove. The woodstove faced one of the beds.

*There was a sliding glass door that led out to the back porch,
which faced the Miles River. The river was so wide at this
point that Kim thought they were on the Chesapeake Bay.*

*The room was very cold and the wind was whipping
across the river. The water was very choppy and Kim even
saw some whitecaps. Steve was hungry, but it was too early
to go to dinner, so he left and drove to a convenience store
in St. Michaels and bought several hot dogs and Cokes. While
he was at the cash register, he noticed the latest issue of* Playboy *behind the counter and decided to purchase it and
sneak it back to the room, so Kim wouldn't see it.*

Steve liked to keep some magazines like Playboy *around,
but Kim always gave him a hard time about bringing them
into the house because she was afraid Sarah would find them.
However, Steve still bought them and hid them in his golf
bag, suitcase, truck, or anywhere he thought Kim wouldn't
find them.* (Again, contrary to Rosenberger's speculation, Mike and Maureen Miller, however, said nothing could be further from the truth. They said the
only *Playboy* magazines Steve ever had were collectible
editions that had belonged to his dad.)

*Steve brought the snacks back to the room, and Kim and
Steve settled in on separate beds. Steve took the bed directly
in front of the woodstove. There was a complimentary fire
log and matches on top of the woodstove, so they decided to
light it to warm up the room. Once the log was burning, they
left the stove doors open to get as much benefit from the heat
as possible. There was no screen covering the opening.*

*Kim noticed the slacks she was wearing had a stain on
them, so she decided to rinse them out and hang them outside on the porch to dry. When she opened the sliding glass
door, the wind and cold air coming off the water took her
breath away. She managed to hang her pants up in the corner
of the porch and in no time they were frozen stiff.*

There was some champagne in the room, so Steve and Kim

each had a glass. Kim didn't like the taste, so she didn't have any more. The couple then settled in to read the Washington Post *they had brought with them from home before going to dinner.*

At dinner Kim and Steve sat at a table for eight. Steve often felt awkward around people he didn't know, so he just didn't say much. Once the mystery play started, Kim and another guest at the table took an active role in solving the crime. Someone at the table ordered a bottle of wine and everyone had a glass. Steve also ordered a beer or two.

After dinner Steve stopped at the bar and bought two more beers to take back to the room. The couple then stopped at the hotel desk to get another fire log for the woodstove. Back at the room they put the log in the woodstove on top of the first one, which was still burning. Then they turned the television on to watch the movie Tommy Boy.

Steve mixed a packet of Theraflu for his cold. Earlier, he had taken Effexor, Xanax, and Flexeril. The doctor had just doubled Steve's dose of Effexor for his depression, so he hoped it would help. He was taking the Flexeril because he had recently pulled a muscle in his back. When the movie was over, Steve started acting strange. He appeared to be drunk and was slurring his words. Even his movements were odd. Kim knew he hadn't had much to drink all evening, so none of this made sense. (However, this statement directly contradicted the story Kim told police and anyone else who would listen—that Steve was totally sloshed.)

Steve approached Kim for sex, but she wasn't interested. Kim reminded Steve that their counselor had advised them to have a nice weekend—talk and work on their marriage. The couple had agreed in advance that there was to be no intimacy.

Steve was somewhat obnoxious and Kim became upset. She dressed and grabbed her coat, purse, and car keys, telling Steve she needed some space. Steve was still on his bed when she stormed out of the room. He had pushed the bedspread toward the end of the bed. Once Steve was alone, he decided to take out the new Playboy *he had hidden in his suitcase. He didn't know where Kim had gone or how long she would be out. Since she could come back at any minute, Steve decided to lie down between the two beds with his feet facing the woodstove. He took two pillows off the bed to put under his head. Steve figured by lying on the floor, he would hear the door open before Kim could see him.*

When Steve went to get the Playboy, *he also noticed the cigars in his suitcase. They had been lying on the dining-room table at home and at the last minute he threw them in his bag. Steve lay down on the floor and started looking through* Playboy. *Eventually he pulled his pants down. After he was finished, he lit the cigar and put the match inside the woodstove. What Steve had failed to notice was that when Kim opened the front door to leave, the rush of oxygen into the room caused the two fire logs in the stove to flare up. Some sparks had landed on the bedspread and were smoldering. As the sparks smoldered, Steve didn't smell the smoke, because there was already smoke in the room from the cigar, as well as the burning logs.*

As Steve lay back down to enjoy his cigar, the bedspread totally ignited. In an instant the bedspread was engulfed in flames. Steve threw up his left hand to protect his face. (Here Rosenberger was trying to explain why Steve's left arm was bent upward at the elbow when he was found). *The bedspread ignited the two pillows under Steve's head. Because of the speed of the fire and his shock when his head, neck, and shoulders caught fire, Steve never took another breath.* (This was Rosenberger's attempt to explain why there was no carbon monoxide in Steve's blood or soot in his lungs.)

When Kim came back to the room, everything was quiet. She soon realized she had forgotten her room key. She knocked on the door, but Steve didn't answer. She thought he was prob-

ably asleep, since he had taken so much medicine. Kim re-
membered the sliding glass door that led to the rear deck was
probably still unlocked, so she walked around to the back of
the cottage. As she approached the porch, she noticed that the
room was completely dark. She pulled the sliding glass door
open and a huge whoosh of incredible heat knocked her
backward. The smell was horrible. She couldn't see anything.
Kim was scared, so she ran around, trying to get help from
the other guests in the same complex. No one answered, so
she got in her car and drove to the lobby to get help.

"During the entire time since Steve's death, Kim has never changed the facts of the tragedy," Rosenberger said. "It seems to me that after [all these years] it would be hard to continue to keep the story straight— unless it was the truth. Many times I tried to confuse Kim or catch her with her 'story,' but it was always exactly the same."

In fact, Kim's story did change. From the beginning Kim told everyone that Steve had been drinking heavily. However, speculating about what happened the night Steve died, Rosenberger said even though Steve appeared to be drunk when they got back to their room after dinner, "Kim knew he hadn't had much to drink all evening," so his bizarre actions after they watched *Tommy Boy* didn't make sense to her. So which was it—had Steve been drinking heavily as Kim told police, or had he not had much to drink, as she told Rosenberger?

The problem with Cathy Rosenberger's assumptions was that all she knew about Steve's death and the events leading up to it was what Kim had told her. And Rosenberger took Kim at her word. When Rosenberger visited Kim in jail, they would talk about the case and then she would go home, write out their conversations as well as any questions she might have, then she would send her recollections and questions back to Kim so she could add more information.

Rosenberger shared some of that information with journalists covering Kim's case and her appellate attorney, Christopher Griffiths. Kim and Rosenberger spent many hours trying to debunk the testimony the prosecution elicited from witnesses during trial.

While reading this information put together by Rosenberger it's important to note that she believed then—and still does—that Kim absolutely, positively, did not murder her husband. All Rosenberger's explanations and speculation were based on Kim's version of what happened at Harbourtowne on Valentine's Day weekend, 1998.

One of the issues Kim and Rosenberger questioned was the prosecution's theory of how Steve ended up on the floor.

In a letter Kim wrote to Rosenberger on April 23, 2000, she said that she was still in awe of the prosecution's theory of "the crime"—that somehow she moved Steve onto the floor after killing him. Kim said the prosecution must have thought she had planned everything right down to the last detail. And the prosecution also must have believed she had incredible physical strength.

"What would make them think such a thing? It certainly wasn't physical evidence," Kim said.

Kim said if she had attempted to move Steve, there should have been some evidence of it, like some kind of injury.

"Or do they think I was able to gently place him on the floor? It blows my mind," she said.

And exactly how did Cathy Rosenberger think the fire started? A spark from the woodstove could have started it, she said. Rosenberger said Kim's trial attorneys submitted a fire log into evidence. She said the issue of the fire log was discussed briefly and then dropped.

About a month after Kim's trial Rosenberger said she was walking through a local pharmacy and noticed a display of fire logs. She purchased three different brands and said they all carried written warnings not to burn them in a woodstove. She said she even called one company that sold fire logs and told the customer service representative that she wanted to burn the log in her woodstove and wanted to know if she should leave the stove door open or closed (the door to the woodstove in the Hrickos' room at Harbourtowne was left open).

The company told her their logs were not to be used in a woodstove, with the door open or closed, she said.

"If you look at the diagram of the room, the woodstove is directly in front of the bed that burned. It is only about three feet away. The [fire marshal testified] that the doors were wide open and there was no screen," Rosenberger said. "Could the fire log [in the woodstove] have thrown a spark that landed in the bedding?" she asked. "It could have smoldered for a period of time unnoticed before it finally created a flash fire."

Rosenberger didn't put much stock in the state's theory that Kim injected Steve with succinylcholine to paralyze him before she set the fire.

"The prosecutor's position is that Kim used the drug on her husband to stop his breathing before the fire," she said. "Because the drug was available to Kim, she therefore used it."

And how did Kim, who weighed 155 pounds, convince Steve, who weighed 245 pounds, to cooperate and allow her to inject him with the drug?

"Three minutes is a long time when you're on the receiving end of a needle," she said.

Rosenberger also questioned Judge Horne's decision to allow the medical examiner to offer his opinion that the cause of Steve's death was probable poisoning and the manner of his death was homicide.

"If Dr. Fowler could not determine how Steve died, why didn't he call in someone for a second opinion?" Rosenberger asked. "Should he have conducted more tests? Why did he release the body for cremation? It seems to me the autopsy report should consist of exactly what the medical examiner sees and the test results performed. Period. Fowler's opinion was based on interviews with witnesses and the defendant."

In a letter to Rosenberger dated June 27, 2000, Kim wrote about a book, *Actual Innocence: When Justice Goes Wrong and How to Make It Right* by Jim Dwyer, Peter Neufeld, and Barry Scheck, that talked about miscarriages of justice in the American court system.

"I think it will be very helpful to us," Kim said. "It is supposed to highlight the things that can cause a trial to be unfair. Like bogus testimony from a coroner. I think it will be information that we can use, as well as inspirational. . . . All of [the cases] are reversed decisions."

Rosenberger put a lot more credence in the testimony given by defense witness Dr. John Adams than that of Dr. Fowler. She said Adams examined the autopsy and police reports, toxicology report, witness statements, and he examined the microscopic autopsy from duplicate slides.

"His professional opinion was cause unknown and manner undetermined," she said.

However, she admitted his testimony could have been better.

Wanting a second opinion, Rosenberger shared some of the information regarding the succinyl-choline with her surgeon, who often testified as an expert witness in various trials.

"He stated that with a small-town jury, such as in Easton, he would have put the drug in a syringe and actually injected ten to twenty cc's into a slab of raw meat," she said. "He said that would closely mimic the shot going into a human muscle. It would also visually show the jury how long the victim would have had to be still and cooperate with the injection."

Rosenberger also had some real issues with the testimony of Kim's friend Rachel McCoy. Referring to the night that Kim told Rachel about her plan to kill Steve, she commented, "If Rachel was so scared for Steve's life, why didn't she wake him up?"

Once Rachel talked to Maureen O'Toole-Miller and Kim about the circumstances of Steve's death, her story to police began to fit the crime scene, Rosenberger said.

"Would the story have been so similar if she had called the police before she talked to Maureen and Kim?" she asked.

Rosenberger wanted to know why Kim's friends, who got on the witness stand and told their stories about how she had plotted and planned the entire murder—and told them every detail—didn't go to the police with this information.

According to Rosenberger, there was a perfectly innocent reason to explain why Kim told her friends she wished Steve were dead. She said it started when Kim was just a child and living in Hollidaysburg with her mother and stepfather. Rosenberger got this information from Kim and Kim's friend Rachelle St. Phard.

"Rachelle St. Phard has been Kim's best friend since

they met at Baptist high school. They were like sisters and spent many hours together and at each other's houses," Rosenberger said. "[Kim's] stepfather, Jim, did drink and yell at everybody all the time and made everyone miserable. Rachelle and Kim didn't like him and spent many hours fantasizing, as teenagers might, about things they could do to him, or wishing he would get hurt.

"This was Kim's way of dealing with the pain and putting up with a situation that she couldn't control," Rosenberger said, adding that Kim's stepfather had changed since Kim was a teenager, and had apologized to her for all the hurt he caused her while she was growing up.

"During their school years there were two other people that Rachelle and Kim didn't like and talked about all the time," Rosenberger said. "They were both schoolmates. The people they didn't like they would talk about—wishing bad things would happen to them. They never took any action on anything they said. To help deal with it, she did talk with schoolmates. They never took any action on anything they said. Kim's marriage was also a miserable situation that she couldn't change. To help deal with it she did talk with some of her friends about wishing things on Steve. This was a pattern that was started in high school."

Because she really didn't mean any harm to Steve, Kim wasn't very pleased with the fact that her friends turned against her. In her June 27, 2000 letter to Rosenberger, Kim said she had the information from her explaining how to be a good witness and she asked Rosenberger where she came across it.

"I couldn't help but think, though, that my ex-friends probably think that they did all that. They performed just as they were trained to by the prosecution,"

Kim said, adding that it was easy to see just how much they had been manipulated by the prosecution.

In her letter Kim also asked Rosenberger to do some research on a phenomenon called "memory enhancement."

"It is what happened to the people who were at the scene the night of Steve's death," Kim said. "They wrote statements that said one thing, but a few months later, sang a completely different tune."

Kim said what the witnesses at the scene believed happened superceded what they actually saw the night Steve died. She said the same principle also applied to the testimony of her friends.

In another letter dated May 20, 2000, Kim told Rosenberger she never understood what made all her friends feel as though they ought to testify against her. Kim said it was clear to her that one of her friends used guilt to convince the other women to testify.

"I had attributed it to the fact that they were convinced by the prosecutor and themselves that I am guilty, but making them feel somehow partially responsible for Steve's death would be an even stronger tool," Kim said.

Kim also told Rosenberger she never understood why her defense lawyers didn't think it was important to talk to her friends. She said her friends testified for the side that sought them out. She believed that if the defense team had made any effort to get them to believe in her, they might not have testified for the prosecution.

Chapter 21

Several days before Kim's appeals hearing in May 2000, Rosenberger received an e-mail from Texan Gerald Hurst, a Cambridge University–educated chemist who had investigated scores of fires in his career

Hurst was helping Kim's post-conviction attorneys poke holes in the prosecution's case. In the e-mail Hurst discussed the autopsy report, which listed the carbon monoxide level in Steve's blood as normal. Hurst said he had no idea what the pathologist considered normal.

"A heavy smoker will have a level of up to about twelve percent, whereas a nonsmoker will register near zero depending on the environment," Hurst said. "This leads me to the point that one should always get the underlying data for any conclusory report."

Hurst said he was sure the pathologist sent the blood sample to a toxicology lab that reported everything it found in numbers, including the values for ethanol, carbon monoxide and the drug metabolites. Hurst said the lawyer should obtain copies of the lab reports.

Hurst also told Rosenberger he had a "far-out" theory

about Steve's death which he thought Kim's attorneys should consider.

Hurst gave some background from his own life. He said one day when he was in college, he was sniffing around the chemical stock room at college, using his nose as chemists do in order to develop their ability to identify various compounds.

"I forgot what chemical I passed my nose over. The substance was not particularly pungent but one whiff closed my epiglottis like a mousetrap and I was unable to breath at all for perhaps ten or fifteen seconds. It follows that there are vapors which might cause death by asphyxiation," he said.

He then told Rosenberger about two accidental death cases he had investigated. He said although the two people died in a fire, no carbon monoxide was found in their blood.

However, he said because both of the decedents were rather old, it could be argued that they died of heart failure from the excitement rather than from the fire. However, their deaths occurred from some combustion product that had the same effect as that laboratory chemical he sniffed while in college.

Hurst told Rosenberger that he thought there was a remote possibility that Steve died as a result of a toxic chemical released by the fire.

"The police said that the pillows contained a fire retardant. They then ran a silly cigar ignition test," Hurst said.

Hurst called the test silly because any fire expert knew that the elastomeric foam in untreated pillows and mattresses was not very susceptible to a smoldering ignition, but the untreated foam burned fiercely when ignited by an open flame like the open flame that might get kicked out of a stove in the form of a flaming ember.

Hurst said the most common foam in bedding was polyurethane, a nitrogen polymer, which produced, among other things, some small quantity of cyanide gas under fire conditions. If a fire retardant was added to the foam, its combustion products would become more toxic. Therefore, he said, it might be worth looking into the toxicology of the products of combustion of that particular fire, especially with regard to the foam in the pillows and mattress.

The fire expert also said he just couldn't understand how Kim could have injected Steve with the succinylcholine without his cooperation.

"It seems to me that a needle prick would lead to some rather violent reactions before the plunger could be depressed, unless he was passing-out drunk—which the blood test appears to rule out," he said.

Maureen O'Toole-Miller said Steve's sister Jenny had a theory about how Kim was able to inject Steve with the drug. Jenny speculated that when Kim swiped the succinylcholine from Holy Cross Hospital, she also took some ether, which comes in a bottle and is highly flammable and odorless.

"What we think is she put the ether down on the pillow and got him to lie down and she massaged his back until the ether took effect, then she injected him with the succinylcholine and used the ether to light the pillow on fire," Maureen said.

On May 5, 2000 Kim's appellate attorney, Christopher Griffiths, argued before the Maryland Court of Special Appeals that her life sentence should be overturned and a new trial granted. But Kim's friend Cathy Rosenberger said the hearing did not go very well for Kim. Rosenberger said she didn't like the judges' body language or their attitudes. She said one of the judges even made jokes about Monty Python during the hearing. It seemed to Rosenberger that the judges made up their minds even before hearing Kim's arguments.

Griffiths first argued that there was insufficient evidence to prove homicide beyond a reasonable doubt because the prosecution didn't prove cause of death. He also argued that the trial court erred in allowing the medical examiner to testify that the cause of death was probable poisoning. He said without a specific cause of death the medical examiner shouldn't have been allowed to offer his opinion about what killed Steve.

Finally, Griffiths argued that there wasn't sufficient evidence to convict Kim of arson because the state was unable to present evidence that the fire had been set.

"The state's evidence was insufficient to overcome the presumption that the fire in this matter was accidental," Griffiths said.

Kim wrote to Gerald Hurst in June 2000, thanking him for taking an interest in her case. In the letter Kim told Hurst that his special talents and knowledge might be able to help her, even though no one else could. "Mr. Hurst, I did not murder my husband. Yet proving my innocence seems to be an impossible task," she said, adding that she had been incarcerated for two years. She told Hurst that Sarah needed her home and she needed to be with her daughter. She begged Hurst to help her and said she was praying for a miracle.

But even with Hurst's help, Kim's miracle didn't come.

In an opinion, dated September 27, 2000, which upheld Kim's convictions, Maryland Court of Special Appeals judge Charles E. Moylan Jr. used quotes from William Shakespeare, Fyodor Dostoyevsky, Sir Walter Scott, Miguel de Cervantes, and others to dismantle Kim's arguments and grab the attention of readers.

Moylan began his opinion with this quote from *Hamlet:* "The play's the thing, wherein I'll catch the conscience of the king."

Then he wrote, "Taking that version of the facts most favorable to the state, what unfolds is the melodrama of an estranged wife, desperate to free herself from a marriage gone stale, leaving a trail of false clues and staging her husband's death so as to make it appear a random act. As with the murder of Gonzago in *Hamlet* or Pyramis and Thisbe in *A Midsummer Night's Dream,* there is with this real-life drama a play within a play. In the real-life drama, the husband was lured to the scene of his fatal poisoning by the reconciliatory promise of a romantic St. Valentine's weekend at the Harbourtowne Resort in St. Michaels."

Moylan said the highlight of the getaway weekend was the dinner theater murder mystery that the dinner guests were invited to solve. That play was called *The Bride Who Cried.* The real-life drama involving Kimberly might well be called, *The Widow Who Lied,* he said.

In the real-life drama, the last hours of the ill-fated marriage began with a bottle of champagne provided by the host to each couple when they arrived at the inn, the judge said. In *The Bride Who Cried,* the wedding feast ended with a champagne toast proposed by the groom to his bride and shared by the actors and participating guests alike. The bridegroom died as he drank from the poisoned chalice. In the real-life drama, the husband died of poison within an hour of returning with his wife to their cottage, he said.

While the audience identified the culprit of *The Bride Who Cried* within an hour of the staged murder, Kimberly Michelle Hricko, was not indicted for her husband's murder until three and a half months after she contrived his accidental death. Moylan said, "Truth is both stranger and more complicated than fiction."

And then he quoted *Richard III:* "Thus hath the course of justice whirled about."

Moylan said Kim raised three contentions in her appeal: that the evidence was not legally sufficient to support the conviction for arson; that the evidence was not legally sufficient to support the conviction for murder; and that the medical examiner should not have been permitted to testify that the cause of death was probable poisoning.

Before getting into the background of the Hrickos' marriage, Moylan quoted the opening line from *Anna Karenina,* by Leo Tolstoy: "Happy families are all alike; every unhappy family is unhappy in its own way."

Then Moylan talked about how Kim and Steve met and married and how "the domestic skies had been brighter" than they had in late 1997 and early 1998.

Next Moylan explained what happened after Kim reported the fire including the efforts of Philip Parker and Elaine Phillips to save Steve. He said what was obviously called for was some explanation from Kimberly about where she had been and what she had been doing between leaving the dining room at approximately 10:30 P.M. and reporting a room fire to Elaine Phillips at approximately 1:20 A.M.

To introduce the section detailing Kim's statements to police about the events preceding Steve's death, Moylan referenced this line from *The Dunciad,* by Alexander Pope: "Explain a thing till all men doubt it."

Moylan said that Kim gave a full account of the missing three hours to Maryland State Trooper Clay Hartness around 2:30 A.M. Hartness accompanied Father Paul Jennings, who notified Kim of Steve's death. However, Moylan said Kim gave the most complete explanation to Maryland State Trooper Keith Elzey at approximately 5:00 A.M. The judge then recounted Kim's story of what happened before Steve died.

Moylan said Kimberly's attempted explanation became part of the proof of her guilt. He said that it was a forensic fact of life that if a statement designed to prove that a person was not guilty of a crime was not believed, it then became highly incriminatory. In prosecutorial jargon, Moylan said that was called the "false exculpatory," and it served to prove the consciousness of guilt. Indeed, her explanation began to unravel even as it happened, he said.

The first improbability was getting lost—not just getting lost, per se, but getting lost for two hours, Moylan said. The fact is that Easton is no more than a fifteen-minute drive from St. Michaels—a thirty-minute round trip. It probably didn't make sense to the jury that Kimberly would get lost for such a long period of time in such a confined area, especially since Kim had driven to the Millers' house in Easton just ten weeks earlier, he said. And, he said, Kim's brother lived just two blocks away from the Millers.

Moylan also questioned why Kim just didn't call the Millers or her brother for directions. The judge said when Kim told Maureen O'Toole-Miller that she was trying to find her house for nearly one and a half hours, Maureen asked the question the jurors would have asked themselves and received an improbable answer – that she didn't want to call because it was too late.

Kim's explanation just didn't make sense, the judge said. Moylan wondered why Kim didn't want to wake up the Millers with a telephone call when she fully intended to wake them up by ringing the doorbell.

Moylan also noted that Kim's attempted explanations that Steve was drinking heavily before he died simply generated greater and greater disbelief, especially since the medical examiner's report indicated his blood alcohol level was 0.00.

Before beginning to address the incongruities in Kim's story as well as her behavior, Moylan quoted from "To A Mouse" by Robert Burns: "The best laid schemes o' mice and men gang aft agley; an' lea'e us nought but grief and pain."

"Even before telling a story rent with incongruities, the well laid scheme of Kimberly had begun going 'agley' within minutes of going operational," Moylan said.

First, her behavior was inappropriate and therefore highly suspicious, he said. A reasonable person who discovered that her husband was trapped in a burning room would not have displayed the remarkable composure exhibited by Kimberly, he said. In fact, he said her screams should have awakened other occupants in building 500—but they didn't.

"Where one would have anticipated screams to pierce the very fabric of the night, none of the other occupants of building 500 was even awakened," he said.

Moylan noted that Kimberly's arrival in the lobby of the resort was even more "bizarre." As Elaine Phillips testified, there was neither excitement, nor for the longest time, even an indication that her husband was still inside the burning room, he said. Moylan said Elaine's cousin, Philip Parker, also testified to Kim's preternatural calm. Moylan noted, according to the testimony, the fact that her husband was in the burning room seemed almost an afterthought to Kimberly.

"As a tell-tale reaction, Kimberly displayed a 'sang-froid' about her husband's fate that was macabre, unless, of course, she already knew that the time of the response was not of the essence," he said, adding that at trial Philip Parker gave a characterization of Kimberly's almost icy demeanor, saying she appeared "really calm."

Next Moylan talked about how Kim's behavior after Steve's death betrayed sometimes-telling indications of consciousness of guilt. He led off this section with a line from *Hamlet*: "Foul deeds will rise, though all the earth o'erwhelm them to men's eyes."

Moylan said even for the most hardened professional, it was difficult not to be anxious after committing a crime. He said Kim's behavior after Stephen's death betrayed a number of sometimes arguable, but sometimes telling, indications of consciousness of guilt.

He then pointed to the comment she made to Bonnie Parker that "I want to go see his body." Although it was an ambiguous statement, Moylan said it could be interpreted as revealing a concern about whether the charring of the victim's skin adequately obliterated a puncture mark made by a needle. Such a reading takes on greater plausibility in conjunction with Kimberly's later concern to learn the autopsy results and her strong desire to have Steve's body cremated, he said.

Moylan said the fact that Kim asked Maureen to call several of her friends to find out what, if anything, they said to police, also sent up a red flag. He said it wasn't normal for someone who had just lost her husband to want to know what her friends had been saying to the police.

In addition, the judge said, several conversations Kim had with Teri Armstrong shortly after she was taken into custody also betrayed a consciousness of guilt. In one of those conversations Kim told Teri that she was feeling a lot of remorse about what happened at Harbourtowne over Valentine's Day weekend.

And in a conversation Kim had with Jennifer Gowen shortly after her arrest, Kim said, "I don't care what anyone says, it wasn't for the money."

Moylan said that statement was a revelation as to

her motivation and the rhetorical question that needed no answering was, "What wasn't for the money?"

The judge then referred to the meeting with Troopers Elzey and Alt at Harbourtowne on February 23, 1998. He said Kim's statement to the troopers, "I really want to tell you the truth," clearly implied that she had not told them the truth earlier.

Then Judge Moylan took a swipe at the Maryland State Police, saying that the department was apparently not as relentless as popular legend would sometimes have people believe. The reason, he said, was that at that point Kimberly, who was obviously ready to break, was allowed to go home.

Next the judge introduced his discussion of the testimony from the prosecution's expert witnesses with this quote from *Don Quixote*, by Miguel de Cervantes: "The proof of the pudding is in the eating."

Moylan said Kimberly's appellate contentions were obsessed with the expert testimony. He said two of her contentions went to the legal sufficiency of evidence to prove the corpus delicti (the proof that a crime has been committed) of arson and the corpus delicti of murder.

He said Kimberly would like to look at the evidence supporting the corpus delicti of arson in a vacuum, as if only the physical examination of the fire scene by the fire marshal had pertinence and as if all of the other evidence in the case had no bearing on the question of arson.

Similarly, her contention over the murder charge assumed only the physical examination of Stephen's body by the medical examiner had pertinence and all of the other evidence in the case had no bearing on the question of murder, he said.

"Unfortunately, from the state's point of view, that is not the case," Moylan said. "The state's case on all charges is an intertwined totality."

The evidence of arson and the evidence of murder were not mutually exclusive, watertight compartments, he said. That meant that, in evaluating the evidence of arson, Moylan had to factor in all the evidence of murder, which indicated that the fire itself might have simply been part of the murder scheme, because of the bearing it had on the question of arson.

Conversely, as Moylan evaluated the evidence of murder he had to factor in all the evidence of arson, which indicated that the fire was deliberately set in an effort to conceal the true cause of death, because of the bearing it had on the question of murder.

"In determining the legal sufficiency issues, we will look to the expert opinion as to the cause of death that came into evidence, not simply to the evidence that Kimberly agreed should have come in," the judge said.

Next Moylan discussed the purely physical phenomenon of the fire in room 506. He led into this section with this *Julius Caesar* quote: "Those that with haste will make a mighty fire, begin it with weak straws."

In this section, Moylan referred to the trial testimony of Deputy Fire Marshal Mike Mulligan. Moylan said a significant aspect of the fire scene investigation involved the process of elimination. Mulligan testified that lightning and spontaneous combustion could be ruled out as causes of the fire and also said the fire did not have an electrical origin.

So two possibilities remained—careless smoking and a spark from the fire log in the woodstove, Moylan said. Mulligan eliminated the woodstove as the possible source of fire because he didn't believe it was possible for a spark to leap from the stove, travel to the pillows and ignite them, Moylan said. Ultimately Mulligan also eliminated careless smoking as the cause of the fire.

Moylan went on to say that even though Mulligan had

eliminated a number of possibilities as the causes of the fire, Judge Horne would not let him offer his opinion that the fire was set because there were other possibilities he did not consider. In arguing that the state's evidence was not legally sufficient to sustain the conviction for first-degree arson, Kimberly relied entirely on that evidentiary ruling by Judge Horne, Moylan said. He said Kim argued that she shouldn't have been charged with arson because Judge Horne wouldn't allow Mulligan to say that the fire was set.

Again Moylan said Kim's argument didn't distinguish between Mulligan's opinion and the state's total case. He said Kim's brief confused what was before Deputy Mulligan with what was before the jury, which was not limited to a physical examination of the fire scene and was not asked to render an opinion based upon such a physical examination.

Moylan said Kim's argument was a "leap of faith" that fell far short of the mark, because the jury heard evidence of arson above and beyond the physical examination of the scene by Mulligan. And, Moylan noted, at the end of the third day of the trial as well as at the end of the trial, Judge Horne denied the defense motion for a judgment of acquittal and ruled that the totality of the evidence was enough to justify submitting the charge to the jury.

The bridge between Mulligan's physical examination of the fire scene and the evidence of arson developed beyond that examination began when he eliminated careless smoking as a possible cause of the fire, according to Moylan.

Kimberly had told Trooper Elzey that Stephen smoked when he was drinking and investigators recovered an open package of Backwoods cigars from the scene, so they immediately thought a carelessly smoked cigar caused the fire, he said. But try as he might, Mulligan couldn't get the cigar to ignite a variety of materials found in the room, Moylan said. Initially Mulligan eliminated the Backwoods cigars as a possible source of the fire, the judge said. However, they would take on far greater significance as affirmative proof of both arson and murder, he added.

Ultimately, investigators showed that the cigars were the centerpiece of an elaborate ruse carefully staged by Kimberly to make it appear that Steve had died in an accidental fire caused by careless smoking, Moylan said.

"The setting of a false trail is strong affirmative evidence of guilt," he said.

In addition, Moylan said the Hrickos' friends and co-workers all testified that Steve did not smoke. Moreover, the Hrickos' room, room 506, was a non-smoking room, he said. And within weeks of Steve's death, police uncovered evidence that Kim purchased the cigars at Astors Liquor shortly before the Valentine's Day weekend getaway.

Moylan added there was evidence to show that in staging the scene to make it look like Steve died in a fire, Kim lied to the police about Steve's drinking; lied to police about Steve's smoking; and planted the cigars to make it look like the fire was started by careless smoking. He said the ruse of an accidental fire had two purposes—primarily it was to serve as the apparent cause of Stephen's death or, if all went well, it was to be the actual cause of Stephen's death. The fire was also meant to obliterate, by charring the skin, any puncture mark left by the needle through which poison was injected, he said.

But the ruse failed miserably because there was no soot or carbon monoxide in Steve's lungs or in any other part of his body and it was conclusively established that he was already dead before the fire started, he said.

In arguing that there was no evidence from which the jury could infer that the fire was set, the defense conveniently ignored that the most conclusive support for such an inference was that the fire was an integral part of a larger murder scheme, he said. The evidence throughout the trial overwhelmingly showed that Kim murdered her husband, he said.

"The evidence abundantly supported the conviction for arson in the first degree, corpus delicti and criminal agency alike," he wrote.

Before introducing his opinion on whether the evidence presented was legally sufficient to establish the corpus delicti of criminal homicide, Moylan quoted *Hamlet* again: "Murder, though it have no tongue, will speak."

Moylan said on this point Kimberly also chose to look at the post mortem examination in a vacuum, arguing that if the autopsy didn't reveal a trace of succinylcholine or any other poison, then the jury shouldn't have been able to consider poison as the cause of Steve's death.

"She would deny the jury the prerogative of looking at mountains of other evidence, extrinsic to the post mortem examination," Moylan said.

The judge said all one needed to do was put oneself in the shoes of a reasonable and inquisitive juror to realize that Kimberly's argument was absurdly self-refuting.

Moylan then asked if Kimberly's frequently expressed desire to kill her husband; her detailed intent to poison her husband; her ready access to the poison; her flawed attempt to disguise the poisoning as an accidental death in a fire; and her quasi-admission that she had done exactly what she intended to do, helped the jury to conclude that the cause of the otherwise mysterious death was probable poisoning?

His answer was yes.

Once again, Moylan noted, Kim ignored the totality of the prosecution's case, which consisted of much more than the post mortem exam. He said if proof of the death itself could be circumstantial, then proof of the cause of death could be circumstantial as well.

In fact, he said, there have been cases where someone had been convicted of murder even though no body had been found. In those cases the lack of a post mortem examination wasn't an impediment to a conviction. In Kim's case, the medical examiner's post mortem examination and his trial testimony corroborated all of the state's other evidence proving that she poisoned her husband with succinylcholine.

"The two tributaries of proof converged into a single and inexorable stream of guilt," Moylan wrote.

The medical examiner, Dr. David Fowler, explained that Stephen's body was initially brought to his office simply to confirm whether or not Stephen had, in fact, died in a fire, Moylan said. However, the examination revealed that he had not. In court Fowler testified that he had eliminated all the normal causes for a natural death and added that all of Stephen's organs were also normal. In addition, the report from the toxicology laboratory showed there was no alcohol present in his bloodstream, and that finding was repeatedly rechecked and reconfirmed, Moylan said.

And because of Kim's statements that Steve had been drinking, Fowler had a second specimen of his blood and as well as his urine and liver tested, Moylan said. The results remained the same.

Fowler then eliminated most poisons and operating room anesthetics because they could be detected in the blood and because he didn't find any traces of them in Steve's body, the judge said.

"His focus turned to succinylcholine," he said.

Because the delivery method for succinylcholine would be through injection with a hypodermic syringe, Fowler examined Steve's skin for a puncture mark, but couldn't find one, mainly because the upper part of his body had been charred, Moylan said in his opinion. The autopsy and the subsequent toxicology tests did not reveal the presence of succinylcholine because the drug wore off naturally in the body, he said.

After a vigorous legal argument, Judge Horne ruled that Fowler would be permitted to give his expert opinion as to the manner and cause of Stephen Hricko's death, Moylan noted. Fowler testified "with a reasonable degree of scientific" certainty that the manner of death was "homicide" and the cause of death was "probable poisoning."

"Although in a separate contention Kimberly challenges the admissibility of Dr. Fowler's expert opinion that the cause of death was probable poisoning, that opinion is nonetheless part of the indubitable evidence as we assess its legal sufficiency," Moylan wrote. "We hold that the evidence was legally sufficient to establish the corpus delicti of murder."

Moylan also held that the evidence was sufficient to support the murder conviction in general.

Citing the quote, "When you have eliminated the impossible, whatever remains, however improbable, must be the truth," from *The Sign of the Four*, by Arthur Conan Doyle, Moylan discussed Kim's final contention that Judge Horne abused his discretion when he allowed Fowler to offer his expert opinion that the cause of Steve's death was probable poisoning.

Moylan said Kim's argument rested on the supposition that the evidence from the post mortem examination alone did not support such an opinion. But, he said that was not the case. Moylan said the totality of the physical examination eliminated all reasonably foreseeable natural causes for Stephen Hricko's death and Fowler's examination also eliminated all external trauma to the body.

Moylan said Kim was reluctant to acknowledge that the careful process of eliminating possible causes of death could provide proof of the actual cause of death.

"We do not share that reluctance," Moylan said.

The judge explained that after eliminating natural causes, as well as causes of death based on physical trauma, Fowler, an experienced medical examiner who had conducted over 5,000 autopsies, offered his opinion that Steve's death was caused by probable poisoning, an opinion that was allowed by law.

However, he said, Kimberly still stubbornly relied on the fact that the autopsy itself showed no trace of succinylcholine to prove there was no succinylcholine, even though various experts testified that the drug generally left no trace.

"A negative, moreover, may sometimes have positive significance," Moylan said. "Like the dog that did not bark in the night in Holmes's [short story] 'Silver Blaze,' the utter absence of evidence may proclaim guilt as loudly as an affirmative clue. Although it does, to be sure, partake of the paradox of *Catch 22*, the best proof of a substance that leaves no trace is the complete lack of any trace."

Finally, Moylan said the court had not yet resolved Kim's evidentiary contention because it had "a chameleon-like quality," and just when he thought he had pinned it down, it took another form.

Moylan said that sometimes Kimberly seemed to argue that Fowler's medical opinion was based on too little, while at other times, she seemed to argue that Fowler's medical opinion was based on too much.

"The too little argument—the absence of affirmative

traces of poison in the post mortem examination—
we have now disposed of. The too much argument is
that Dr. Fowler may improperly have taken into consideration extrinsic evidence from sources other than the
post mortem examination itself," he said.

Moylan said in ruling to allow Fowler to give his
opinion as to both the manner and cause of Steve's
death, Judge Horne properly looked to the three necessary requirements: the proposed witness must be
qualified to testify as an expert; the subject matter
about which the witness will testify must be appropriate for expert testimony; there must be a legally sufficient factual basis to support the expert's testimony.
Moylan said Horne satisfied the first two criteria, leaving only the third issue before the court.

Kim's argument, Moylan said, was that the evidence
extrinsic to the post mortem examination itself might
not contribute to that "factual basis." Kim argued
that in giving his expert opinion about the manner
and cause of Steve's death, Fowler relied on other evidence in the case—non-medical evidence—rather
than on the science, or medical evidence. But Moylan
said the court's review of Fowler's testimony didn't suggest he relied, even in part, on extrinsic evidence in
arriving at his conclusion. But there would have been
no legal problem even if he had, Moylan said. In fact,
he said, Maryland law mandated that when the medical examiner was investigating the manner and cause
of a suspicious death "the police or sheriff immediately
shall" give the medical examiner "the known facts
concerning the time, place, manner and circumstances of the death."

And in one final "grasping at a straw," Kim argued
that because Fowler may have relied, in part, on extrinsic evidence and because such extrinsic evidence, if
relied on, was evidence readily comprehensible by

the jury, the expert opinion, therefore, invaded the province of the jury.

"The argument is so speculative in several regards and without merit in so many regards that responding to it is like trying to catch a moonbeam in your hand," Moylan said.

Though much more could have been said, the judge said it was enough to note that the jury could have been helped by the expert opinion of the experienced medical examiner that the cause of death was probable poisoning.

Moylan said that in ruling that there was an adequate factual basis for Dr. Fowler to render an expert opinion as to the cause of death, Judge Horne did not abuse his discretion. So Kimberly's third and final contention would not fly, he said.

And in this quote from *Macbeth*, Moylan once again turned to Shakespeare to drive home his point: "Thus even-handed justice commends the ingredients of our poisoned chalice to our own lips."

Then Moylan said, "We hereby affirm the convictions for a crime that can only be described as 'twas one described by the ghost of old king Hamlet, 'Murder most foul, but this most foul, strange and unnatural.'"

Kim was back to square one.

Chapter 22

Her appeal denied, Kim decided to seek a new trial, claiming that her two trial attorneys did not represent her effectively, in part, because they failed to cross-examine properly the state medical examiner and deputy state fire marshal.

In preparing for Kim's request for a new trial, fire expert Gerald Hurst crafted a report for Kim's new attorney, Robert Biddle, debunking the prosecution's theory that the fire started at or near the pillows under Steve's head.

Based on his review of both prosecution and defense materials related to the fire in the Hrickos' room, Hurst said it was his opinion, to a reasonable degree of scientific certainty, that the point of origin was not the floor area adjacent to the bed, as Mike Mulligan testified. According to Hurst, the more probable point of origin of the fire was the burned bed that was located next to Steve's body.

Hurst said it was his opinion, to a reasonable degree of scientific certainty, that the fire was more likely caused by a flaming ember traveling from a woodstove

to the bed adjacent to the victim than it was a deliberately set fire.

After reading the trial transcript, Hurst said he identified several areas of Mulligan's testimony that could
have been subjected to cross-examination by Kim's
defense attorneys, but were not. Hurst said the defense
did not challenge Mulligan's testimony regarding the
fire's origin during their cross-examination of him.

Hurst said Mulligan placed the fire's origin at or near
the pillows under the victim's head on the left side near
the foot of the bed, based on his opinion that there was
heavier burning on the left side of the bed, charred
wood near the left corner of the foot of the bed, and
a soda bottle on the night stand that was bent somewhat in the general direction of the alleged origin.

Hurst said one common mistake that fire investigators often made was failing to take into account burning debris that fell to lower levels during the progress
of a fire and then burned upward from that spot. He
said that the asymmetrical burning of the bed was sufficient to establish that the fire originated to the left
center of the bed, but it could not establish the exact
point of origin.

"Given the clear photographic evidence of irregular
drop down from the left side of the bed, it is clear that
a fire on the left half of the bed would have spread to
the pillows below and that the subsequent rapid ver-
tical fire would adequately account for all of the observations made by the investigator (charred wood, bent
soda bottle, asymmetric bed damage)," Hurst said.

Challenging Mulligan's opinion about the fire's
point of origin would also have helped Kim's defense in other areas including debunking Mulligan's
cigar tests, Hurst said. Hurst said in those tests Mulligan tested only the materials in his alleged area of

origin, but he didn't test the mattress, the sheet and the blanket. Under cross-examination Mulligan did testify that not all the materials had been tested, but Hurst said that information was worthless if the jury believed those materials were not present at the point of origin of the fire.

Hurst also questioned the medical examiner's conclusion that Steve didn't die as a result of the fire because there was no carbon monoxide in his system. He said fire investigators and analysts understood that the majority of fire deaths occur because the victim had inhaled carbon monoxide of other toxins. But, he said, anyone who had investigated numerous fire deaths was aware that "low-carbon-monoxide" deaths did occur reasonably frequently and that the mechanism of death was not always determinable to a high degree of scientific certainty.

One well-known cause of death associated with fires was the phenomenon sometimes referred to as "laryngeal spasms" induced by the hot gases produced by a flash fire, according to Hurst. In those cases medical examiners often found that the respiratory systems had been partially or totally seared and reported this type of death as death by asphyxiation. In Steve's case there was no flash fire, Hurst said. However, Steve was lying on the floor directly adjacent to hanging bedclothes, as well as near the carpet and a synthetic pillow, all of which produced toxic vapors when they burned.

He said it was possible that Steve inhaled either hot or chemically laden gases early in the fire either by turning his head in his sleep toward the toxic vapor or having a flaming piece of synthetic fabric fall across his face from the bed clothing hanging along the side of the bed.

Although there was not much published data on low-carbon-monoxide deaths, Hurst said Kim's attorneys should have carefully established, through cross-examination of the medical examiner, the limitations of the written material of both thermally and chemically induced laryngeal spasms as they related to low-carbon-monoxide deaths. At the very least this would have created another issue for the jury to consider, Hurst said. But left unchallenged the medical examiner could appear to be near infallible in death cases, he said.

Another area of concern for Hurst was Mulligan's testimony concerning the alleged inability of a fire log to propel a flaming ember a few feet and set the bedding material on fire. Hurst said it was apparent from reading the trial transcript of a sidebar between the attorneys and the judge that the defense understood some of the basic weaknesses of Mulligan's testimony concerning flying embers. Hurst said the defense clearly explained those issues to Judge Horne, who also seemed to understand the problem and seemed willing to at least take some remedial action.

According to Hurst, Kim's attorneys blew their chance to plant a seed of doubt in the jurors' minds about how the fire started.

"Unfortunately, the defense attorney completely failed to impart the information he understood to the jury during cross-examination or to timely object to blatant supposition by the expert," Hurst said.

Hurst said Kim's attorney also failed to challenge the expert concerning the technical or rational basis upon which Mulligan based his opinion.

"The end effect on the jury would have necessarily been to leave them with the false impression that the expert had unrebutted scientific bases for his speculations," Hurst said.

Hurst added that early in his testimony Mulligan essentially conceded that the doors were open wide enough to allow one or more embers to be ejected from the woodstove. However, in order to eliminate the possibility that the fire could have been started by a flying ember, Hurst said Mulligan found it necessary to offer his opinion that the fire could not reach the fuel source because the fire log somehow lacked the power or energy that might be found in some other types of logs. Hurst said Mulligan continually offered his opinions without foundation and without objection from the defense.

Hurst pointed to this testimony from Mulligan about the wood-burning stove to prove his point: "I eliminated [the wood-burning stove]. The doors were open but as I said the only source of fuel in there, the last source of fuel, was the store-bought easy-light log. When I got there, it was still warm, but it had been out, obviously it had been out for some time and you had the crust of ash there with the paper match stuck into the ashes. And I don't believe it's possible for a spark to have generated from that log and come out the doors and travel that distance to those pillows and ignited those pillows. It's physically impossible."

Not only did Mulligan repeat his earlier opinion that the woodstove could not have been the fuel source, Hurst said he added speculation that the fire log was the last fuel source added to the stove.

"Again the defense failed to object to the foundationless expression of opinions that might have had the effect of convincing the jury that the last possible accidental cause has been eliminated," Hurst said.

Hurst added that the fire dynamics Mulligan testified

Linda Rosencrance

to was pure junk science, devoid of any connection with reality. He said the defense attorneys should have hired their own expert to teach them how to expose the bogus nature of Mulligan's testimony, especially since they knew in advance that the dispersion of embers or sparks was going to be an issue at trial.

Kim's two-day hearing for a new trial began in Kent County, Maryland, on June 16, 2004. The hearing was held in Kent County because each county has only one judge, and if it were held in Talbot County, she would once again be in front of Judge Horne, the trial judge.

At the hearing, Kim's new attorney, Robert Biddle, asked the court to grant her a new trial because her trial attorneys, Harry Trainor and Bill Brennan, did not represent her effectively. Biddle told Kent County Circuit Court judge J. Frederick Price that Kim should get a new trial because her former attorneys didn't pursue information that could have shown that she didn't murder her husband or set the fire in room 506 at Harbourtowne.

In the petition for postconviction relief, Biddle claimed Trainor and Brennan failed to object to testimony that should have been ruled inadmissible, including statements Steve made to other people, as well as extremely prejudicial letters Kim wrote to Brad Winkler. Kim's new attorney also said that at trial her defense team didn't properly cross-examine Deputy Fire Marshal Mike Mulligan and the state's medical examiner Dr. David Fowler.

Biddle also contended that the state did not prove its assertion that Steve died from an injection of succinylcholine. He also challenged the evidence used to convict Kim of arson. Hurst testified via telephone from his Texas home—he was ill and unable to travel to Maryland—that a spark from the woodstove in the Hrickos' room most likely caused the fire. Biddle said Kim's defense team made a mistake by deciding not to call a fire investigator to the stand at her trial who could have testified that the woodstove could not be ruled out as the cause of the fire.

Bob Dean called his own fire expert from the Federal Bureau of Alcohol, Tobacco and Firearms to testify. The expert told the court that he had conducted several tests with woodstoves just like the one in the Hrickos' room, and even when surrounded by flammable materials, none of them sparked a fire.

In preparation for the hearing Biddle had written to Dr. Edward Friedlander, a pathologist from Kansas City, Missouri, asking for his assistance in refuting the state's theory that Steve was poisoned and that he did not die from some other cause. After providing Friedlander with background information on Kim's trial and conviction, Biddle reminded him that "as this hearing is not a substitute trial, the defendant's burden is to show that material issues relating to her innocence were not properly addressed in the original trial such that prior counsel provided ineffective assistance of counsel."

For example, Biddle said that Gerry Hurst was prepared to testify that there were witnesses and approaches that could have been taken on the fire issues that would have provided the jury with a compelling, alternative view of the evidence suggesting that Kim was innocent. Biddle was hoping that Friedlander's testimony would accomplish the same goal.

In his letter Biddle told Friedlander that the state's principal evidence against Kim at trial was her presence at the crime scene near the time of the crime, her access to the poison that could have killed Steve—even though no poison whatsoever was found in Steve's body—and the testimony of several friends and co-workers, including Ken Burgess, Jennifer Gowen, Teri Armstrong, and Rachel McCoy. Biddle told Friedlander that those witnesses testified that Kim had confided to them her desire to kill Steve and a couple of them testified that she had told them exactly how she planned to do it, which the state argued matched exactly the way he was killed.

Biddle said the state's evidence of events outside room 506 of the Harbourtowne Inn was stronger than their evidence of events inside the room. He wrote that the crime scene itself was heavily contaminated before the state decided to view it as a crime scene. In addition, he said the state never clearly explained how Kimberly could have injected Steve with the succinylcholine while he was laying on the floor, set up the crime scene to look like an accident and then start a fire with the characteristics shown by the evidence.

Biddle told Friedlander that even though Kim never confessed to the police, the jury heard the state troopers testify that she said she would tell them what really happened if they would let her see her daughter.

"The trial attorneys, Brennan and Trainor, tried the case relying on reasonable doubt," Biddle said. "They did not offer a single unified theory of the defense. Mr. Brennan argued in summation that the husband killed himself."

Biddle then summed up the defense's case for Friedlander.

Brennan and Trainor introduced the husband's medical records and asked the witnesses about his exposure to toxins and other chemicals as a golf-course grounds superintendent, Biddle said. The trial lawyers were successful in keeping out the fire marshal's opinion that the fire in the Hrickos' room had been set, although he was allowed to testify that he had eliminated all accidental causes for the fire that he knew of, Biddle told Friedlander. Biddle explained that the defense medical expert, John Adams, testified that the medical examiner should have listed the cause of Steve's death as undetermined, although he testified that Steve was poisoned. Kim's uncle, David Woleslagle, told the jury that Steve smoked cigars and her mother, Lois Wolf, briefly testified that Kim was upset at Steve's death.

Biddle said there were several medical issues raised by the facts of the case. For one thing, even though the autopsy report stated that the cause of death was probable poisoning, no poison was found in the Steve's body. And even though there was a fire in the hotel room, Steve's carbon monoxide levels were normal, according to the autopsy. Biddle told Friedlander that Gerry Hurst was going to testify at the hearing that Steve could have died as a result of the fire despite his nominal carbon monoxide levels. On the other hand, Biddle said he was also reviewing whether, coincidentally, Steve died from a natural cause.

There was a variety of medical testimony at trial, including testimony from Dr. Neil Meade, a family-practice physician who last saw Steve eighteen months before his death, Biddle told Friedlander. Meade prescribed medication for Steve for a rash and insomnia and also provided him with a patch to help him stop chewing tobacco.

"The principal reason to call him seemed to be to show that the deceased did not smoke tobacco, which based on the presence of cigars in the room in which he died, was possibly a cause of the fire," Biddle wrote.

Biddle told Friedlander that David Fowler, the medical examiner who performed the autopsy, was the state's chief medical witness. Fowler testified that the low carbon monoxide levels in Steve's blood showed that he died before the fire started because he did not breathe any of the products of the fire. Fowler testified that the absence of soot in Steve's nose, mouth, trachea, windpipe, and lungs also confirmed that Steve died before the fire reached him. Biddle told Friedlander that Fowler admitted that there was nothing in the toxicology results that indicated the cause of Steve's death. Biddle explained that because Steve worked on a golf course, Fowler claimed he looked for evidence that Steve's death was caused by overexposure to pesticides, but there was nothing to indicate that was the case.

Biddle said Fowler admitted there was an issue with Steve's "q" waves something that couldn't be confirmed without a stress EKG, which Steve never took—although he was told to get one.

The prosecution also called FBI toxicologist Marc LeBeau, who tested Steve's blood and urine for the presence of succinycholine, but didn't find any, Biddle said. Barry Levine, the toxicologist for the medical examiner's office, tested for the presence of alcohol in Steve's blood and found that the level was normal.

In contrast to the numerous experts paraded out by the prosecution, the defense called only one key expert, Dr. John Adams, who told the jury that the cause of death should have been listed as unknown on the autopsy report. Adams also testified that the type of fire was consistent with fatal fires where death occured despite a low level of carbon monoxide in a deceased's blood, Biddle said. In addition, Adams told the jury that given the mechanics of injecting succinylcholine, Kim couldn't have injected Steve with the drug without his cooperation, Biddle told Friedlander.

At Kim's hearing Friedlander, who had gone over Dr. Fowler's autopsy results, testified that the autopsy alone was not enough to rule out natural causes. Friedlander said Fowler did not record the condition of Steve's heart during the postmortem and also couldn't determine the exact cause of his death.

At the two-day hearing in June, Biddle called Kim's lawyers, Harry Trainor and Bill Brennan, to the stand to ask them about the decisions they made to call or not call certain experts during Kim's trial.

Now, five-and-a-half years after Kim's conviction, Brennan and Trainor talked about their preparation for her trial.

"As part of our trial preparation we went down to Harbourtowne and went into the actual room where the fire occurred and examined it with our investigator. We took photographs. We did that type of on-scene, hands-on investigation in the case," Brennan said. "The issue in this case was the cause of death of Mr. Hricko. The medical examiner of the state of Maryland basically opined that Mr. Hricko was an otherwise healthy individual. He said there was no sign of cancer, no sign of heart disease, no sign of any other illness that would have killed him. So we were faced with an otherwise healthy thirty-five-year-old individual who died suddenly—what causes that—was there a criminal agency behind that or was it a natural death? So the ME said they did a complete autopsy and all of his organs were otherwise healthy. We called Dr. Adams to show that this flash fire would have caused heat to go down his lungs and cause his sudden death and it wouldn't necessarily leave a lot of charring. I believe that was the issue we had Dr. Adams opine on."

However, the defense team had another expert who worked with them on the case, according to Trainor.

"That was our fire reconstruction expert who worked for us, consulted with us, and advised us, but did not testify," Trainor said. "Why didn't he testify? Well, we liked where the facts were—you don't call an expert to testify if his opinion would not change the facts."

Brennan said, "I think the fact that the judge wouldn't let the state fire marshal opine that it was an incendiary fire—that it was a set fire—and once the judge struck that opinion and wouldn't let him give that opinion, that's about as good as we were going to get on that issue."

Trainor said there was a strategic element to not putting their fire expert on the witness stand.

"If we put our expert on, then Mr. Dean would have had him on cross-examination and could have asked him leading questions on that issue and we open up that issue that we've already closed," Trainor said. "We certainly wouldn't put on someone and open him up to cross-examination on an issue that has already been closed by the judge in our favor."

As far as the cause of Steve's death, Brennan said there was no evidence of succinylcholine in Steve's body.

"We clearly objected at trial that the medical examiner was speculating that it was poison because there was no evidence of succinylcholine," Brennan said. "And it was pure speculation that a poisoning or something caused the death because there was no scientific or medical evidence to substantiate that opinion. I remember cross-examining him on it, saying he was considering things outside the record to arrive at his opinion that it was poisoning. But I think he said if he confined his examination to just the science or the medicine, there really was no cause of death. But when the medical examiner looked beyond the medicine and took into consideration all the other stuff, he then got to poisoning as the cause of death."

Brennan said, "I think our legal issue was you're the doctor, you confine it to medicine or you confine it to science, then tell us what you have. I think if he confined it to that, he wouldn't know what killed Steve. The law in Maryland is that the medical examiner can look beyond the science and consider other issues. We were fighting over that issue, but the appellate court judge ruled that the medical examiner could look beyond the pure science and get into other issues. Our objection was that once he got beyond the pure science, he was making value judgments as to who was telling the truth; who was not telling the truth; was succinylcholine really used? There was absolutely no evidence that there was any succinylcholine in Mr. Hricko's body."

In a ruling dated November 4, 2004, Judge Price denied Kim's request for a new trial. Price ruled that Kim was not denied effective counsel during her trial. Price said according to case law a defendant must show that the performance of her lawyer "fell below the standard of reasonableness under prevailing professional norms." And if a lawyer's performance was ruled professionally unreasonable, then the defendant must also show that there was reasonable probability that the result of her trial would have been different.

In both cases Judge Price ruled that the actions of Kim's attorneys at trial were not unreasonable, but even if their decisions had been unreasonable, the outcome of the trial would not have changed.

Despite the unfavorable outcome of the hearing for a new trial, Kim still has a sliver of hope that her sentence could be reduced.

"After Kim was convicted and sentenced, we did file a motion for reconsideration of sentence, which is still pending [as of this writing]," Trainor said.

Under Maryland law, trial attorneys can file a motion within ninety days of sentencing asking the judge to modify or reduce the sentence, Trainor said.

"That has been taken under advisement by the judge, and, as far as I know, is still pending and could, in the future, mean she might get a hearing on that motion," he said. "The law is in flux, but, as it stands right now, I believe the judge can act on it almost at any time in the future."

However, the law has been changed since Kim was sentenced, Brennan said.

"As of July 1, 2004, the law changed and now the court only has five years to modify a sentence. Prior to that, there was no limit and the judge can hold it for one year, five years, or ten years," Brennan said.

"When you look at Kim's sentence—Judge Horne sentenced her to life in prison because she was convicted of first-degree murder—although he wouldn't be able to change the life imprisonment sentence, he would be able to suspend some portion of it," Trainor said. "That means he'd have the power, if he chooses to exercise that power, to change it to a life sentence and suspend all but a set term of years, but it hasn't yet been ruled on, as far as I know."

As it stands, Kim is eligible for parole consideration after fifteen years, less good time, but the judge

AN ACT OF MURDER

has the authority to suspend any portion of that, Brennan said.

"He could suspend all but thirty years, or all but twenty-five years of her sentence, but it's purely at the judge's discretion," he said. "But that motion is still pending."

In December 2004, Kim also filed an application for leave to appeal to the Maryland Court of Special Appeals asking that the court take another look at her case. Such requests are called applications for leave to appeal because the granting of a hearing by the Court of Special Appeals is discretionary, not mandatory. Kim filed this application "pro se," or representing herself, because Biddle, who prepared the application for her as a gesture of good will, said he couldn't continue to represent her because she couldn't pay him.

The Court of Special Appeals denied Kim's request for leave to appeal. After Kim's friend Rachelle St. Phard put up an additional $22,500, Biddle filed a post conviction petition for relief of the state court's decision in the U.S. Court of Appeals for the Fourth Circuit in Richmond, Virginia. Biddle told Kim he planned to argue that state court's denial of her appeal was based on an unreasonable interpretation of the federal ineffective assistance of counsel law. That petition was pending as of this writing.

Cathy Rosenberger, however, isn't so sure anything is ever going to help Kim.

"Through this entire legal process with Kim I have learned so much about the legal system," she said in a letter to Robert Biddle. "From an outsider it looks like a 'good old boys club.' The members of the club consist of judges, police, prosecutors, medical examiners and investigators."

Still firmly believing that Steve died accidentally in the fire at Harbourtowne, Rosenberger said the exact details of his death would always remain a mystery. In the beginning, Rosenberger said she had faith in the system and thought if a person presented enough reasonable doubt people would listen.

"That's why I put up about $40,000. But I stopped contributing because it doesn't appear to me that there is any way that a judge is going to listen," she wrote. "Even if we uncovered the exact cause of death, the judges would turn a deaf ear," she continued. "After sitting through Kim's trial and hearings—I have watched a total of five judges during proceedings— [judging by] their facial expressions and body language it was so obvious to me that they are practically laughing at us. The smirking, rolling eyes, smiling, etc., [sent] a very clear message [to us]."

Loyal to the bitter end, Cathy Rosenberger is unwilling to accept the meaning behind that message— that Kim Hricko did, in fact, kill her husband.